CIVIL WAR WRITINGS OF GOVERNOR HENRY WATKINS ALLEN OF LOUISIANA

Civil War Writings of Governor Henry Watkins Allen of Louisiana

George Bagby

Tall Men Books

Contents

Henry Watkins Allen

The editor dedicates this volume to the late Roger Busbice:
scholar and lover of "the true Louisiana, the honorable
Louisiana."
His patriotism burned bright, and he endured scorn for his
love.

ISBN: 9798869361226

EPUB ISBN: 9798869361233

This book was edited entirely in Brunswick, Georgia,
by George Bagby.
tallmenbooks@gmail.com
Spring of 2024

Forward

The impetus for this little volume was the need for the republication of Allen's important investigation of Federal depredations in Western Louisiana. This rare document, assembled by sworn testimony, was republished in Lafayette, Louisiana by one David Edmonds several decades ago, but this small printing is vanishingly rare, and the facsimile editions of the original are very difficult to read. That difficulty is remedied in this reprinting.

Allen's biography was originally preserved by one Sarah Dorsey: a friend and intimate who published the *Recollections* to preserve his memory in 1866, only months, apparently, after Allen's death. *Henry Watkins Allen of Louisiana*, published in '64 by Cassidy and Simpson, is an academic biography that may serve as the last word on Allen's life. The sources on Allen and his administration remain obscure due to the capture and captivity of the state archives with the surrender of Shreveport in 1865, which have left these records in a permanently disordered and inaccessible condition when they are extant. No resources have yet been dedicated to their organization.

Allen, in the words of Roger Busbice, "accomplished miracles," and was one of the ablest administrators of the Confederate states. The formidable Douglas Southall Freeman wrote that Allen could have impacted the outcome of the War had his talents been sooner recognized. Elected governor after the catastrophic collapse of Confederate authority on the Mississippi and the abandonment of both Baton Rouge and the refuge capitol of Opelousas, Allen took office in January of 1864. His incredible industry and ability to inspire was essential to Gen. Richard Taylor's late successes in the Red River Campaign, and all of this in spite of his grievous wounds suffered in the Battle of Baton Rouge, which made him unfit for further military service. He sponsored and encouraged various manufacturing efforts, relieving the crisis of war supplies and civilian necessities. He used old business connections in Texas and Mexico to import vital raw materials, and even paper, which had become impossible to procure. His indispensable efforts to relieve the poor and especially the war widows and orphans won him the deep regards of his countrymen. Dorsey tells piteous tales of widows relieved by Allen's personal funds, which so exhausted his finances that he arrived in his Mexican exile virtually penniless. Of great interest to modern historians is Allen's commission on Federal atrocities in Louisiana: the testimony of which was legally sound but the physical evidence, especially that of the catastrophe of Tiger Island, need to be investigated and substantiated.

The plight of the Freedmen is an untold story of the Civil War. Some historians, such as Jim Downs in *Sick From Freedom*, have delved into the suffering that resulted from the sudden and unplanned emancipation that left thousands as desperate dependents on an army totally unprepared to provide the necessities of life. Tiger Island, the site of modern-day Morgan City, Louisiana, was reportedly the site of a large contraband camp decimated by starvation and cholera in sight of the Yankee depot and garrison. Allen's report recounts the story, and Allen's addresses, included here, allude to this enigma of the War and emancipation. Provision and planning for the future of the African was seldom the goal or thought of the prosecutors of the War.

Allen's bibliography is larger than what is collected here. He assembled a charming volume of correspondence from his travels in Europe before the War, and we have tantalizing evidence from Dorsey of lost correspondence and poetry. Dorsey has collected far more than what is included here, and her sources are obscure or lost. Of Allen's official productions, all that is extant and known to the editor is collected here.

George Bagby,
Louisiana, Spring of 2024

1

The Conduct of Federal Troops in Louisiana

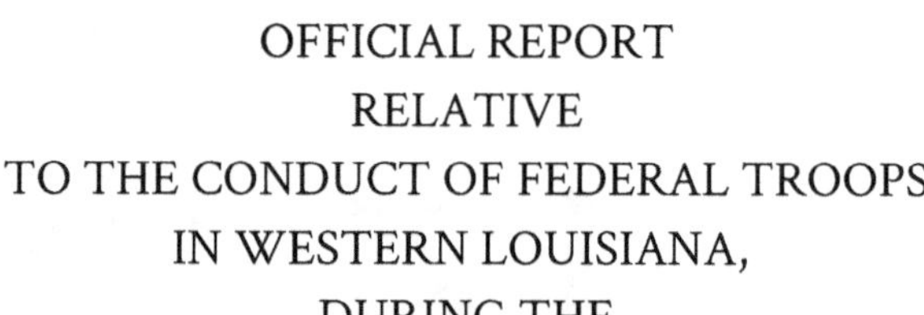

OFFICIAL REPORT
RELATIVE
TO THE CONDUCT OF FEDERAL TROOPS
IN WESTERN LOUISIANA,
DURING THE
INVASIONS OF 1863 AND 1864.

COMPILED FROM SWORN TESTIMONY,
UNDER DIRECTION OF
GOVERNOR HENRY W. ALLEN.
SHREVEPORT, APRIL 1865

EXECUTIVE OFFICE, SHREVEPORT, LA., March 20, 1865.

In June I appointed commissioners to gather and collect testimony concerning the conduct of the enemy during their brief and inglorious occupancy of a part of West Louisiana. I addressed to each of them the following letter:
EXECUTIVE OFFICE, SHREVEPORT, LA., June 20, 1864.

SIR - I desire to obtain for publication and historical record a careful, accurate, authentic statement of the atrocities and barbarities committed by the Federal officers, troops and camp followers during their late invasion of Western Louisiana.

Confiding in your known industry, your love of truth, and your judgment in discriminating between that is important and what is not, I appoint you an agent and commissioner for the purpose a both set forth. I wish you to spare no pains in getting statements in writing from eye-witnesses and sufferers, signed and sworn to. Hearsay reports should be carefully sifted before being received and incorporated in your statement.

It will be borne in mind by you that the testimony thus taken will be *exparte,* the accused not having the privilege of introducing evidence to explain, mitigate or rebut what will be published against them; hence it is important that the publication when made should contain intrinsic evidence of its own credibility. It may be well therefore to introduce such details as will corroborate the general statements of your report. If you hear of any special acts of kindness that may have been done to our citizens by Federal officers or soldiers, please report them, with the names, rank, &c., of those who acted thus creditably. I hope, for the honor of human nature, that some such instances may be reported by you.

When your report is completed, forward it to this office with the affidavits on which it is founded, together with an account of your necessary and reasonable expenses while actually employed under this order, which will be repaid to you in addition to an equitable compensation for your services.

Commissioners will be appointed for other invaded parishes, with whom you may do well to communicate.

Very respectfully,
your obedient servant,
HENRY W. ALLEN,
Governor of Louisiana.

Hon. T. C. Manning, of Rapides; Gen. John G. Pratt and Col. John E. King, of St. Landry; Hon. J. W. Butler and Col. Phanor Prudhomme, of Natchitoches; Hon. E. North Cullum and E. de Generes, Esq., of Avoyelles, were appointed for their respective parishes. Only the commissioners for Rapides and St. Landry have sent in their reports. Should the others be received before the printing of the reports of Messrs. Manning, Pratt and King is completed, they will be added; otherwise they will be issued in a supplement.

1 have thought proper thus to obtain a verified statement of the occurrence which gave to the late invasion an atrocious, savage and most execrable character, while they were still fresh in the recollection of our people. I do not expect that this statement will be seen by many of our enemies, or that it will arouse them to a sense of the disgrace which impartial history will attach to them; nor can I expect that it will awaken much interest with the few strangers into whose hands it may chance to fall. But I hope the publication of a few hundred copies of this report will preserve for the future historian many facts which might otherwise be forgotten.

The commissioners have performed their task with praiseworthy fidelity and with great ability. Within the limits of the State their high character and personal merit command implicit confidence and belief;

but they have done their duty so well that their reports will stand secure on their own external evidence in the mind of every discriminating and enlightened foreigner, while the scholar will be pleased with the accuracy, dignity and classic elegance of the language and style in which they are compiled.

HENRY W. ALLEN,
Governor of Louisiana.

REPORT OF MESSRS. PRATT AND KING.

To His Excellency, Henry W. Allen, Governor of the State of Louisiana:

SIR-Appointed in June last by your Excellency, Commissioners, to make a full, accurate and authentic report of the barbarities and atrocities committed by the officers, troops and camp-followers of the Federal army, during its several invasions of South-western Louisiana, we, soon after the reception of the commission, proceeded carefully and industriously to collect the necessary materials. How far we have succeeded will best appear from the body of our report. The objects had in view by your Excellency, we thought; would be best accomplished, by giving such statistical, geographical, and local information, as might be necessary to understand fully the details. If many of the facts enumerated in these pages seem incredulous, from their offensiveness to the moral sense of mankind, they will be found to be supported by an array of distinguished names among the eye-witnesses and the sufferers, by the personal observation of your Commissioners, and by undisputed notoriety.

The district within which our investigations have been made, extends from the southern boundaries of Rapides and Avoyelles to

Berwick's Bay, and includes the Parishes of St. Landry, Lafayette, St. Martin and St. Mary. Few countries were more highly favored by nature, and embellished by art, than the belt of land lying on either side of the water-courses of this fertile region, and which, in St. Landry and Lafayette, spreads out in high prairies, intersected by woods. The productive oil and genial climate here favor the growth of the fruits of tropical and temperate regions; and to these natural advantages had been added the labor of art and industry, in the development of its resources. The great staples of the country were profitably cultivated on the opulent soil of this belt. While there were no cotton plantations of any great magnitude, innumerable small ones produced an annual aggregate crop of about thirty-eight thousand bales. Some two hundred and eighty-eight sugar estates, many of them employing expensive machinery, and using all the modern improvements, yielded annually, for export, about forty thousand hogsheads of sugar, and sixty thousand barrels of molasses, besides what the villages and people of the country consumed. Added to these products of the soil, there were annually driven to the plantations on the coast and to New Orleans, some thirty thousand head of cattle, taken from the numerous herds which range, summer and winter, on the luxuriant prairies and the wild cane, lands of the adjacent swamps. The total value of these products amounted to about five million dollars, which, in an aggregate population of sixty-five thousand one hundred and seventeen, (see Auditor's report for 1858,) of which population, thirty-five thousand seven hundred and thirty-seven were slaves, gave more ore than four hundred dollars in value, of surplus exportable products, for each family of five persons-a result which is seldom obtained in any agricultural district of the same area and population.

These parishes, including Vermilion and Calcasieu, formed the ancient counties of Opelousas and Attakapas, which, in 1810, had an aggregate population of 12,417, of which 4,802, were slaves. The same district had, in 1858, an aggregate population of 73,368, of which 37,737 were slaves. It is a remarkable fact, that this unexampled increase of population, which, in every decade has more than doubled its number, and maintained almost an equilibrium between the races, is due less to accretion from abroad, than to the patriarchal habits of the people and a salubrious climate. Absenteeism has never been the vice of this country: like the ancient patriarch, the proprietor has always lived in the midst of his family, his servants and his flocks, content to fulfill the simple duties imposed upon him by his condition.

Before this fair land had been wasted, and the labor of years destroyed, the planter's spacious mansion was surrounded by fields of waving corn and cane, and overlooked broad prairies animated with flocks and herds, and checkered with farms of cotton, whose trim and careful culture recalled the husbandry of the patient Hollander. Around the planters' dwellings were seen the numerous out-buildings used for agricultural purposes, and the negro cottages, always enlivened by groups of happy children. When the labors of the day were over, the scene was ever animated by the loud laugh, the rude sports, and the merry faces, indicating the happiness of the returning laborers. In the midst of these evidences of contentment, the planter enjoyed a more elevated pleasure, in communion with his family, in literary pursuits, or in the entertainment of his friends, - his highest social enjoyment consisting in administering the rite of hospitality under his roof. The master and the slave were alike happy, in their respective vocations. Such a condition naturally suggests the reflection, that the system which has produced them could only be in harmony with the wise designs of a beneficent Providence.

The insulated district we have described, enclosed within a narrow territory, and separated from the parishes bordering the Mississippi, by an intricate net-work of bayous and lakes, presents, it would seem, no grand route for the passage of armies, and no strategic point for their concentration; and it might reasonably have been anticipated, that it would have escaped the ordinary havoc of war, if conducted on principles recognized by the civilize in world. Had the poverty of this district been as a parent as its isolation, it cannot be doubted that it would have remained free from invasion. But unhappily, we are engaged in war with an enemy who recognizes only such principles of warfare as suit his caprice, his convenience, or the gratification of his vindictive rage; who does not scruple to recruit his soldiers from the felons of penitentiaries and prisons; who appoints Generals often without conduct, without honor, and without humanity; who wages war upon our hospitals, on peaceful citizens, and on women and children; who riots in robbery and pillage, in devastation and destruction; and who sympathizes with the demoniacal joy exhibited by Gen. A. J. Smith, at Alexandria, where, surrounded by the flames of a peaceful village, in the midst of falling timbers, crumbling walls, and flying women and children, he waved his sword in an exultation inspired by so congenial a scene, exclaiming - "This, boys, is something like war!" That such is the character of the warfare of the enemy, the history of the several invasions of Attakapas and Opelousas will abundantly show.

In the spring of 1863, Gen. Banks, suddenly abandoning the siege of Port Hudson, threw his army across the Mississippi river, and marched through the parishes watered by the Lafourche to Berwick's Bay, which is an enlargement of the Atchafalaya river near its mouth. The Bay was then in possession of the enemy's gunboats, which had free communication with the waters stretching along the parishes of St. Mary and St. Martin. Crossing the Bay, and marching a few miles above the junction of the Têche with the Atchafalaya, his army, numbering about twenty thousand men, of all arms, found itself confronted by the Confederate forces, numbering about thirty-five hundred men, leader Gen. Taylor. The later occupied a slightly intrenched position across the peninsula through which the Têche flows, in the lower part of St. Mary. Repulsed before this position, Gen. Banks sent a column by transports to operate in Gen, Taylor's rear. Finding it impossible with his small force, to keep open his communications, Gen. Taylor concluded, reluctantly, to evacuate the country. Holding in check the column which numbered more than his whole force, and which had effected a landing some fifteen miles above his position, with a small force and several detached sections of artillery, the Confederate General effected his retreat along a line of road which ran within cannon, shot of the Federal column, without the loss of any of his material. From this time the advancing columns of the enemy met with no obstacles to impede their progress, except occasional skirmishing with his advanced guard, until they reached the Bayou Vermilion. While the enemy was effecting the crossing of this bayou, defended by less than five hundred Confederate troops-(magnified by the apprehensions of the enemy into the dimensions of an army,)-Gen. Banks was writing, from the Cote Gelée, his first official dispatch, in which he asserts, with the characteristic mendacity of Federal war bulletins, that his army had fought *half a dozen pitched battles* between Berwick's Bay and the Vermilion.

Gen. Taylor having skilfully conducted his army beyond the indefensible boundary, the beautiful and wealthy district of Opelousas and Attakapas was left an open prey to the ravages of the enemy. Meeting with no opposition, the progress of his columns was marked by scenes of spoliation and devastation unparalleled in civilized warfare. His advanced guard maintained some degree of order, as it penetrated into the country; but it was followed by a confused mob of officers and men, horse and foot, spread out in every direction, plundering and destroying whatever came within their reach. While some were attacking with sword and bayonet the domestic animals, and shooting into the poultry yards, others penetrated to the negro quarters, and endeavored, with inquisitorial ingenuity, to extract from the slaves the secret of the buried treasures of their masters, or to excite them to revolt.

From the many statements of eye-witnesses to these scenes of plunder and pillage, we select the description of a venerable and accomplished lady, living by the way-side. "I was" she says "watching from my window, the apparent orderly march of the first Yankees that appeared in view and passed up the road, when, suddenly, as if by magic, the whole plantation was covered with men, like bees from an overthrown hive; and, as far as my vision extended, an inextricable medley of men and animals met my eye. In one place, excited troopers were firing into the flock of sheep; in another, officers and men were in pursuit of the boys' ponies; and in another, a crowd were in excited chase of the work animals. The kitchen was soon filled with some, carrying off the cooking utensils and the provisions of the day; the yard with others, pursuing poultry, and firing their revolvers into the trees. They penetrated under the house, into the out-buildings, and went into the garden, stripping it in a moment of all its vegetables, and trenching the ground with their bayonets, in search of buried treasures. This continued during the day, as the army was passing, amid a bewildering sound of oaths and imprecations, mingled with the clatter of the poultry and the noise of the animals. At one time during the day, passing through the house, my attention was attracted to a noise in the parlor. I opened the door, and was just in time to see two soldiers springing out of the window, in possession of some books and daguerreotypes they had taken from the table. Securing the windows, I turned to other parts of the house. In the children's room, I found a trunk broken open, and its contents strewn upon the floor, and I discovered that some articles had been taken. When the army had passed, we were left almost "destitute." Another lady confessed to us her inability to describe the scene. "I can only say," said she, "it was bedlam let loose." Though varied in particulars, many of which will be given in the sequel, the testimony of every eye-witness on the enemy's line of march, is to the same purport. A gentleman of high character, and distinguished in the political annals of the State, was arrested at his residence near Vermilionville, and carried, on the line over which was passing this motley crowd, twelve miles to the Carencro, where the head of the Federal column was then resting. The country through which this line passed was thickly dotted with farms and plantations, intersected by the public road and lateral lanes. Though we cannot reproduce his graphic description of what he witnessed, in his own words, we take the liberty of giving enough of it, from memory, to convey an idea of this licentious march. "The road," said he, "was filled with an indiscriminate mass of armed men, on horseback and on foot, carts, wagons, cannon and caissons, rolling along in most tumultuous disorder, while to the right and to the left, joining the mass, and detaching from it, singly and in groups, were hundreds going empty-handed and returning laden Disregarding the lanes and pathways, they broke through fields and enclosures, spreading in every direction that promised plunder or attracted curiosity. Country carts, horses, mules and oxen, followed by negro men, women, and even children, (who were pressed into service to carry the plunder,) laden with every conceivable object, were approaching and mingling in the mass from every side. The most whimsical scenes presented themselves, at every step: horses and even gentle oxen, were pulled, pushed, and beaten along towards this seething current, with pigs, sheep, geese, ducks, and chickens swinging from their backs, fluttering, squealing, and quacking, while the burthened animals, in bewildered amazement, were endeavoring to escape from their persecutors. These scenes, repeated at every step on my way to Carencro, was only varied on my return, by the diminished objects of plunder left for those that came after."

The Federal a my established, on its route, military posts at Franklin, New Iberia, St. Martinsville and Vermilionville, with sufficient "transportation" to carry out what seemed to be the main object of the campaign. Halting at Opelousas. with its right resting on the Courtableau at Washington, adequate preparations were made to gather the fruits of its manifold victories. Immediately, the Commissary and Quartermaster's wagons, with all the teams which could be pressed in the country, were put in requisition to collect cotton and sugar, to carry to the different landings on the bayou, thence to be taken off by steamers. Horsemen were sent to scour the country in every direction for stock. The less philosophic of the astonished proprietors, rushing to Head Quarters to remonstrate against being deprived of their property in so summary a manner, were insultingly told that "receipts would be given, and if after the war, they could prove their loyalty, they might be paid." Even the lip service, which has sometimes passed current, would not be received, in exchange for property. The work of spoliation went on. The finest blooded stock, imported at great expense, and every living thing of value, were indiscriminately appropriated for transportation or slaughtered, papers ransacked, locks picked, strong-boxes broken open; and all exportable commodities, convertible into money, were shipped as fast as they could be transported by steamers.

While matters were progressing thus favorably, with no enemy within a hundred miles, General Banks was summoned to a new scene of action. The intelligence having reached Opelousas that Admiral Porter had forced the defences of Red River, and was steaming towards Alexandria with his fleet, it became necessary for the Federal General to put his army in motion, to share with Porter the glory of the conquest of an interior undefended town. He accordingly undertook a forced march to that point. *En route*, he passed up the Bayou Bœuf, through a planting district, lying on either side of that stream, remarkable for its exuberant fertility, and ornamented with extensive plantations, cultivated by proprietors of education, refinement and wealth. - So effectually was this wealthy region laid waste during this Vandal march, that the few inhabitants who remained clinging to their desolated homesteads, amidst the ruins that surrounded them, were spared the presence of the Federal army, when the autumn brought it back to consummate its work of destruction.

Whatever agreeable visions may have occupied the mind of General Banks, during his occupation of Alexandria, were rudely dispelled by a summons to less congenial duties than those of reducing helpless citizens to poverty. Giving his weary soldiers but little time to rest, after their forced march to Red River, he precipitately withdrew from Alexandria, crossed the Mississippi, and resumed the siege of Port Hudson. Meanwhile, the several small corps, strung along his rear, retreated by way of Berwick's Bay, carrying with them loads of plunder, and thousands of negroes, as will be more particularly noticed in another place.

After the Federal forces were thus withdrawn, in the spring of 1863, for four months these parishes were left in peace. Many of the citizens believing that the storm had passed, set about repairing their damaged fortunes; while others less confident and more wise, gathered up what was left of the wreck, and removed beyond the borders of the district. In the month of September, 1863, the Federal army again crossed Berwick's Bay, advanced leisurely along the route taken in the spring; and rested the head of its column, on the Courtableau, at Washington. After having remained in this position several weeks, it fell gradually back, sweeping, as with a drag-net, everything in its way, until it massed itself along the Teche, on the Peninsula embraced within the limits of St. Mary, where it remained encamped during the winter months,

The Red River campaign, which terminated so disastrously to the Federal arms at Mansfield and Pleasant Hill, opened in March, 1864, just one year after the expedition undertaken for the devastation of Opelousas and Attakapas. The larger portion of the army, which had fallen back upon the Peninsula, was withdrawn from time to time, during the winters of 1863-4, leaving but a remnant to complete the destruction of that beautiful Parish. But in the early spring, it was joined by the several corps and commands, which were to compose "The Grand Army of Louisiana and Texas." This grand column of invasion commenced the blunders, which culminated in its disaster and route in North Louisiana, by marching through the country which it had previously stripped of the means of furnishing subsistence or forage, when it might have reached Alexandria in twenty-four hours by river transports from New Orleans. On the 22d of March, the rear guard of the "grand army" passed the northern limits of St. Landry. -Since then, with the exception of occasional visits to the wooded outskirts, from Military posts on the Mississippi, by marauders who came to open a ballot box, in which to deposit their own votes; or to capture or murder an unoffending citizen, this district has been free from the tread of the enemy.

From this general description of the country, and the operations of the invading forces, it will be seen how far the Federal General may congratulate himself, on the accomplishment of his congenial mission, viz: the impoverishment of the people, and the destruction of the resources of the country. Gen. Banks found this district a garden; he left it a desert. By his hand, the fruit of the patient labor of half a century has been destroyed. The flocks and herds that ranged upon its verdant praries have been wantonly swept away. Citizens, whose means once enabled them to dispense a liberal and heart-warm hospitality, have been reduced to poverty and destitution. Families, who had enjoyed a cultivated ease in their elegant homes, have been forced into voluntary exile, to seek immunity from Federal persecution in a land of strangers. The contented and happy negro, who had grown upon the soil, fulfilling the destiny that God had prepared for him, and through which He might have been leading his race to higher destinies, has been recklessly driven, with the family, from a once peaceful and happy home, to a life of degradation, want, and painful death. For the proper fulfillment of the duties assigned to us, under the commission with which we have been honored by your Excellency, we have traversed the high-roads, on which are grouped the most considerable plantations of this district, from the lower limits of Rapides and Avoyelles, to the junction of the Teche with the Atchafalaya; and although it was in the early autumn, and on the approach of the harvest, with the exception of occasional half-cultivated "patches," enclosed by the wreck of former field fences, we saw, along this whole route of 180 miles, but a few meagre vestiges of the treasures of the earth, cultivated by the hand of man. Along the entire route could be traced the melancholy monuments of the devastating march of the enemy. Uninclosed fields were covered with the rank luxuriance of weeds and wild vines, which encroached upon the very thresholds of the mansions, still standing, as memorials of former prosperity. Some of these dwellings were occupied by families. living upon the wreck of their former fortunes. Others were entirely deserted, presenting, with their unhinged doors and broken windows, a gloomy picture of decay. The sites of others were marked by charred ruins, from the midst of which arose the blackened remains of crumbling chimney stacks. The large and costly structures erected for the manufacture of sugar, as well as the less expensive buildings of the cotton planter, we found in every stage of decay, dilapidation and ruin, owing, either to the absence of the proprietor, or the destroying hand of the enemy. But no less remarkable than these general features, was the absence of the domestic animals. Through St. Landry and Lafayette, where the broad prairies sweep down to the road, may yet be seen a few castle that have wandered in by the way side; but along the Teche, animal life diminished at every step, until, below Franklin, even the most necessary domestic animals disappeared. For miles nothing could be seen but the vulture brooding, from some shattered tree top, over the desolate scene; or the hawk, flying low, in search of his prey, over the tangled thickets usurping the once cultivated fields. But the exuberance of nature, as if in mockery of man's desolation, was still prodigal of its bounties. The vine of the pumpkin, overleaping the thicket, deposited its golden treasure, even by the way side; and we saw them, in one instance, gathered by the girls of the adjacent village, who gleaued over this desolated field for bounties thus spontaneously bestowed. An exception to this scene may be found in some Lends of the bayous, some curvatures of the 1oad, or some sequestered nooks on the lakes, protected by their situation from waste and destruction; but these places are few, and their combined products, tor the present year, will not equal what has been produced annually by a single large plantation on the Têche.

But out of the calamities with which the scourge of war has afflicted the people of this ill-fated district, has come some good. Like gold purified in the fire, they have become more ardent in their patriotism, in the midst of their adversity. They have been inspired with a new zeal in the cause of our independence. More men have girded on their armor for battle; and more mothers have sent out their husbands and sons, to defend their homes and firesides against the tread of the Vandal, and the torch of the incendiary.

It might have been anticipated that the exactions of a hostile army, occupying a rich agricultural country, would fall with peculiar severity on its inhabitants; that the foraging parties would not nicely balance between their military rights, and the right of property in the proprietor; and that many acts of hardship and oppression would occur from the exercise of unrestrained power. A just appreciation of the evils incident to a state of war, might have taught the reflecting citizen to brave such hardships with becoming equanimity; and the reflection that invading armies are not always entirely free from the presence of the dissolute and the depraved, might have led him to anticipate some rule attempt upon his purse, or some aggravated assault upon his person. -But the outrages committed by the enemy did not flow from the ordinary sources of the calamities of modern warfare, as the facts embraced in our narrative will fully demonstrate.

We have been commissioned by your Excellency, to prepare "for publication and historical record, a full, accurate, authentic statement of the atrocities and barbarities committed by the Federal officers, troops and camp followers, during their late invasions," and we will more clearly subserve the purposes of the commission, by first enumerating, under their respective heads, the charges brought against the enemy, and afterwards under corresponding heads, corroborating them by details.

The Federalists not only robbed the planters of the produce of their fields, and plundered the goods of the merchants; but they destroyed the libraries and depositories of professional men.

They sacked private dwellings, and while reveling upon the contents of the pantries and wine cellers, they grossly and indecently insulted the unprotected females, and wantonly destroyed their last remnants of food and clothing. They shattered the crockery, glass-ware, and mirrors, strewing the floor with their fragments; they stove, with the buts of their muskets, the doors of side-boards and closets, prized open drawers with the points of their bayonets, and slashed with their sabres prized objects of taste, or ornaments consecrated to pious uses; in cooler blood, when their intoxication, or the excitement of a general licence had subsided, they dashed to pieces and burned for fuel costly articles of furniture, and prized heir-looms from former generations.

They violently plundered the rich of their money, the poor of their necessary effects, the women of their jewelry, and even the children of their trinkets. Nor did they spare the dead. They sacrilegiously ravished from them the last covering which enclosed their mortal remains.

They fired volleys among passing citizens, and groups of women and children, in the streets of a peaceful village.

They violated the sanctuary and the tomb.

They arbitrarily arrested peaceful and unoffending citizens, whom they dragged though the country like felons; whom they confined under guard in exposed situations, or lodged in jails from which they had loosed the depraved and the criminal; or, whom they transported to a distant city, to languish for months in prison, a prey to the cares and anxieties haunting the victim thus rudely torn from his family.

In violation of the decencies and proprieties of life, they unnecessarily occupied private dwellings, or surrounded them with their camps, so that helpless ladies were driven to seek refuge in interior rooms, where, besides the annoyances of interrupted privacy, and the apprehension of more serious intrusion, they were deprived of the comforts, and, sometimes, of the necessaries of life.

They not only razed to their foundations, or wantonly burned plantation buildings and dwellings, from which they had driven the inmates; but they tore down, over their heads, the sheltering root of the widow and the orphan.

They destroyed not only the poultry, the flocks and herds, the fields, the gardens, and the orchards, and attempted to destroy the sources of salt, all essential to sustain and preserve life, but they also destroyed the medicines and surgical instruments, indispensable to restore health. They not only chopped to pieces or burned the aratory instruments, the carts and wagons, the corn and sugar mills, necessary for the production of a new supply of food; but they hacked in pieces the cards, the spinning wheels, and the looms, required to furnish the necessary clothing; and, as if this were not sufficient to gratify the most refined malignity, they introduced loathsome diseases among the people whom they had previously bereft and despoiled.

While thus violating, on the one hand, the law of the christian, and, on the other, the precept of the Mohammedan, they set at naught both, by neither keeping faith nor covenant with those whom they drove to accept their protection, on the condition of professed allegiance, nor with the credulous negroes, whom they had perfidiously drawn into their toils.

We have already alluded to the fact, that means of transportation was put in motion, in the words of the worthy commandant of the post at Opelousas, "to collect the valuable products of the country;" and his report will show the result of the operations in the Parish of St. Landry.

What was collected at the other Federal military posts, we have no accurate means of judging; but, as we find the same complaints throughout the district, we presume that the officers commanding them, if less diligent, had a success at least commensurate with their efforts. With regard to the merchants, as the suspension of foreign commerce had reduced their stocks of merchandize to a low ebb, (except in a few instances,) the only articles of value they still retained were the exchangeable objects of the country, such as hides, tobacco, flour, &c. These, with such goods as were left on the shelves, were generally taken; none escaped but the very few who were covered by foreign protection, or who had made some particular interest with the enemy, and even those were sometimes plundered. The iron safes, possessed by most of the merchants in the country, unless they were emptied and purposely left open, as in some instances they were, were forcibly entered, and their contents taken or destroyed. Mr. Hine, of the Parish of St. Mary, had replenished his stock of goods; and, on the second advance of the enemy, he had, probably, a larger supply than had been in the possession of any one merchant in this district, since the close of the first year of the war. His store was sacked by a New York regiment, under the command of a Col. Love. This officer, however he may have illustrated the tenderness of his name, while engaged at home in his handicraft or other peaceful pursuit, sadly belied it here, as Mr. Hine testifies. Under his superintendence, this store was broken open, and those articles which could not be taken away, such as hardware, were thrown into the Teche, which ran nearby. After thus disposing of the contents of the building, his men attacked the iron safe which was very large and strong. Working faithfully eight hours without success, with a battering ram constructed with bars of iron lashed together, they were about ceasing their labors; but encouraged by the Colonel, who cried, "Go on, boys, don't give it up so!" they persevered and finally accomplished their object. Finding the contents to consist only of merchants' account books and papers, which though of the last importance to the owner, were of no possible value to them, they gratified their disappointment in the destruction of the fruits of years of unremitting industry. Not content with plundering and destroying his visible effects, they now annihilated the evidence of his credits, Turning his account books inside out, they trampled the leaves in the mud; and tearing asunder his bundles of valuable papers, they scattered them in the street; then, to crown their malevolence, they "besmeared," to use the words of Mr. Hine, "the house from top to bottom, and left it."

This account which we have from this gentleman, corroborated from other sources, well illustrates the Federal mode of proceeding with the merchant; with those of the learned professions, the proceedings were no less summary. We have witnessed this, in the torn and charred remains of libraries which are scattered broadcast in the villages; and in the broken and mutilated safes which once enclosed their important legal documents and papers, -for the lawyer's strongbox shared the same fate with that of the merchant. Major Anderson, a Representative in the State Legislature from the Parish of St. Landry, bad a valuable library which was consumed as fuel under the boilers of his engine, "set in operation" to grind meal, by the Forty First Massachusetts regiment.

In entering upon the subjects appropriated to this head, we are met at the threshold, by a mass of testimony, written and verbal, so voluminous and so alike in general character, that we find it difficult to make proper selections. It would appear from this testimony that the general license accorded to the Federal army, on entering the country, was restricted after passing the Vermillion. We may judge that this restriction had been necessary to prevent the entire dissolution of the bonds which bound the army together in a controllable mass; but, be this as it may, we find, as it approached St. Landry, that there was a prohibition against entering private dwellings, which was attempted to be enforced; while below dwellings were entered with impunity, and sacked under the eye of the officers.

As the Federal column advanced up the banks of the lower Atchafalaya and the Teche, its gunboats, which moved a little in advance, threw shells to the right and left, over houses and among the buildings of the plantations. The startled inmates, overwhelmed with terror, rushed wildly, taking with them nothing but the clothes on their persons, in search of places of shelter and protection. When the imminent danger was over, or after the column had passed, they returned to their homes to find themselves bereft of every article of luxury, of comfort and necessity.

We have before us a statement from the family of John M. Bateman, Esqr., an aged and wealthy planter, who lives on the lower Atchafalaya, nearest the Bay, the starting point of the Federal advance, which we shall use in this and other places, to illustrate the character of the Federal outrages. Admonished by a shell "which passed through the dining room and exploded in the yard beyond," this family abruptly filed from their dwelling. Returning the next day, they found a scene of desolation difficult to be described. "Fences were broken down; shrubbery broken and trampled under foot; corn husks, fodder, hay and broken glass, and table ware. were scattered over the yard: without all was disorder; within, all ruin. A company of Federals had occupied the residence, fed their horses around the house, from the provender of the place, while they had helped themselves from the garden, store-room, closet and dairy. Making the servants cook for them, they had feasted on all they could find to gratify their appetites. With their bayonets they had split open the panne's of a costly side-board, and broken into a closet, from which they had abstracted the liquors, preserves and jellies. Nor was feasting and drinking all the damage they had done. With bayonets and kicks, they had broken the glass in the windows, the large parlor mirror, the glass in the doors of the dining room safe, and the fine cut-glass table ware, with a beautiful set of china, imported from France before the war. They had carried off knives, spoons, kitchen utensils, table cloths, napkins, and dairy bowls, in fact, everything portable about the house."

Mr. Fortier, a highly respectable gentleman from the coast, with his family consisting of a wife and nine children, the youngest an infant, had taken refuge in St. Mary. He occupied a dwelling on a plantation between Franklin and Jeanerette. At this time, hearing the firing below, he, with his family, fled in consternation for safety and protection, to a neighboring plantation. In his absence many soldiers, including officers, from the advancing columns, fell out, and taking possession of the premises, they gathered in the servants of the plantation, whom, while administering to their pleasures, they incited to plunder. Then commenced a regular bacchanalian carouse. Drawing out the hoarded luxuries of the family, dashing open side-boards and closets, to come more readily at their contents, they drank wassail amid the clashes of glasses, which were thrown over their shoulders as fast as emptied, and with stentorian voices calling for more, they danced in mad glee among the fragments. While their wants were being supplied by servants, with whom to hear was to obey, they varied their entertainment with feats of dexterity against mirrors and such other objects as afford sport to the licentious. At length, in the fervor of excitement, an officer, it is said, mounted the table and commenced auctioning off the furniture and other objects, which could not be conveniently carried away. The servants, participating in the excitement, brought in their little hordes of silver, and an active bidding immediately ensued. Pianos, armoirs, side-boards, &c., were knocked off on the most liberal terms, amidst peals of wild laughter, and the low chuckle of the grinning negroes. These deluded victims thought, undoubtedly, that the world had turned upside down, and that, by a happy chance, they had come uppermost. The grossest African bought articles adapted to the most refined taste, and even the more discriminating loaded themselves with objects unsuited to their wants or condition. While this was going on, the more prudent of the soldiers, those who perhaps, in Massachusetts, had been early taught that the pleasures of the bowl were always subordinate to the "main chance," were making perquisitions for "the valuable products." Learning from the blacks, or conjecturing from the circumstances of the family, that plate and jewelry were concealed in the house, they penetrated into every supposed hiding place. They tore down the wainscot from floor to ceiling; and in the ardor of their search they hardly spared the roof. Whatever may have been their success here, it is certain they found in the house a large amount of "valuable product," which, with every other portable object they carried away. When this family returned, they found themselves suddenly bereft of every thing they had not a morsel of food, none of the luxuries or conveniences of life, not even a change of clothing for the infant, was left to them, in their destitution.

Mr. Eugene Olivier, living below New Iberia, was driven from his dwelling by the apprehensions which impelled so many to leave theirs. On the near approach of the gunboats, taking his child in his arms, and followed by his shrinking wife, he ran up on the banks of the bayou, trusting that no ball would be directed towards him as long as he remained with his family in view of the gunners. Presently he was halted by a soldier from the opposite bank, who, leveling his gun, cried: "I only want to shoot you, put down your child!" Mrs. Olivier, with the characteristic generosity of her sex in similar situations, flew to interpose her own person between her husband and the menacing gun. The gentleman, while holding off his wife with his disengaged arm, scornfully taunted the ruffian for his baseness [*lachete*]; the soldier, dropping his weapon, churlishly ordered him to go on. He did so, and at every step the wild sounds of revelry, proceeding from his dwelling, reached his ear. He could hear, blended with the sound of his piano, which sent forth notes such as could only be drawn from it by the heavy hand of a drunken dragoon, the sound of heavy tramping, and clanging scabbards, mingled with the rude laughter and ruder imprecations of the licentious soldiers, who were desecrating his household with their mad dance. He returned to his residence to find it entirely denuded. Furniture, beds and bedding, food and raiment, and cooking utensils had been alike appropriated or destroyed.

Mr. Hau, residing in St. Landry, not apprehending danger, had gone with his family to visit a daughter, who resided a day's journey from him. When he returned the Federal army had passed. Like the angel of death, it had rested but a moment to leave ruin in its track, From kitchen to parlor, from cellar to garret, all was empty; even the bucket had been taken from the well.

But if freer scope was given in houses untenanted, those whose inmates remained were, in many instances, violated with the same indecency.

The dwelling of Capt. F. O. Darby, situated above Franklin, was sacked in the presence of his family, by a regiment of Gen. Dwight's division, which was then acting under the command of one Captain Frederick. Ordering his men to shoot Capt. Darby, if he should attempt to resist, he proceeded with a deliberateness of design that discovered his instincts as well as his expertness. While some of his men secured the animals used for the purposes of luxury or convenience, others fell upon the carriages and carts, destroying such as could not be readily taken away, while others were employed in chasing the flocks and the poultry with which the premises were abundantly stocked. But the larger portion were engaged in more agreeable occupations. They brought out the wines and liquors from the well-filled cellar. The medicines they trampled under foot. They appropriated the silver plate, the bed and table linen, the articles of the toilet, and the entire family wardrobe, and destroyed all the furniture of the table and of the house. Captain Frederick then left the family standing on their bare floors.

The dwelling of Mr. Davisan Olivier was searched in his presence, though fortunately in the absence of the female members of his family, by the Second Rhode Island Cavalry. While a lusty dragoon thumped upon the piano, his fellows whirled around in the excited mazes of a dance, which was enlivened by the clank of scabbards against the floor or the furniture, by rowdy songs, obscene exclamations, and resounding whoops, which would have delighted a band of Sioux or Pottawatamies. Had this entertainment ended here, the proprietor of the house might have been compensated for his lacerated sensibilities by the safety of his effects; but when the war dance ended, the pillage commenced. A party, attacking an armoir with their sabres, were spared the hazard of breaking by Mr. Olivier, who promptly presented the key, and stood by to witness all his clothing and the contents of his pocket-book distributed among the licentious soldiers. Parties penetrating other rooms, soon came forth laden with the spoils of the parlor, the dining room, the bed chamber, the closets and other receptacles of household effects. Nothing, which could be carried away, was left behind-not even a supply of food for the evening meal.

On the Olivier estate, in the parish of St. Mary, resided a venerable lady, the head of that numerous and highly respectable family, the relict of a distinguished gentleman, who was the connecting link between an honorable ancestry and descendants noted for the qualities which enlighten the council-board and adorn the social circle. But neither age, nor worth, nor position, could protect her against insult. As the column of Gen. Banks trailed its slow length along, like the serpent which carries its venom within its coils, the dwelling of this venerable lady was filled with riotous soldiery, whose sounds of revelry might have been distinctly heard by the trailing masses as they passed along the road. Her dining room, and the various offices connected with her menage, were situated on the lower floor of the dwelling. This portion of the building was occupied all the day by a ribald rout, who, while they were reveling on the contents of the plentiful pantry, store-room and wine-cellar, called in the female servants of the plantation, whom they compelled to share in their debaucheries, to assist in the pillage, and to minister to their pleasures. The more refined maid servants of the house fled for protection to their mistresses, to whose private apartments they were pursued by intoxicated ruffians, who, with drawn sabres, and using indecent and opprobrious epithets, drove them forth. To the weeping ladies, whom they abused with ribald tongues, and whose tears they derided, one of them, with menacing gestures cried: "Dry up; we've seen enough of you Southern women's tears." The venerable lady of the mansion, thinking perhaps that her presence might inspire respect, had gone below, to exert her influence on the rout, to cause them to cease their orgies, and to spare at least something on which to subsist the family. Upon entering the dining room, she was accosted by an intoxicated soldier, who rushed towards her, thrusting to her lips a goblet of the lees of wine, brutally exclaiming: "Drink, you damned old rebel, drink to the Union!" The precipitate retreat of the lady was followed by jeers and taunts, and shouts of drunken laughter. She gained with effort the apartment to which her family had withdrawn, where overwhelmed with bitter tears, she sank exhausted in the arms of her despairing children. During the ensuing night these ladies were guarded by the feeble arm of a private soldier, whose conduct would be more particularly noticed except for the reason given in the sequel. The next day the soldiers, after having broken what they could not carry away, and destroyed what they could not consume, left the premises; and the family, on re-occupying them found only a disordered mass of broken fragments lying around.

The last instance we shall give of this species of outrage, occurred in the family of Major G. La C. Fusilier, who resides on the lower Teche, in the same Parish. Maj. Fusilier, the representative of one of the most distinguished creole families of Attakapas, was as noted for his munificent hospitality, as for the chivalric character which impelled him, at an advanced age, to encounter the hardships of the camp, and to brave the perils of the field. His lady, who united refinement of manners and dignified deportment, with the quality of an accomplished manager of a large domestic establishment, was left, like a chieftainess of old, to manage her numerous dependents and servants, while her husband stemmed the heady fight, or joined in the toilsome march. -One day a company of Federalists halted at the front gate, and from it a detachment rode to the door of the house. Hastily dismounting, some threw their reins to others who remained behind, and rushed in, as if to carry by assault a defended place. Meeting the lady in the hall, they passed her rudely, without remark or explanation, and immediately commenced ransacking the house. Without waiting for keys, or even demanding them, they violently broke open doors, armoirs, drawers, and whatever interposed an obstacle to their search, indulging in boisterous oaths and obscene language, and pillaging every article that could be conveniently bestowed about their persons. The terrified domestics, running through the house, were pursued, with indecent and menacing exclamations, which added to the general confusion. One of the party, perhaps touched by the distress of the mistress of the mansion, addressed her in French, suggesting that his party were unauthorized to search for arms in this manner, and that she should appeal to the Colonel, who was with the main body. The Colonel presently appeared in person. She represented to him her situation, and demanded the protection which is due to every lady. "Protect you!" he cried, rushing by her, the hilt of his sword catching in her dress and whirling her around; "Protect you, a rebel; never! -No protection to rebels !" The presence of the Colonel only increased the rudeness of his followers. They found, up stairs, some brandy, which rendered them still more boisterous. Some of the party, coming down, presented him a travelling bag, remarking, "Here, Colonel, is something that will suit you." It contained Major Fusilier's clothes, on perceiving which, the Colonel turned to the lady and said: "I shall pass here this evening, and I want this bag. If I don't find here, you'll see what'll happen." He then peremptorily ordered breakfast for his command, which, being provided by the servants, and eaten, the party rode off. Two hours after, the sergeant, who conducted the search in the morning, returned and demanded the travelling bag. -Madame Fusilier answered by informing him of the threat of his Colonel. "The Colonel has sent for it," he answered. "What is the name of your Colonel?" responded the lady. "That's none of your business," he replied. She then asked him for a receipt. He gruffly refused and snatched the bag from her hands. Going to the front of the house, he delivered it to one of his men on horseback, and went round the house to the rear, where he found the gardener, a Frenchman, advanced in years, and who could not speak the English language. Him he ordered to get a brand of fire to burn the house. The man, only understanding the menacing looks and gestures of the Sergeant, shrunk back, terrified. The Sergeant drew his pistol and felled him to the earth, and immediately jumping upon him commenced rifling his pockets. Having thus robbed the poor fellow of what money he had. he dragged him to the kitchen, put a fire brand in his hand, and hauled him back to the house. Meeting the lady in the hall, he exhibited to her the fire, which he ordered to be thrown upon the floor. -Then presenting his pistol to her breast, he demanded all the clothes she had hidden. While she was denying and expostulating, one of the men without called to him. He went out; and, after a brief consultation, the party hurriedly rode away. The fire, which was left kindling on the floor, was soon extinguished. The federalists, at this time, were in undisputed occupation of the country; and the only protection which could be sought was that of the Federal commander. -Madame Fusilier, finding, not only her dwelling, but her life in jeopardy, abandoned her home to the charge of faithful domestics, and sought this protection. While she remained in Franklin, then the Federal head-quarters, she lodged at the house of a friend, from whence, every day, she saw her carriage and horses driven, with insolent bravado, under window, conveying officers smoking cigars, and reclining in every attitude in the stolen equippage. And while these scenes were enacted under her eye, her elegant house in the country was occupied by federal officers, who outraged the sensibilities of the christian, and the obligations of common decency, by desecrating her private chapel, and breaking down the altar with all its appropriate decorations, and by breaking to pieces and burning, on her hearthstones, her splendid furniture; thus destroying the objects associated, in her mind, with the most pleasing and holiest recollections of her domestic life. She was compelled to remain in Franklin until the work of destruction had been completed. Not until then could she receive a "pass" to return. "Then," says she, "I found my house empty. The little furniture that had been saved, my servants had secreted in their cabins. My carpets had been cut to pieces, my curtains torn down and destroyed, and my furniture broken up and burned for fuel. The windows and doors were broken, and the hall, covered with litter, appeared as if it had been used for stabling horses. My cooking range, and cooking utensils even, had been broken or carried away." Furniture, it would appear, was found in many places a convenient substitute for firewood. The Rev. Mr. Rand, of Vermilionville, was arrested in the dead hour of night, on some frivolous pretext, and conducted to an officer, who was comfortably stretched before a fire, made of tables and chairs taken from a neighboring house.

We have already described the perquisition for concealed treasure, on the march; we shall have occasion, in another place, to refer to the robbery of the negroes. But we may observe here, that while the success of the latter was commensurate with the effort, that of the former was not inconsiderable. On the approach of the enemy, most of the families, with a well-grounded distrust, or a distinctive apprehension of the Union-savers, concealed or buried their valuable plate and ornaments. Sometimes by the treachery of the servants, and sometimes by accident, these treasures were discovered and seized: A lady in St. Mary had sent to a relation in St. Landry, her plate and jewelry, of no inconsiderable value; and the relation, not venturing to keep what he could not protect, buried it, with his own, in a remote place, and, as he thought, with great secrecy; it was found, disinterred, and carried away. In trenching a garden near Opelousas with the bayonet, not an unusual proceeding, a lucky soldier threw up a thousand or more dollars in gold and silver, which amply rewarded him for his virtuous labors. In an island of woods near the same town, after diligent search a valuable deposit of gold and silver, and jewelry, was brought to light and appropriated by the robbers. Plundering was universal; and, as the impunity offered to the soldiers was not sufficient, suitable auxilaries were employed to make it more thorough. -The arts used to obtain treasure, were such as have been employed by the unprincipled in every age; delusive promises, violent seizure, terror, the cord, and the baton. At Mr. Joseph Frere's, in St. Mary, the proceeding was a *l'aimable*. A party of officers, leaving their command at the gate for the appearance of the premises promised higher game than was suited to the common herd-entered the house. Meeting Mr. Frere in the hall, after complimenting him on the general appearance of his mansion and the surrounding property, they suggested in the mildest manner, the possibility of its being protected; indeed, if properly remunerated, they had no doubt they could afford all the protection necessary. Mr. Frere was not in funds. Had he not some articles of value -a watch for instance? One of the party was immediately made happy in the possession of the gentleman's watch. Another thought such an appendage would gratify him; and another watch was produced. -The others, charmed with the appearance of their fellows, with their newly acquired property, would each like a watch. Fortunately, among the ladies of the family, a sufficient number were found to gratify those whose wants were the most pressing. But they were not restricted in their fancies. They had sweethearts and wives. Chains, broaches, bracelets, diamond and even plain rings, it was insinuated, would be acceptable. In fact, on reflection, they had pressing need of those articles, and would be obliged to take them. The ladies of the family, in consternation at the increasing demands, which now assured them that personal violence would follow refusal, divested themselves of their ornaments, and handed them over to these gentleman of the Federal army. But as they could not appear in ornaments only suitable for ladies, at the entertainments given by the Commander-in-Chief and other officers, in the confiscated houses in New Orleans, they thought it desirable to have some which would be more appropriate and better adapted to the dignity of their rank. One of them gently insinuated his fingers into the bosom of Mr. Frere's shirt, and extracted a diamond stud. No further ceremony was now necessary, and no more was attempted. Proceeding directly to the business in hand, they broke open the gentleman's armoirs, bureaux, and other receptacles, and abstracted such articles of clothing and taste as suited their fancy. They were particularly gratified in finding several dozen fine Parisian shirts, which, with the other little articles of *bijoutrie* they had picked up, no doubt made them objects of envy, at the promenade concerts of the ensuing winter, in the metropolis.

In other instances, they disregarded the *suaviter in modo*, and resorted to the most summary means. At Mr. John D. Hudspeth's, in St. Landry, they placed a negro on guard over the person of the venerable proprietor, while they conducted the search. They found some money. But the supply not corresponding with their expectations, they were indecent in their abuse, and gratified their disappointment by appropriating all Mr. Hudspeth's wearing apparel.

At Mr. Boudreau's in Lafayette, they robbed the gentleman, who was infirm and confined to his bed, of every thing in the house and on the premises, taking even the covering on which the invalid was lying.

At Mr. Delhomme's, in St. Martin, the lady of the house had recently died; they pillaged the effects of the dead. The servants of the family begged them, with tears in their eyes, to leave them some memorial of their old mistress, but they were inexorable. vino oil)

On Petite-Anse Island, they entered the house of Mr. Hayes, then in the ninetieth year of his age, and forcing from him the key of his iron safe, they opened and robbed it of all the papers it contained. -Fortunately his money had been taken from it the evening before. -Passing from this, they opened all his trunks, and abstracted their contents of clothing and other articles; then, robbing the beds of their covering, they departed, after bestowing on the aged man a volley of abusive epithets.

At Mr. Antoine Goulas', in St. Mary, they not only stripped the family of all their wearing apparel, even the infant's clothing and all the bedding, but they presented their pistols to Mrs. Goulas' head, threatening to shoot her if she did not reveal the hiding place of her money. Afterwards another squad came along, and leveling their guns on Mr. Goulas, demanded his money.

At Mr. Sandoz's, near St. Martinsville, while plundering the plantation, they assaulted Mr. Sandoz, and tore his watch from his pocket. They afterwards came in the night, and first arresting the gentleman in the house, demanded his money. On being answered that he had none, they told him they would search, and if any was found they would shoot him. The tone and manner of the menace assured him that it was no idle threat; but he answered, "You may search, and I will abide the consequences." They dug under the floor of a basement room, but met with no success. While they were thus engaged the lady of the house came in; and they immediately placed their cocked pistols to her head, demanding that she should discover to them the place where her husband's money was buried. She stood the ordeal as firmly as her husband, and the ruffians were foiled.

At Mr. Kemper's, in Cypres-mort, after robbing the house of every object of value, they took from the persons of the ladies their breastpins and rings.

At Mr. Alexander Vilmeau's, in Fausse Pointe, they not only robbed him of a large sum of money, but plundered him of everything he possessed. While the party were pillaging the house he heard his wife loudly crying for help. Running to her assistance, he found several ruffians scuffling with her; one had wrenched a ring from her finger, after biting it so severely that she suffered many weeks from the effects; another had snatched her ear-pendants, tearing away the end of one ear. While attempting to rescue her, Mr. Vilmeau was shot at twice, and grazed by the bullets. On leaving the premises the ruffians fired several shots from the gate, at the house, among the family, but the balls not taking effect, they were spared from further harm.

At Mr. Dasincourt Borel's, near New Iberia, they pillaged his house, taking from it every article, his own and his children's wearing apparel, all his blankets and bed-covering, leaving him completely stripped; and, on going away, they took his only horse. Mr. Borel went to Gen. Banks, who was then on the Olivier Estate, and applied for his horse. "It is the only means of support I have left me," said he, "and if I do not get it, I cannot support my family. My children will starve." Gen. Banks replied: "The horse is no more your property than the rest. Louisiana is mine. I intend to take everything." "But I have a right to be protected," answered Borel, "I have taken the oath." "When you shoulder your musket," retorted the General, "you may receive further protection." The poor man went back sorrowing to his destitute children. He had accumulated the little sum of five hundred dollars in specie, which he had hidden; it was all he had left.- He may probably have made this remark, for the news soon reached the Federal camp. A day or two after the interview with Gen. Banks, an officer rode up to his door and commenced a sympathizing conversation with him. He expressed great regret for the loss Mr. Borel had sustained, and great indignation at the perpetrators of the outrage. Taking his departure, he rode down the lane, and meeting a negro, began to question him about Borel's money. "If you can find out where it is hidden," said he, "I'll manage the business and share with you." The negro promised, but immediately informed Borel. That night, four men came to his house at a late hour, and arrested him, as they said, to take him to the Provost Marshal at New Iberia. Getting him to the bottom of the lane, a pistol was put to his head, and he was told that if he did not at once reveal where he had hidden his five hundred dollars, he would be instantly shot. "I know," said Borel, "you are capable of everything. You have taken the last morsel from my children's mouths. You would kill me as remorselessly. Let us go back; you shall have the money." They went back; and Borel delivered to them his last dollar-his last means of supporting his children.

At Mr. Cesair Deblanc's, on the Bayou Petite Anse, they found the proprietor and his wife, an aged couple whose grey hairs should have commanded respect, if their feeble condition had not inspired pity. They had money; and in the pursuit of such spoil, the Federal soldiers neither regarded age, nor condition, nor infirmity, nor any of the obligations which bind man to man in civilized society. A large party surrounded the house; and employing every means that ingenuity could devise to inspire terror, drew from the aged couple their hoarded wealth. But in the conflict, the venerable lady succumbed. By her anxious and sorrow-stricken servants she was carried to the bed, from which she never arose.

At Mr. David Berwick's, on the Bayou Salée, the residence of another gentleman far stricken in years, the representative of the family which gives its name to Berwick's Bay, occurred another scene, which, if it was not so fatal in its consequences, exceeded the one just mentioned, in atrocity of design. This gentleman was aroused at a late hour in the night, by the noise of crushing blows upon his door, which brought him, hastily appareled to answer the rude summons. He was met by a party of cavalry from the adjacent camp, whose horses were held in the yard. They demanded his money-used threats to extort it-and then resorted to more potent weapons. A pistol presented to his breast was knocked down, when in the act of being fired. Another, raised over his head to strike, was turned aside by one who suggested a better expedient. Going to his horse, he returned with a lariat, which he skilfully tied in a noose, as he traversed the yard. The noose was at once, and without further parley, put over Mr. Berwick's head, the end of the rope drawn around a column of the gallery, and then pulled tight. In a moment it was loosened, and the demand reiterated. While the old gentleman was recovering his faculties, and before he could answer, the rope was again drawn tight-this time bringing him to the verge of suffocation. The ingenuity that was exercised in guaging the extent of suffocation, as well as in applying the means, betrayed a practiced hand; the success which followed was no doubt as nicely calculated from the effects observed on previous experiments. They drew from their victim about six thousand dollars, and then left him both tortured in body, and a prey to serious apprehensions. That night the road was full of inebriated troopers riding furiously, and robbing every one by the way. Though they did not again attack Mr. Berwick, the fear of such an event impelled him to abandon his house, and take refuge in an out-building. Before morning, an officer penetrated his hiding place, who said he was seeking his men; but, from the attendant circumstances, was doubtless an accessory seeking his principals in crime.

Mr. Narcisse Thibodeau, at Brough's bridge, near four-score years of age, was taken from his house by Federal soldiers accompanied by negroes, and beaten with sticks, until he confessed where his treasures were hidden. They took from him many thousand dollars in gold; but not satisfied with this, or incited by their unusual success, they pursued their robberies from house to house. Some citizens, gathering courage from the magnitude of the danger, united in pursuit of the marauders. They found them at Grande Pointe, in the act of laying violent hands on an aged lady-Mrs. Guidry, to compel her to disgorge her money. Arresting them here, they returned, and on their way home were themselves robbed of their prisoners, and the money they had recovered, by a body of Federal troops they met on the road.

But it is unnecessary to multiply these sickening details. Nothing was too little, nothing too great, nothing too sacred, to stay the Federal hand. While robbing the rich and the provident, it pillaged the poor, cutting, as we have seen, from their looms, the cloth woven by their hands. But its rapacity was not satiated upon the living; it fell even upon the dead. The men who brutally invaded the domestic sanctuary, did not scruple to desecrate the ashes of the departed. At Brashear city reposed the remains of the late Dr. Brashear, long distinguished in the councils of his adopted State, the cherished associate of great men, the friend and countryman of Henry Clay. The sacrilegious invaders, with the instincts of the hyena, ravished his tomb, and appropriated to their own use, and carried off, enclosing their own dead, the metallic coffin which had contained his mortal remains.

Gen. Bank's policy embraced the use of auxiliaries, when the harvest was not too great for his own reapers, as was exemplified at Opelousas. On the western confines of St. Landry and Lafayette, where the extended prairies are fringed by the pine forests, there are but few cultivated fields. The occasional huts of the herdsmen only, as in the wilds of Australia, for many miles are here sparsely scattered around. For more than half a century, this country has also been the refuge of the idle and the depraved, who have avoided the haunts of civilization, to enjoy in solitude the pursuits which society rejects. Subsisting upon the cattle belonging to more industrious proprietors, they have never wished to enjoy the fruits of their own industry. So long as their depredations were confined to the herds on the prairies, but few were interested in suppressing them. Some attempts it is true, had been made; but the difficulty of detection and the consequent immunity from punishment, seemed only to confirm them in their incorrigible habits. With the same instincts that lead the vultures to gather around the carcass, these men flocked to Gen. Banks at Opelousas. They were armed at once, and sent ostensibly to gather in the stock; but, seeming intuitively to apprehend the full design of the Federal commander, they commenced plundering the houses of the citizens, who repaired to head quarters in crowds to enter their complaints. In the temporary absence of Gen. Banks on a visit to New Orleans, Gen. Emory was then in command of the army. With the promptness of a soldier trained to the duties of his profession, he undertook to remedy the evil. He arrested the marauders within reach, and issued the following proclamation:

HEAD QUARTERS UNITED STATES FORCES,
Opelousas, April 27, 1863.

It having come to the knowledge of the General temporarily in command of the United States Forces, that unauthorized persons are temporarily banded together, and committing plunder and outrage on the peaceful inhabitants of this country, it is hereby ordered and declared to be without the authority of the United States, and all the United States troops are commanded to shoot down at sight, and disperse, all such bands of robbers and thieves.

(Signed)   WM. H. EMORY,

By the General Com'd'g.,   Brig. Gen. Com'd'g,

(Signed)   RICH'D B. IRWIN, A. A. G.

Gen. Banks on his return from New Orleans, disavowed the order, and annulled it, by reinstating the robbers, furnishing them again with arms and ammunition, and sending them forth to plunder and destroy. The creatures, as cowardly as they were depraved, hesitated in the performance of their task. Halting on the outskirts of the village, they sent back for succor; and the 41st Massachusetts regiment was mounted, and sent out to guard them against the outraged citizens. Thus was Inaugurated and organized that band of "jayhawkers" who have since become such a pest to the country. In the very midst of the depredations of these armed marauders, and the daily accumulating spoils plundered by his own orders from unoffending citizens, Gen. Banks, with characteristic duplicity, issued a proclamation reflecting upon plunderers, and inhibiting conduct derogatory to the honor (!) of his army.

The town of St Martinsville is situated on the right bank of the Téche, which, at its narrow point, is but a stone's throw from hank to bank. Its streets intersect at right angles, those fronting the stream running to the water's edge perpendicularly. For some time after the Federal army had fallen back to New Iberia, this town occupied, in the bend of the bayou, a neutral territory between the Confederate and Federal lines. The pickets of either party sometimes entered the town, as, by tacit consent, the neutrality of the position was recognized. The citizens, unmolested, pursued their ordinary avocations; and on the Sabbath, gathered, as usual, at the church. According to the customs of the Catholic towns of Europe, which they inherited from their ancestors, after church services they met in groups upon the streets to indulge in friendly conversation, or to interchange social civilities. On one of these occasions, a bright, joyous Sunday morning had invited unusual numbers to the open air of the streets. In the midst of their friendly greetings, they observed a Federal regiment filing up on the opposite bank, which, being no unusual occurrence, attracted but little attention. The column advancing, covered the principal streets; when, suddenly facing to the front, it enfiladed them with volleys of musketry. The scene which ensued baffles description. An instinctive impulse directed the feet of every one to the nearest shelter. Families thus became separated, and soon the shrieks of mothers, the cries of children, the frantic exclamations of husbands and fathers, all a prey to the most agonizing apprehensions, rent the air. After the volleys ceased, the streets were filled with men, women and children, seeking their lost loved ones. Fortunately, with one exception, all were found. As if more strikingly to indicate the peculiar victims of Federal persecution, the bullets of the regiment took effect only upon a man of hoary head and tottering step, while he was receiving the kindly greetings of a passing friend.

Col. Robison, who commanded this regiment, bearing the name of Louisiana, unblushingly avowed the act, and declared that he would repeat it every time his regiment passed the rebel town. The inhabitants sent an express to General Green, then the nearest Confederate commander. He immediately sent notice, under a flag of truce, to the General commanding at New Iberia, that if the act was repeated, he would retaliate on the prisoners he held. The act was not repeated; but the conduct of the Colonel passed without censure.

In the early days of the French Revolution, when, in the fervor of new ideas the altars of God were thrown down, and the reason of man enthroned, the churches of France were devoted to base uses, but the sacrilege has justly received the reprobation of mankind; and among nations, whether Christian or Infidel, that recognize the supremacy of an overruling God, the edifices consecrated to His service are universally respected. An exception was found in the Federal army. The Catholic church at Opelousas, after having its enclosures torn down and destroyed, was saved from further desecration by the Irish Catholics in the enemy's ranks, who rose in mutiny against the sacrilege; while the Protestants of that army permitted, without murmur or protest, the desecrating hand of Massachusetts to make of the Protestant Episcopal Church a den of infamy. They stole the sacred vessels from the Catholic Church at New Iberia, and danced in the robes of the priest who served at its altar. They struck with the flats of their sabres, and kicked the venerable priest who ministered at the altar of the Church of St. Martinsville, while his fingers were yet moist from the sacred symbols of the body and blood of Christ; and they violently took away the humble conveyance which carried him to the bedsides of his parishioners, to administer the consolations of religion. They ravished from the Methodist Church at Franklin the chairs, the pews, the chancel, the lamps and the chandelier, to furnish a theater in a billiard saloon, where ribald farces might be represented. But further, they shocked the sensibilities of the human race, which lead even the savage to approach with awe the graves of the dead. They broke down and burned for fuel the enclosure around the cemetery at Opelousas; they used the materials of the tombs and monuments at New Iberia for chimneys and hearthstones; they picketed their horses among the graves, and spread their forage upon the tombs in the cemetery at Franklin. In the vain search of treasure, they threw out the freshly buried or mouldering remains of the dead. They ransacked family vaults under the eye of the family, breaking and shattering the coffins they enclosed; and so often were these revolting scenes enacted, that some citizens, brought, as a last refuge, the bones of their ancestors under the sheltering roof of their dwellings.

In the parish of Lafayette resided Basil C. Crow, Esq., who, in former years, was distinguished as one of the prominent men of Opelousas and Attakapas. Bred to the bar, he was engaged, in the vigor of manhood, in the active practice of his profession; but as his sons and daughters grew up, he retired to his estate on the banks of the Vermilion, and devoted the energies of a robust age to the cares of a large domestic establishment, and to settling them around him. One by one they had left the paternal roof, until, either on neighboring estates, or in the adjacent village, they had separate establishments. with a new generation of children growing up around them. Understanding, on the approach of the enemy, that the line of the Vermilion would be defended, which would expose their dwellings to the fire of the opposing forces, these families, with loaded wagons and carriages, hurriedly started for a place eight miles distant, to await the result of the anticipated conflict. Learning, presently, that the Confederate forces had retreated without giving battle, and that the Federalists had crossed the Vermilion, they set about returning to reoccupy their homes. Approaching the village of Vermilionville, they were met by a New York regiment that had come out in line of battle to meet them. Advancing at a charge, its wings speedily enveloped the train, and the soldiers, as exultant as if they had captured an opposing force, fired guns over the carriages, and subjected the inmates to their coarse jests and ridicule. Leading the train in triumph to the village, they sent the ladies and children to their empty dwellings, without permitting them to retain either food, raiment or bedding; and confining the gentlemen in jail, they ordered the carriages and wagons containing the personal and household effects to Opelousas, twenty-five miles above. The gentlemen were soon sent after, to report, under the charge of an officer, to the "Military Governor," then engaged in "collecting" at Opelousas. While these families were at home, suffering in the deprivation of the most necessary articles, they were kept here many days. At length, through the intercession of an officer, a written order was obtained to release them. As they were leaving the "Governor's" office, he stopped them. "By the by," said he, "there is some silver plate among those things; this must be confiscated. Come back here tomorrow morning at 10 o'clock;" and he turned aside to other business. The gentlemen left, with the written order in possession, which they were not slow to render available. Before ten o'clock the next morning they with their effects, including the silver plate, worth several thousand dollars, were beyond the jurisdiction of the Military Governor, and out of the reach of his collectors.

While the Federal army was passing by the Cote Gelée, in the disarray we have described, some soldiers in the rear of a division, in quarreling over their spoils, killed one of their number, and leaving the body by the wayside, rejoined their command. As the next division passed the body was discovered, and the officer in command sent to the nearest house and caused to be arrested its only inmate, a man well stricken in years, and who did not understand the language of his captors. Without investigation, enquiry or ceremony, he was dragged to the corpse and made to kneel before it. A firing party was drawn up in front, and as the word was about being given to fire, it was arrested by the arrival of a burying party from the division in advance, who had been sent to inter the body. The old man, thus rescued from the jaws of death, was released and with menacing gestures ordered back to his home.

As the army marched up the Bayou Boeuf, a Capt. Dwight, following in the rear, was shot from the opposite bank of the bayou by some Confederate scouts. Under the circumstances, as they have been related to us, the act was according to the usages of war. But whether it was or not, it was done by soldiers of the regular army acting in their line of duty; and this fact was made apparent to the Federal general commanding. Yet, notwithstanding, to retaliate he caused to be arrested the next day all the male citizens dwelling on the bayou over a line of forty miles. Sixteen, from St. Landry, grandfathers, fathers and sons, from early youth to four-score, respectable citizens, accustomed to the comforts and luxuries of life, were forced along twenty-eight miles of road, and guarded at night in an open enclosure on a dung heap. The next morning, part of the way on foot, part of the way in open wagons without seats, they were carried back forty miles, to Washington. On the way, none were permitted to stop at their homes, to bid farewell, or explain their position to their families; and but one was released, Mr. Jesse Andrus, aged eighty years, the head of a numerous and respectable family, after being dragged on foot over fifteen miles, hauled in a wagon forty, and confined and guarded as above stated, all within the space of thirty hours, was permitted to return home. The others were taken the next day to Opelousas and confined four days in the common jail, from which felons had just been loosed upon the community. They were then brought out, formed in line, and marched between lines of soldiers to Port Barré; from thence they were shipped to Brashear City, and on the passage had only the cotton bales with which the boat was laden to sleep upon. At Brashear they were placed on the railroad, in a box car without seats, which had last carried stone coal, and were thus transported to Algiers. Here they were imprisoned in a deserted iron foundry for three weeks and then sent across the river to New Orleans. Here they remained confined two months, after which the survivors were released to make their way. home as well as they could. The trials of the march had brought Mr. James Hicks, an old man, to the verge of the grave, and he remained in the hospital during the time the others were confined. Two died in prison: Mr. Hiram G. Roberts, aged 46 years, and Mr. Solomon Link, aged fifty. It is a simple story. We have read before of a similar fate befalling a party of men-they were shipwrecked mariners thrown upon a barbarous coast.

When Gen. Burbridge was repulsed in an action at the Bayou Bourbeux, in the parish of St. Landry, and thrown back to New Iberia, he, by the common impulse of ignoble souls, retaliated his shameful disaster on the defenceless citizens of that place. He compelled the entire male population, old and young, at the point of the bayonet, to work fifteen days on his line of ditches, and he arrested and held under guard young and delicate ladies, who had preferred not to walk under his disgraced brigade flag.

Before the first invasion of Gen. Banks, a raid was made on the Rentrop estate, on the lower Atchafalaya, by a portion of the 21st Indiana regiment, under the command of Col. McMillan. The command was brought up by the gunboat Estrella. The men on landing committed the customary depredations, conducted in the usual licentious manner. Mr. Rentrop was then lying very ill, and his wife, leaving the bedside of her husband, sought the officer in command and implored him with pathetic eloquence to do his untimely work as quietly as possible, as she felt assured that the least excitement would prove injurious,. if not fatal to the invalid. Her supplications were treated with contempt. The depredations went on with increased boisterousness. The men fired their guns among the poultry and flocks, under the window of the dying man. They even entered his room, and taunted and jeered him at the very portals of death. After continuing this inhuman conduct all the day, at night-fall they departed. Before the morning dawned the suffering invalid, overcome by the excitement, had breathed his last. The next morning the Estrella brought back the depredators of the preceding day. The family were gathered around the corpse of the husband and father. Their mournful wailing issued from every opening of the dwelling; but disregarding these sounds of grief, the soldiers with rude and boisterous mirth rioted on the luxuries of the orange groves and indulged in unrestrained license on the premises. In the very midst of these discordant sounds of affliction and ill-timed mirth, Lieut. Harwick entered the house, arrested the two sons of the deceased while kneeling before the body of their murdered father, and dragged them away amidst the shrieks of their sisters and the heart-broken groans of their agonized mother. The boat returned again the next day, and the men, landing, renewed the boisterous scenes of the previous days. Nor was this all: persecuted in the body, his bones were not permitted to remain quiet in the tomb. They were disturbed by other robbers from the same army, and as they were not permitted to rest in peace in the home allotted to the dead, the family were compelled to bring them back to the home of the living. The two boys who were so rudely arrested while weeping over their father's remains-one a mere youth, and the other discharged for disability from the army-were not soldiers then: they are soldiers now.

But the indulgence of private animosities was undoubtedly a prolific source of arbitratry arrests. The Federal army was followed by vicious and lawless men of the country, who had not the principles to attach them to any government. As like bodies gravitate towards each other, they have been drawn to the Federal ranks, and with the zeal of converts and the malignity of their kind they directed the Federal hand against every citizen whose prominence excited their apprehension, or who had been instrumental in restraining their vicious conduct.

The house of Dr. Francis Mudd, a practicing physician of Vermilionville, was surrounded one evening by Federal soldiers, under Capt. Martin, who conducted the affair with a method which could only have been acquired by experience. The doctor was quietly sitting, conversing with his wife, on the gallery, when the officer approached and announced that he was his prisoner. Startled at the summary proceeding, he enquired the reasons, or what might be the charges against him; but the officer could only show the order of arrest, which came from Gen. Washburne, and which was couched with that military brevity not calculated to assure the mind. The gentleman begged to be permitted to remain at home that night, as his wife would be alone, and the next morning, after making proper provision for her protection and comfort, he would report in person at the general's headquarters. The officer had no discretion; he could only wait to examine his papers, and for this purpose he demanded his keys. The search being fruitlessly made, the doctor was conducted to headquarters, some two miles from his residence. There he found several other citizens, who had just been dragged from their families without any assigned cause. Not being permitted to see the general, they were given what was said to be six days rations, which consisted of hard crackers and black tea, and were confined and strictly guarded in a neighboring cooper's shop, which was open and exposed to the inclemency of the weather. Here, among deserters, criminals of the army and negroes, besides suffering from the discomforts of their situation and the nauseous filth of their fellow prisoners, they were subject constantly to the vulgar abuse of the guard, and of those whom curiosity attracted to the place. They applied to Capt. Gorsuch, the Provost Marshal, for the charges on which they were thus ignominiously confined. He replied that he knew of no charges; he was simply acting under orders. They could get no satisfaction here or elsewhere; but at length after thirteen days confinement, another order, signed by a Major Morgan, an officer of Washburne's staff, came for their release. When Dr. Mudd returned to his house he found, what others similarly situated had found, that his substance had been made way with or destroyed.

One morning, while St. Martinsville was occupying the neutral position we have described, a body of about four hundred Federal soldiers, with two pieces of artillery, drove in the Confederate pickets above that town, and proceeded to the residence of Mr. Olivier Duclosel, which was not far distant. After forcing off all his negroes, who had been proof against the seductions of the Federal missionaries, and stripping the premises of everything, not excepting the clothing of the family, they took Madam Duclosel, who was sixty years of age and afflicted with aneurism, and forcing her to kneel among them, they gratified their fiendish rage in abusive and indecent epithets, and disregarding the blood that flowed profusely from her dilated arteries, they rocked her backward and forward, pushed her to the right and left, and threw her down and raised her up, until exhausted nature could bear no more, and she sank in a swoon. Then arresting and carrying away her husband, her son and her daughter, they left her prostrate on the floor. Some two hours after, this aged lady recovered to find herself alone, surrounded by a scene of desolation. Her first impulse was to fly to seek her family, but her physical energies being overcome by exhaustion, she fell prostrate in the yard, where she was afterwards found insensible by one of her grand-children. Her husband, Mr. Duclosel, was aged, gouty and obese. He had not been known for years to walk a hundred paces at a time; yet his inhuman persecutors pushed him on foot, at the point of the bayonet, over a mile of muddy road to St.

Martinsville, where in mockery of his sufferings they made him stand the remainder of the day in one of the streets.

Recently a raid was made in that part of St. Landry which stretches along the upper Atchafalaya, by a body of Federal troops from Morganza. A party of soldiers from this body, conducted by a *soi-disant* Union man who had been driven from the country for his crimes, went at midnight to the house of Mr. John Lyons, once well known as a popular and skillful commander of steamboats on the inland waters of this district, then a respectable planter, and calling him out from his bed, cruelly murdered him on the threshold of his own door.

The citizens of every town and neighborhood were subject to arrest, confinement and release, under the Yankee system of *lettres-de-cachet*; but many prisoners were dragged to New Orleans, and languished in prison or on parole for months without any assignable cause.

On the first advance of the enemy, the Hon. Alexander Mouton, ex-Governor of Louisiana, while quietly occupying a private station, was taken from his home. sent to New Orleans, kept six months, and then released as abruptly as he was arrested. Many others were sent there at the same time, and languished for months in close confinement. Subsequently a large number of prisoners fell into the hands of Gen. Taylor, on the Lafourche and at the Bay, and a correspondence under a flag of trace ensued between the Confederate and Federal commanders in reference to them, or on the general subject of the exchange and treatment of prisoners. In this correspondence there were expressions used by the Federal commander which led Gen. Taylor to infer that he had entirely changed his policy, and that no more non-combattants would be arrested by him. Assuming this to be the future Federal policy here, he advised those gentlemen who were preparing to fly from their homes to escape Federal persecution to remain in the quiet pursuit of their ordinary avocations, and one of the undersigned commissioners, who was not then in the military service, and also a sufferer from ill health, acted upon the advice. He was arrested and sent to New Orleans. On his way thither he met, in an unfurnished guard house without even a bench for the weary, several citizens of Lafayette, who had been arrested by Gen. Ord, at the instigation of a Union man, a worthless fellow, who had been under the ban of the law for crimes not political. Your commissioner took occasion to inform Gen. Ord that these men had been in the militia, and at the time they were proceeding as charged they were acting under his orders, and that he alone was responsible for the act, not to any Federal authority, but to. the Governor of the State. They were however sent down, and one of them at least, perhaps more, died in prison in New Orleans. At this time there was no parish in the district but had its representatives, (arrested under similar circumstances) in the prisons of that city-indeed they were full of them.

Soon after, a correspondent of the New York Herald was made prisoner at Bourbeux, and the pressing instances of the proprietors of that journal induced Gen. Banks to make an effort for his release. He accordingly enclosed the Herald's correspondence and wrote himself to Gen. Franklin, from whose headquarters flags passed between the belligerents. Gen. Banks did not venture to sully his character before his enemies, by preferring a request for this person's release, in the terms of his commander's letter; he simply forwarded it with the accompanying correspondence, to have all the weight to which it was entitled. One of us has read this letter, characteristic of the writer. In it Gen. Banks comments on the impropriety of *making prisoners of non-combatants*, and concludes with the assertion that he always scrupulously avoided such practices! On the receipt of this extraordinary communication, and without requiring the usual parole, Gen. Taylor sent the Herald correspondent, with such other non-combatant prisoners as he held in possession, to the enemy's lines, and demanded at the same time the return of our prisoners held in New Orleans. It having come to the knowledge of your commissioner, then a prisoner, that these persons had arrived in the city, he, fully under the impression that they could not have been released without provision made for the release of non-combatants in Federal hands, wrote lac note to Gen. Banks, which, while it assumed a compact between the belligerents, demanded his immediate release. The reply of Gen. Banks, through his chief of staff, denied the compact, but ended by saying "that Gen. Banks had concluded to permit you [him] to return home on giving a parole not to do any act hostile to the government of the United States until released from the effect of the parole by some officer of the United States Government." Considering that if there was no obligation to release, the manner of imprisonment only would be changed; and if there was that the parole would have no binding effect, either in conscience or in fact, he accepted the conditions, and was immediately sent out of the Federal lines. Messrs, Voorhies, O'Brian, Broussard, and perhaps others, were not released until nearly eight months after. These facts require no comment, and we pass to another subject.

In a country abounding with shady groves overshadowing a smooth sod the Federal commanders selected for their headquarter encampments the smiling parterres, or the verdant lawns, tastefully embellished, and spreading out in front of the private dwellings. Female modesty was often shocked at the indelicate exhibitions of camp life immediately in view of their private apartments. Half-dressed officers and their indecent menials did not hesitate in language and manner to violate all the proprieties due to the inmates of the domestic circle. If their conduct only offended delicacy of offered inconvenience, it might have been tolerated, as in consideration of greater calamities it might have passed only with a partial notice. But like other Federal this carried with it material destruction, b discomfort, and starvation and death. We have, in our note bodily book, many instances where opulent families, surrounded by luxuriant fields and gardens, with enclosures filled with poultry, flocks and fatted oxen, with magazines bursting with stores of provision for man and beast, were subjected in a day to extreme destitution, and who were compelled to subsist for many days on the corn snatched from under the feet of the horses, or on the scanty provision surreptitiously taken by faithful servants from the luxurious tables of the officers.

A banquet was one day provided, in the dining room of Madame Olivier, for Gen. Banks and his staff, who feasted on the lower story, waited on by the servants of the estate, while the ladies above were suffering for the necessaries of life; and after the banquet was over, as if in mockery, the field negroes were called in to consume what remained.

Mrs. McKerral, with her three daughters, without any male protector, was residing on her plantation near Franklin. Her premises were occupied for a camp; the rooms of her dwelling were taken for quarters; and she, with her three daughters, after her servants had been forced away, was confined to the occupancy of three rooms. She had secured some poultry in an upper room of the house; every fowl was taken; her provisions were consumed; and she saw from her window, not only the last outbuilding on her place destroyed, but her last milch cow shot in the yard. Surrounded by a noisy, vulgar, profane crowd, she suffered there, for the camp was removed she found that even the family all the tortures of shocked delicacy, apprehension and want. When carriage had been maliciously taken to pieces, and the necessary parts either thrown away or destroyed.

Gen. Burbridge occupied the enclosures around the residence of the Hon. John Moore, in New Iberia, and flaunted his brigade flag over the entrance gate. He was not satisfied with occupying the kitchen and all the out-buildings, thus depriving the family of the conveniences of the household, but he took possession of the lower rooms of the dwelling. Mrs. Moore, a lady far advanced in years, belonging to a family distinguished in the annals of the nation, accustomed, not only to the conveniences, but the elegancies of life, was driven, with the ladies of her family, to the upper apartments, where she was subjected to every privation. Gen. Franklin, with his military family, arriving shortly afterwards, fell into possession of the quarters. His presence, however, did not ameliorate the condition of the family; on the contrary, his continued occupation daily increased its privations. No relief was obtained none offered. Gen. Franklin says, none was asked. Mrs. Moore succumbed in the midst of these manifold privations. She died-died, imprisoned in her own dwelling, deprived of the comforts she would have bestowed upon the humblest of her servants; and, as at the Rentrops, Federal persecution followed her to the grave; her tomb was desecrated to furnish brick for Federal hearths.

We desire to do justice to Gen. Franklin. Though an enemy, his character and former associations entitle him to consideration. We have reason to believe that he fell into these quarters, as he would have fallen into them had they occupied any other place, without enquiry, and without being aware of the distress his occupancy caused; and we think his sin was rather one of omission than of commission.

Not so of another officer of the old U. S. Army. When Gen. Weitzel's division encamped on the Rentrop estate, his camp extended to the enclosures of the dwelling. Mrs. Rentrop, the afflicted lady of the mansion whose sufferings on another occasion we have noticed, being alone with five other ladies of the family solicited the General to occupy one of the rooms, or at least to encamp near, as a protection against the rude intrusion of his soldiers. He not only refused this reasonable request, but he pitched his tent at the lower extremity of his camp, as it, and as the ladies believe, to give a freer scope to the licentiousness of his followers. We have before us a communication from a member of this family, which would make a chapter of itself- a chapter of inconceivable atrocity. Omitting many details, we give the substance in the language of the lady who relates them: "As he must have expected, and as he no doubt wished, the men immediately commenced depredations. They broke into the sugar house, and helped themselves to all the sugar they could devour or carry away; they drank all the water of the cistern; they shot down all the work oxen, and killed the hogs in the pen; and they tore up the fences and burned them in their camp fires. Mrs. R. went to Gen. Weitzel and begged for a guard. He sent her two men to guard the house; but it was all a sham. One said he would not use his gun to prevent what his words would not. Some chickens had been saved, to be used only for the sick: these were hastily secured in a room of the dwelling. While Mrs. R. was absent, her daughter and another young lady guarded the door; unconscious of danger they felt no fear, until vile oaths and obscene language met their ears. Crowds had approached, and it would have been evident, to less suspecting ears that evil was intended. -Ere the vile purpose was carried into effect, an officer came with orders to search the house for rebel uniforms. This officer dispersed the mob, reached the house, and was satisfied the report was false. -But before the usual time for retiring another came, followed by a half dozen of the most ragged and dirty which hang around an army. They proceeded from room to room, peeping into this and into that, evidently to see what the house contained. After passing a sleepless night, at early dawn, Mrs. Rentrop again returned to Gen. Weitzel to beg for a more efficient guard. Soon the black-smith's shop was discovered to be in flames, and soldiers prowling about said that this was to be the fate of every building on the rebel place. The plantation bell which had long been unused, now pealed forth a summons long and loud. One would have supposed this to be a signal that help was needed to extinguish the fire. This, how-ever, was not intended. The building burned to the ground without an effort to extinguish the flames. It was a signal of another kind-to assemble a mob!- Soldiers collected in crowds around the house. The ladies becoming alarmed, closed and fastened every opening of the dwelling. Those alone who have seen a mob collecting, can form an idea of what they witnessed, as they stood tremulously gazing through the window blinds. Some rushing into the kitchen; others into the store room, breaking, destroying, or carrying away, whatever they could lay their hands on; while hundreds surrounded the house, yelling, cursing, swearing, and making most fearful threats, as they tried to open the doors, climbed up outside, or crept underneath the floors. The ladies within knew not what to do. Trembling in every limb, they walked from room to room, or paused to beg aid of the only source of help, the God of Heaven! The mob broke open the door of the room in which were the chickens. They cursed, swore, and squabbled for them; this scene might have been ludicrous to the ladies at any other time, but now they were filled with horror at seeing themselves in the power of beings so utterly depraved. They had hastily secured the door between the robbers and themselves, and were now in momentary dread of that being broken. Mrs. Rentrop's sister, being in terror as to the probable fate of her daughter and nieces, determined to risk herself to save them. She bravely passed out at the front door, which was quickly closed by the frightened inmates, and walked through these crowds unmolested. They were startled by the sudden appearance of a lady in their midst, and momentarily awed by her dignified manner. She hurried down the road until she met an officer on horseback. She begged him to fly to the rescue of the innocent females shut up in the house. He listened to her earnest appeal, and God obliged him to grant it. He rode on with his company and dispersed the mob. Seeing the flames bursting forth, between the wing and main building, he cried, 'Your house is on fire.' Yet he made no effort to extinguish it-he did not even order the soldiers to bring water from the bayou for that purpose. Fortunately the day previous the ladies, finding that all the water of the cisterns was going, had filled all the pitchers, buckets and tubs in the house; and now with their own hands they brought it out and extinguished the fire."

After the family were thus saved, Mrs. Rentrop returned with a guard. Her daughter 1an out to meet her. "O mother!" she exclaimed out of breath, "what a dreadful time we have had! What would my dear brothers say, if they knew what we have endured this day? Could they have seen that ruffian with raised club, curse me and call me a vile name, and swear he would knock my head off, if I came out with the water, would they not feel that they had rather die in the cause of independence, than to be united with such a vile race as this?" While this work was going on-while the fire-bell was sounding the alarm, Mrs. Rentrop, a lady delicately reared, of education and manners belonging to an elevated station in society, was compelled to dance attendance before Gen. Weitzel's tent. He did not deign to see her, as she expresses it, "until he had eaten two breakfasts" -until, in fact, complete time had been given for the contemplated destruction of the dwelling sheltering these feeble and unprotected women.

But we find this officer again, on the Tarlton estate. He here followed the more usual custom. His camp was pitched within the enclosures, and under the windows of the dwelling; his officers and men occupied the out-buildings, where they committed the ordinary depredations and excesses; and he, personally, as the evidence discloses, by his coarse manners and language, and by his indecent behavior, drove the ladies of the family to their most secluded apartments. Generally intoxicated, he exhibited himself openly and shamelessly in fond dalliance with negro servant girls. His staff imitated their chief in vulgarity of speech and behavior. Finally his camp broke up; when he rode out of the yard calling out, "Come on boys, there are other rich plantations here to sack!"

There were instances of protection being offered by officers high in command; but the policy of the Commanding General prevailed over them, if they were sincere in their offers or their efforts.

Gen. Lee requested permission to take apartments in the dwelling occupied by Mrs. Smedes, on her plantation near New Iberia; and as an inducement to her compliance with his request, he suggested that his presence would be a protection to her property. She very gladly acceded to it, and the gentleman and another officer established themselves very comfortably. But presently, the lady found herself deprived of the use of her servants; that her provisions were gone; and that her gardens, orchards and fields were being wasted, her fences burned, her plantation buildings destroyed, and the building attached to her residence consumed. She saw at last the fire put to her cornfields; and she indignantly asked the General if this was the promised protection. He recoiled in shame, and humbly confessed his inability to protect her.

But the instances were rare where inhabited dwellings were occupied in this manner; whenever caprice or convenience suggested a want, no motive of delicacy restrained the Federal hand. The country was full of deserted houses from which families had fled; yet inhabited dwellings were remorselessly taken for purposes which exposed the inmates, not merely to inconvenience or deprivation, but sometimes to disease and death.

The residence of Mr. Ledoux, situated in the country, near St. Martinsville, was, in opposition to his earnest remonstrances, taken for a Federal hospital. His family were reluctantly permitted to occupy one room in their own dwelling-the room of his wife-the room in which she had been confined for many years by ill health, and in which she was then lying, too low to be removed without endangering her life.

As the enemy advanced through the country he devastated and tortured; as he retreated he used the torch. The lower waters of the Teche and Atchafalaya, while the Federalists have occupied Berwick's Bay, have been open to their gunboats; and under their protection advances have been undertaken, and sudden retreats made; without leaving some evidence of their presence, in chimney stacks arising out of the charred ruins of costly edifices. These still stand, marking the places where once stood the elegant and hospitable mansions of the Rhodes', the Bateman's, the Stirling's, the Wilcoxon's, the Fusilier's, the Carpenter's, the Corney's, the Perkins', the Bethel's, the Smith's, the Harding's, the Burns', and others. And but for a happy accident, a quick discovery, and an active effort, the site of Franklin, the thriving commercial town of the Teche, would have been thus marked. As the pressed rear of Chickering's column fled through the town, his soldiers fired the warehouses on the wharf; but the sharp crack of Fournet's rifles ringing in their ears. paralyzed their arms; and their work, bunglingly executed, was soon discovered by the citizens, who subdued the rising flames.

But the hand of the destroyer fell no less heavily than that of the incendiary: wherever directed by caprice, convenience or wantonness, wherever the materials could serve a temporary purpose, or offer a momentary gratification, it fell upon the most costly and valuable edifices.

On the wooded banks of the Vermilion, whose waters are shaded by timber trees, which, when felled, would stretch across them, the sugar house of Mr. Crow was pulled down, and the materials transported half a mile, to construct a bridge across the bayou. The destruction of this building for that purpose, not only involved its loss to the owner, but the loss of many thousand dollars worth of seed cotton, left in the open air to waste and decay. The neighboring dwelling house of Major Sosthene Mouton, after being partly torn down to provide tent floors, was wantonly burned to the ground; and other buildings in the neighborhood were, in the same manner, destroyed. The wood work of Governor Mouton's sugar house, even the lintels over the doors, were torn out, and consumed, with the materials of his corn cribs and barns, at the enemy's watch-fires on the banks of the Vermilion, and in the midst of its forest trees. In fact, on all the farms and estates where the enemy encamped, though transportation was abundant and forests near, the most valuable buildings and other costly material were consumed for fire-wood. On the Olivier estate, not only the barns and a large sugar house were torn down and used in this manner, but a large cotton gin, which contained in seed cotton what might now be considered a fortune, was torn to pieces and its contents thrown into the bayou, while the valuable machinery of the other buildings followed the same destination. On the Brashear side of Berwick's Bay, many citizens have been driven away by the continued presence of the enemy; and those who remain, though accepting his protection, under the correlative obligation of obedience to his laws, are subject to every species of persecution. In the winter of 1863-4, all the unoccupied buildings here, were torn down and consumed for fuel. Even the house of a poor widow, on the Young estate, was torn down over the heads of herself and her children; and she with them was driven to one roof-less room, with a part of its gable down. In this miserable abode she and her children were left to shiver over a meagre fire of faggots.- Mrs. Martha Collins, another poor sufferer, shared the same fate.- Robbed of everything she possessed, and her house burned down by the Federal soldiers, she and a large family of children were reduced to want, and turned adrift without food, raiment or shelter.

The Koran of the Mohammedan enjoins that. in warfare, the cattle and the harvest of the husbandman be spared, except in so far as they may be used to supply absolute wants; the Divine law of the Christian requires that the evils of war be mitigated, by sparing peaceful men and feeble women and children; but the men of the "higher law," in the Federal army, will be found to illustrate a code of morals peculiar to themselves.

General Bank's auxiliary robbers, assisted by the forty-first Massachusetts regiment, swept the prairies around Opelousas, bringing in every animal that could be driven-the milch-cow that yielded her daily supply of nourishment-the gentle ox that received his food from his master's hand-the horse for the family- the light horses of the herds-man; the hack-horses of the plantation-the ponies that carried the children to school-the Devons, the Durhams and Ayreshires, from the cultivated pastures-the Meriuos, the Cotswells, and the South-downs, from the fleecy flocks, and every animal adapted to the sustenance or service of man. They were penned in and around the village, and as no care was bestowed upon them many died there and on the road as they were driven away. They were drawn out as they were required, and 80 many were slaughtered, that not only a superfluity of beef remained in the camps, but it was thrown out to all comers without stint. Horses were distributed so freely, that every camp-follower was provided.- Had these animals been required for the use of the Federal army, the inhabitants might still have justly complained of the manner in which they were taken, and consumed; but, on the contrary, few in comparison to the number taken, were consumed or used by it. Thousands were driven off as booty, and sold at prices such as only the robber can afford to receive for his plunder. Such were the number of animals thrown upon the Lafourche and the city of New Orleans, that they became comparatively valueless. From Opelousas to the Bay, wherever this army encamped, or wherever it left a detachment, a squad, or a courier station, animals, far exceeding the number required, were daily slaughtered, and parts of the carcasses with the offal, were left upon the ground to fester and poison the air. At a courier station below Opelousas, where there were five soldiers, they slaughtered for themselves each day, a beef, a sheep, or a hog, and the parts left to decay poisoned the air of a populous neighborhood. During the time that a division encamped near Mr. Elise Thibodeaux', on the Vermil-ion, cattle were driven up by hundreds and butchered before his door; and so recklessly were they shot down that the bullets used penetrated his dwelling. He was an old man-he could not speak the language of his enemies; and therefore, he could not remonstrate-he could only suffer. While cutting up the carcasses, they warmed their feet at fires kindled with his wife's handcards, and fed with his plough beams and her loom. The atmosphere around was infected by the stench of offal and putrified carcasses; and as soon as the division moved away, his neighbors gathered to bury the festering remains. While engaged in this work, they counted one thousand seven hundred cattle heads, lying around, in every stage of decay.

Stragglers over the prairies would kill calves for their tongues; and foraging parties, too, destroyed animals in mere wantonness. A large party were foraging on the Kemper plantation, in the Cypres-mort.- The depredations of the soldiers reached the dwelling, and threatened to invade it. Mrs. Kemper ran out to find the officer in command to obtain, if possible, a guard for her house; but she was turned back before reaching him, by the shocking and sickening sight that met her eye. She made three efforts, but she says her heart sickened and her brain reeled--she could not go forward. The sight of slaughtered cows and hogs, of rude soldiers breaking the backs of calves with billets of wood, and tossing sheep and pigs upon their bayonets, was too revolting. The Federal army also killed colts following their dams, in order to get rid of them; and numbers of these carcasses were found after the evacuation of the country.

The fields, the gardens, the orchards, the fruit, and even the shade trees, were destroyed as ruthlessly, as wastefully, and as wantonly, as the animals. The gardens were rooted up and their fences consumed for fuel; the orchards were broken down, limb by limb; and we have seen pecan trees, the growth of several generations, under which the children of many succeeding families had played, cut down to facilitate the gathering of their fruit. We have seen, too, the pride of the mansion, the venerable live oak, with its evergreen foliage and its extending branches, covering a space where a regiment might find shelter from the scorching rays of the sun, and which had perhaps sheltered the Chiefs, in council, of the Attakapas and the Opelousas, at the time Columbus was answering the doubts of the learned men of Cordova, burned at the roots, and its branches hacked away to make fuel for camp-fires.

They would have destroyed, as previously stated, the sources of the supply of salt, with the same wantonness. They tried their feeble hands upon it, but failed; for God had planted it there, as He had the alluvion of Attakapas, in masses too great to be destroyed, or rendered sterile; and their hands were as impotent to destroy it, as they would have been to exhaust the granite rocks of New England.

To destroy the limited store of medicines hoarded by families, and purchased at incredible expense by druggists, cost but little labor; and their destruction was pursued with as much ardor and vigor, as if they had been magazines of defence. They appropriated and destroyed them, wherever found-in the household, or in the shop. They were made a particular object of search, and when found were thrown into the dirt, if not appropriated. The 114th New York regiment, under Lieut. Col. Purlee, forced open the drug store of Mr. Duchamp, at St. Martinsville, and carried away or destroyed all the medicines, the lancets, and other instruments useful to the surgeon or the physician. It was necessary for the druggists to conceal their stores to save them. In opposition to the usages of the civilized world, have medicines been made contraband of war, and destroyed as are instruments of warfare. For the first time in history, do we find a civilized people making war upon hospitals, old men, and helpless women and children, and glorying in it. But the other day, the report of the Federal general, who made a successful raid into an interior town, boasted, not of the guns and cartridges, the cannon and bombs, he had captured, but of the large quantity of quinine, and other medicines, he had destroyed or brought away.

Dr. E. Millard, an experienced and distinguished physician of St. Landry, assures us that, of those who fall sick, particularly the aged and the children, a larger per centage die now, for want of the proper medicines, than before the war, when they were easily obtained. Let our enemies receive all the satisfaction this assurance will give them. The war they make against the feeble, is more successful than that they wage against the strong.

While the means of sustaining and preserving health were being thus destroyed, the same fell spirit directed the destruction of the means of repairing the consummated waste. In pursuing our investigation, we have seen on different plantations piles of the remains of aratory instruments, plows, harrows, cultivators, shovels, hoes; of coopers', carpenters', and blacksmiths' tools; of iron axles, hub boxes, tires, and other iron work of plantation carts, the wood work consumed by fire, and the iron parts bent or broken. We have seen the remains of the corn mills, that had been violently hurled down, the stones broken, the spindles wrenched out, and the gearing broken in pieces. And we have seen the most valuable machinery for grinding cane and manufacturing sugar, that had been broken, and essential parts had been destroyed, carried away, or thrown into the neighboring bayou. The wantonness and completeness of destruction on the Têche, may be no better illustrated than in the memorandum of one planter, Mr. Nelson, which is attached to a protest intended for public record. On this plantation, twelve miles of fence around the place, enough cypress boards for two more miles of fence, the fences around the house, the orchard and the vegetable garden, the gutters around the building leading to two large cisterns, a valuable floating plantation bridge across the Téche, two hundred and fifty sugar hogsheads, two hundred and fifty molasses barrels, and dressed staves and heading for two hundred more hogsheads, were consumed for fuel at the Federal camp-fires. They also tore down for fire-wood the mill-house, two barns, and nine other out-buildings. They took all the corn, fodder and hay on the plantation, leaving none for either the white family or the negroes. They tore up and destroyed the plantation tan-yard; unshipped and destroyed valuable portions of a fine steam engine; tore down the corn mill, and destroyed the running gear; and they cut to pieces, burned or broke the plows, cane carts, harness, axes, hoes, cane knives, and blacksmith's, carpenter's, cooper's and tanner's tools, belonging to the plantation.

But this destroying spirit, like the pestilence, spared neither rich nor poor it fell on all alike on the small farmers of the prairies, as on their more opulent neighbors of the bayous. The quiet and unostentatious manners of these inhabitants, their frugal and industrious habits, and their unaggressive disposition, which they derive, as they do their language, from their ancestors, the persecuted refugees from their northern Acadia-should have secured for them at least, immunity from the ravages of war; but, on the contrary, it only seemed to invite the aggression of the Federal soldiers. They fell upon them with the virulence which animates ignoble minds against the weak, the defenceless, and those whose language cannot offer the poor shield of expostulation, and deprived them, as we have before stated, of even their food and clothing.

It would be supposed that the most refined malignity could go no farther; but God, as if to show the deep depravity of man, when released from the restraint of His law, has permitted this army to sound the depth of human corruption. From the evidence before us, they spread abroad among the citizens a virus, as sure in its effects as the handful of ashes thrown out by Moses before Pharaoh, which brought boils upon the people of Egypt, though its consequences were more terrific. This followed the course of the blood, attacked the finger nails, the toe nails, the joints, the bones, and threw out upon the surface of the body the foulest ulcers.

This charge is so grave, even against those who have proved themselves, as we have seen, so utterly depraved, that we would hesitate to give it place here, were it not supported by such respectable and concurrent testimony.

When the enemy was encamped at New Iberia, the small-pox broke out in virulent form among the troops; and as they were constantly making excursions into the country for foraging and other purposes, the inhabitants of the farms, plantations, and neighboring villages were exposed to taking the disease. They became seriously alarmed; there was no vaccine matter in the country, and their position precluded the possibility of obtaining it outside of the Federal lines. Their physicians, of necessity, sent to the Federal surgeons for it; and they were supplied with a virus which was used upon infants, children, feeble women and strong men with the same results: its results spread with the rapidity of fire. Had this been in some isolated cases, or had the same effect followed among the soldiers who were vaccinated, we might charitably conclude that the result in the country was from an accidental cause. But while no complaint came from the soldiers, at least no general complaint, the country was filled with cases of this kind, the cause not coming from one source, but from many, and all from the same fountain head-the Federal camp. Dr. Sabatier, a physician of extensive practice at St. Martinsville, says: "In December, 1863, when the small-pox broke out among the Federal troops, then occupying New Iberia, it was impossible in our vicinity to procure the smallest portion of vaccine matter. Exposed as we were to the contagion of the disease, by the constant raids made by the Federalists in our town, I used my best exertions to procure some vaccine from the Federal physicians in New Iberia, and through one of my *confreres* succeeded in getting a few points loaded with vaccine, which I immediately inoculated to my own children. The disastrous effects of the poison were as quick as fire. A few days after the operation, one of my poor little baby's arms was hor-ribly swollen and inflamed, and on the second day appeared a pustule which had nothing of the appearance of vaccine. Three days after, the pustule opened, letting out a little quantity of greenish matter, and to that succeeded a terrible ulcer, which kept growing larger and larger, until it came to the size of a dollar. New pustules formed around the ulcer, and followed the same course. I cannot describe the sufferings of the poor little thing. The disease lasted more than six months; the child lost all its finger and toe nails. The lymphatic glands of the neck and groin formed abscesses which had to be opened, and it was only after a regular course of mercurial treatment that I succeeded in curing the poor child. *The description of this case is nothing to be compared with* HUNDREDS OF OTHERS *whom I have been called upon to treat.*"

We leave this horrid recital to speak for itself, and trust. for the sake of humanity, that few such instances are to be recorded.

A captive, it is said, was brought before an Asiatic prince: the scimetar was already raised over his head, when oppressed by intoler-able thirst he begged for water. A cup was handed him: he held it as if apprehensive lest the scimetar would fall while he was in the act of drinking. "Take courage," said the prince; "your life will be spared till you have drunk this water." He instantly dashed the cup and water to the ground. The good faith of the barbarian saved him. The word had passed: it was enough; and the captive went on his way rejoicing. But we would not try the Federal invaders by so severe a test; for their total disregard of all the obligations of faith and covenant would shame even the king of Dahomey.

The few old men and unprotected women who remained in the lower part of this district, were invited by the Federal authorities to accept their protection; and their peculiar situation, exposed as they were to continuous attacks, both on their persons and property, made it in many instances imperative for them to do so. Their fate as citizens was not to be decided by their own actions, but by the event of the war; and they might perhaps with propriety assume an obligation, which in its nature could be but temporary; and they might, with equal propriety, (as indeed they could scarcely do otherwise,) pursue the even path of peaceful citizens, while receiving the protection of the governing power. The Federalists required, for the protection rightly due to peaceful citizens, the oath of allegiance to their government, as if they were to remain in permanent possession, and exercise its functions. The obligation of this oath could only bind the parties taking it, to obedience to the rules and regulations established by this government; and so long as they did not violate them, they were entitled to the protection extended to every citizen. We do not remember to have read of any State that thought it necessary or proper to penetrate the recesses of the mind, to ascertain if obedience proceeded from affection, or from other motives which may control the individual. Obedience to the law, we believe, has been considered sufficient. It was probably many years after this territory was ceded by France, before the affections of the inhabitants adhered to the government; yet there never was a people more obedient to the law, or who performed the duties of citizens in a more exemplary manner. But the rule of practice and the code of morals of the Federalist, is sui generis. He invites, nay, he forces people to assume the obligations of citizenship, then derides their motives, and refuses the correlative obligation of protection to which he has doubly bound himself, by receiving the one and promising the other.

We have already seen how poor Borel (who had taken the oath of allegiance) fared when he applied to Gen. Banks for his last horse-his last means of support: others fared no better. Indeed, but few received any protection for their property; and those who did, it is thought used more potent influences than personal service or allegiance.

A provost guard, under a Capt. Ellis of the 174th New York, was stationed at Madame Olivier's. He took possession of the magazines, corn-cribs, and other out-buildings, and besides prohibiting the negroes of the place from serving the family in any manner, he incited them by his speeches to insurrectionary proceedings against them. They were denied access to their own corn and meal, after having been deprived before of all the provisions (an ample store) which their house contained. Madame Olivier was insultingly told that she owned nothing; that if she wished for meal, she must buy it of the servants, or if they chose, they might give it to her. She had no recourse but in the protection of the Federal authorities. She sought and received the promised protection; but the proceedings of Capt. Ellis continued as before. The only subsistence she could get for herself and family was covertly obtained and brought to her by some domestics who had remained faithful. Aged and feeble, she was compelled to ride twenty-three miles to general headquarters to seek redress. There her representations and remonstrances were unheeded; and she was sneeringly told to apply to the nearest post-to the officer of which she had already complained, and against whom she had such just cause of complaint.

Madame Fusilier had packed up her clothing, silver plate and jewelry in boxes, and sent them away to the house of a friend. They were discovered, seized and carried off in the quartermaster wagons. This lady was subsequently compelled to seek Federal protection: it was promised. She made application for her boxes. On investigation it was found that the box containing the jewelry was missing, though it was on the list held by the quartermaster. The silver plate was valuable, and, like the plate of the Crow family, had to be looked into. She was put off from time to time by evasive answers, but still led to believe that it would be returned. At length she pressed the matter to a conclusion, and was then, for the first time, coolly informed that her husband and her sons being in the Confederate army, *her plate* was confiscated by the orders of the War Department. Paul Jones returned the Earl of Selkirk's, though he had to force it from his soldiers who claimed it as legitimate booty.

Mr. Bateman, whose house was sacked as we have related, had, through his numerous relatives and friends, refurnished his house and collected new supplies of provisions and a little necessary farm stock. The feeble old gentleman, who had reached the advanced age of three score years and ten, had taken the required oath to receive the Federal protection. Though he had pursued the course of a peaceful, quiet and unoffending citizen, his plantation was frequently despoiled by marauders, and at length all his substance was taken away by regularly organized bodies of Federal troops. A detachment from the 18th New York cavalry and some negro troops, under the command of a Colonel Jones, made a raid up the Atchafalaya, protected by two gunboats. They halted at Mr. Bateman's, and the gunboat No. 49, commanded by Capt. Leonard, landed to receive the plunder from the plantation. Mr. Bateman entreated the officers in command to spare him! He exhibited his papers and claimed protection under them; but neither the entreaty nor covenant availed him, nor did his position or his age protect him against their coarse abuse. They both reviled and despoiled him. All his provisions were taken from his store-rooms; the few barrels of mo-lasses he had saved were rolled aboard the boat; his poultry, hogs and vegetables were taken off, and his house was thoroughly eviscerated from garret to cellar. In the former sack, the upper rooms, to which the ladies had withdrawn, escaped; but on this occasion the work was perfect. They prized open the drawers, armoirs and trunks and emptied their contents into sacks, made by ripping open the beds and throwing out their feathers, hair or moss. They destroyed, or carried away, the family portraits and miniatures, private letters, the toys of the children, and every memorial and heir-loom consecrated in the affections of the family. And then, to crown the villainy, they put fire to the large and costly sugar house and burned it to the ground. These evidences of broken faith and covenant are recorded as examples of hundreds of others; but we are yet to present its most striking exhibition, in the treatment of the black race, who became the easy victims of their professed friends and liberators.

The story of the degradation of the barracoons of the Slave Coast, and the horrors of the middle passage, has been told in history and recited in song, everywhere exciting the sympathies of mankind; but it has been reserved for the peculiar friends of the African race to reproduce, in an enlightened age, aggravated scenes of horror parallel to those so eloquently commemorated by the historian and the poet. The public documents of the enemy, characterized by the same disingenuousness that marks his conduct, invariably convey the impression that the negro seeking freedom under his protection is only received from a sense of duty to relieve his suffering condition. The truthful narrator of the exodus of the negroes from these parishes will exhibit in burning characters the falsity of the impression thus sought to be conveyed.

On its march the Federal army, through its emissaries, who penetrated every negro quarter, proclaimed the freedom of the slave. While it occupied the country, its officers and men were spread in every direction, engaged in inciting the slaves to licentiousness and disobedience, and in spreading artfully devised tales designed to excite their imagination and impress them with the desire of leaving their comfortable homes, in quest of the new El Dorado depicted by their friends. Intimately associating with the blacks, and stimulating them to appropriate such of their master's property as gratified their cupidity, these emissaries succeeded only so far as to divert them from their usual pursuits, or to induce them to appropriate articles of trifling value on the plantations. And it is not less remarkable that insurrection and revolt-the object of these machinations of the enemy-evaporated in occasional disrespect to accustomed authority, or harmless displays of vanity resulting from imagined ideas of equality. The tales circulated for the ear of this credulous and somewhat imaginative people were as fascinating as those of the Arabian Nights. The social condition was to be inverted; the slave was to be served by his master, and to occupy his place and condition; he was to enjoy an uninterrupted exemption from labor; fine equipages were to await his bidding, and he was to enjoy his ease in the quiet mansion of the planter, or in the confiscated dwellings of the City, with their rich furniture and their splendid decorations. The faith in such extravagant promises might simply provoke a smile at the credulity of those to whom they were addressed, did not the criminal motives of their propagators excite a sentiment of disgust and abhorrence. The efforts of the enemy might have resulted in driving into his arms the entire slave population, had not his emissaries been as diligently engaged in plundering as in emancipating the poor objects of their solicitude; for the fact is notorious that on all the plantations the negro women were robbed by the soldiers of their trinkets and the men of their little savings of money. Distrusting those who preached so well and practiced so badly, few of the slaves at first left their homes, but at length, attracted by curiosity and by the desire to follow those who had preceded them, others followed, until the depots under the jurisdiction of the provost marshals on the Teche, at Vermilionville and at Opelousas became swollen by the influx. To understand properly the subject of which we are now treating, it will be necessary to describe the inner life of one of those depots, and we select for that purpose the slave barracoon at Opelousas.

Near the centre of the town is an open square, on three sides of which are private dwellings with wide galleries looking upon the front, and on the fourth, warehouses and stores partially unoccupied. From the centre of this square rises the Protestant Episcopal Church, which had but recently been dedicated according to the solemn and imposing rites of the church. It was so placed that at some future day it might be surrounded by luxuriant shade trees on either side of pleasant avenues, where the citizen might enjoy his exemption from toil, and the christian might find a retreat for religious meditation. Little did its builders imagine that the words of our Savior to the moneychangers of the temple would so soon meet with an application here: "My house is the house of prayer; but ye have made it a den of thieves." This square and church were set apart as a slave depot by the Federal commander. At first the blacks were invited to visit the barracoon, were feasted at the expense of their friends, and were permitted to and come as they saw proper. The place soon became popular. The handsome reception with which they were greeted, the free affable manners of the gentlemen of the army, the generous liquors and the tempting food so liberally distributed, the exciting declamation of black and white exhorters within the church, soon collected a dense sable crowd upon the square who found themselves finally under guard, and prohibited from all egress. The poor negro had been told by his white friends that he was free; he had just heard the same fact proclaimed from the pulpit; he had enjoyed the freedom his instincts led him to seek, in the festivities around him, and in the unrestrained indulgence of his appetites; but when his inclination naturally led him to return home, he was met with crossed bayonets and forbidden to leave the place. An inexorable fatality seemed to hold him within the bounds of his prison. One man, more bold than his fellows, rushed past the guard, and was mercilessly shot. This immediately put an end to all attempts at escape, though it did not prevent some from making their way out by eluding the vigilance of the guard. In the meantime, however, many new comers, men, women and children, were drawn into the vortex, until the church, the square and the adjoining warehouses were filled to overflowing. The accomplished officer who presided over the scenes daily enacted in this barracoon was the "Military Governor of Opelousas," Col. Chickering, of the 41st Massachusetts regiment, who occupied the most conspicuous residence, fronting the entrance of the church. From his eligible position he had, as from the royal box at the opera, the most comprehensive view of the scenes passing beneath. Morning and evening, as he promenaded his spacious gallery, in all the glitter of military button and strap, he passed in review the living panorama before him, which was to furnish such valuable acquisitions to the confiscated plantations on the Lafourche and the coast. The scenes which he so complacently surveyed will long live in the memory of the then inhabitants of the town. In one place groups of human beings, with melancholy faces, were crouched on the earth around some decaying embers; in another, men, women and children were moving in some African dance to the discordant chant of a hundred voices; in another, crowds were reclining in listless idleness on the ground, in every attitude that betrays the vacant mind; in another, half clad men and women were feasting and rioting amidst peals and shouts of unearthly merriment; in another, awkward field hands, grotesquely dressed, were being taken through the exercises of squad drill and the manual of arms, while in the midst of all these scenes blue-coated officers and men were seen in amorous dalliance with the colored Aspasias of the town, exhibiting, in their degradation, a contempt for the commonest decencies of life. Nor was the spectacle less humiliating in the church. From its sacred chancel a half crazy negro, with the voice of a Stentor and the fire of Peter the Hermit, declaimed in a barbaric jargon to an auditory whose appreciation was manifested in wild shouts and screams. The declamation of the preacher, in which the name of God was connected with ideas of heathen superstition, seemed to light up in the minds of his hearers the dormant spark of African barbarism which had smouldered for generations.

Col. Thomas Chickering

These degrading exhibitions, which caused the abashed and shocked families of the neighborhood to seek refuge in the inmost recesses of their houses continued, until the removal of the Depot to Port Barre, on the 10th of May, put an end to the scene. At the latter place, in utter disregard of the considerations of humanity, to say nothing of decency and propriety, the miserable wretches taken from Opelousas were promiscuously huddled together in a hollow square, formed by parking wagons and carts around; and here, without any protection from the then scorching rays of the sun, or the weather, they remained until relieved, to unite with the retreating army.

As Gen. Banks fell back from Alexandria, to cross the Mississippi, his emissaries were sent below in hot haste to spread an alarm in the cabins of the negroes. It came to the ear of the poor negro "like the alarm of a fire-bell in the night." "Haste! haste!" was the cry, "Haste, the Rebels are coming. They are slaying the slaves as they advance. Fly! fly!" Agitated by contending emotions, the attachment of home at length

smothered under a vague fear of impending calamity, the poor creatures fell upon everything within their reach, which could convey them
away. Vehicles of every description were hastily packed with household goods and human beings. The aged, the infirm, and the children,
thus provided for, the more robust mounted in the greatest disorder
on males and horses, and precipitately joined the Federal ranks.

Col. Chickering, in the mean time, had arranged his retreat, with the
view of sweeping both banks of the Teche. The 114th New York regiment, under Lieut. Col. Purlee, which had just arrived in Opelousas,
was directed to encamp on a plantation below, owned by a gentleman
then in the military service of the State, and after "cleaning it out," (we
use the elegant language of Col. Chickering,) to proceed by the right
bank of the Teche to St. Martinsville, while the other column would
take the left. His preparations were accelerated by the news of the rapid
advance of the Confederate Cavalry from the direction of Texas, under
Gen. Mouton.

From Port Barre, eight miles from Opelousas, near the upper Teche,
commenced, on the 21st of May 1863, the memorable Hegira, which
will always occupy a conspicuous place in the annals of Opelousas and
Attakapas.

As the fugitives of Damascus, threatened by the "Sword of God,"
"gathered in haste and terror their most precious movables, and abandoned with loud lamentations or silent anguish, their native homes,
and the pleasant banks of the Pharphar;" so the poor negroes, the
victims of a perfidy of which the fierce Saracen would have been in-
capable, abandoned their homes, in wild disorder, and deep despair
of threatened calamity. The flight down the Teche, from its inception
to its termination at Berwick's Bay, a distance of a hundred miles,
was marked by visible evidence of disorder and despair, in abandoned
children and infants by the wayside, thrown from their mother's arms
to perish, or to find some stranger hand to bestow a mother's care. In a
private carriage, taken from a lady living near Opelousas, Col. Chickering led the flight, and directed its movements. A few miles below Port
Barre, Col. Purlee, by a detour which led him through the village of

Grand Coteau and the adjoining plantations, reached the Teche. On the way he had admirably fulfilled his mission, by effectually cleaning out," at the point of the bayonet, the obnoxious plantation; for he brought with him every living thing, and every movable attached to it; and as twenty of the negroes subsequently died under Federal treatment, his success was complete. On his route, many negroes, influenced by the alarm already spreading, fell into the current and swelled its mass, so as to make no mean addition to the flowing stream of humanity in which it was disgorged.

Above St. Martinsville, situated in a Parish which the Federal President had excepted from the effects of his Emancipation Proclamation, is the large estate of a gentleman, descended from ancestors who settled in Louisiana under the Spanish government, and distinguished for the fine abilities and social qualities which adorned the high honors to which he has been elevated in this State. In the alarming crisis which followed the election of Mr. Lincoln, he reluctantly withdrew from an honorable retirement, to represent his fellow-citizens in the Convention, which was to decide the destinies of the State. Vindictive malevolence could not pass near such a person without inflicting injury; and this was best to be accomplished by forcing from the master, the servants who had been attached to him and his family, from their infancy. Two difficulties, however, must have suggested themselves to Col. Purlee's mind: one, the implied security of slave property here, under the proclamation, which forbade force; the other, the apprehension of a hostile force in his rear, which demanded haste. solved the latter, by bringing his flying column, at night-fall, in the neighborhood; he provided against the former, by going with his regiment over the bayou, and off from the line of retreat, to encamp one night among the negro cabins of the estate. The result may be imagined: Col. Purlee joined Col. Chickering at St. Martinsville, with another mass of human beings, led like victims to the slaughter. But before his departure, a scene occurred, highly illustrative of the conduct of the Federals in their eruption of the slaves. An aunt, belonging to a neighboring plantation, who had joined in the flight, taking a fancy to carry with her a little niece, whose mother was absent, and, failing to persuade her, appealed to the Federal officers to apply force. The child flew for protection to the residence of the manager of the estate, and impelled by a natural impulse, clung to the dress of the lady of the house, and in piteous accents implored her to save her. The sympathetic impulses of the manager prompted him to interpose his person, at the risk of his life, against the first military intruders, who sought to enter his house, to tear the child away. Col. Purlee, being informed of the position of affairs, came in person, and with pistol in hand, rushing into the house, he tore, with his own hand, the screaming girl from the protection of the lady, and carried her away.

The sensibilities of the few remaining inhabitants of New Iberia were excited by another scene more aggravated in its character, because its consequences involved higher degrees of crime. The robust males of the negro families here, caught in the Federal toils, were rudely torn from their mothers and wives and children, who parted from them with loud lamentations, and claimed them as the only protectors the boon of freedom had left them. These men were forced into the Federal ranks, unwilling soldiers, to serve in a cause they did not appreciate, against those with whom they had joined in the sports of childhood, with whom they had enjoyed in manhood the reciprocal relations of provident care and attached obedience; and to take up arms against those with whom they had enjoyed all the sympathetic relations of every period of life.

But, impelled by the alarm from the rear that the rebels were on its track, thirsting for vengeance, the flying caravan came plunging in with accelerated haste. On the estate below New Iberia, where a depot had been established, and a provost guard installed, around the mansion we have already described, in the dead hour of night there was a beat to arms, while the bell pealed forth loud summons to the negroes of the neighboring plantations. They gathered by hundreds. -Provoked already by terrifying alarms and excited to phrenzy by the reflection that the ties which had hitherto bound them were rudely severed, their barbarous instincts were further inflamed by liberal distributions of whiskey. Soon their conduct knew no bounds; in crowds they swayed about the house, animated by a raving and incontrollable fury, and uttering shrieks of demoniacal rage. The ladies of the family, like the gentle flock menaced by the howling wolf, huddled together in an upper 100m, in agonies of suffering, and uttering prayers for their deliverance for it seemed to them that God alone could save them. The venerable lady of the mansion, who had borne up under so many scenes of horror, succumbed to this; she was borne by her sorrowing children to the bed, from which her remains were soon carried to that tomb, which had before been so sacrilegiously violated. The hurrying flight of the retreating army only spared this devoted family from the barbaric rage of an infuriated multitude, who in a moment, as it were, under Federal influence, had extinguished in their bosoms the civilizing influences of a century. Retreating in all the disarray of a beaten and pursued host, the Federal caravan hardly suspended its flight for rest or sleep, until it reached the Bay, under the protection of the gunboats.

The remembrance of the scenes exhibited in this flight, will long live in the memory of the inhabitants along its route. It was a moving panorama of strange and incongruous sights. The family coach, the buggy. the village hack, and the caleche, mingled with huge cane-wagons, village wagons, creaking ox-carts, bread-carts, and the small carts of the plantations, drawn by every species of draft animal, hastily caught and hastily attached, were loaded with huge piles of clothing and bedding, in which sat and clung a squalid, filthy, dust-begrimed, anxious looking multitude of human beings. These vehicles were driven and goaded on by impatient, sweating and terrified drivers, by whose sides were men, women and children, by ones, twos, and threes, mounted on plantation mules just from the plow, and on ponies freshly caught from the prairies, spurring and beating on these exhausted creatures, in heated haste. Stalking along by the side of the road were men bearing bundles, women with infants in their arms-despair depicted in their faces. Boys and girls followed along, dodging from time to time, with youthful dexterity, among the panting animals, to get a ride on some overburthened beast, or catch a lift on the projecting parts of the groaning vehicles. The scorching sun was sending down his most ardent rays; and a dense cloud of dust covered, as with a pall, the sweltering mass, which extended eight miles over a closely packed road. Chickering, in the advance, and riding in state in his confiscated carriage, was pressing on; and Purlee in the rear, with his faithful 114th, pushing forward, rolled the heaving congeries irresistably along. Like some dark river swollen to a torrent, and sweeping away with its inundating waters, the flocks and the herds, and the buildings along its banks, this flood of animated life moved along its course. The ravages of the overflow may, however, be repaired; the husband-man may replenish his stores, and increase his flocks, and repair his losses; but can the grave give up its dead? Of the tide of human beings we have described, two thousand perished in six weeks. Their shallow graves lie along the waters of the Ramos. Scooped out with careless indifference, and covered with in-decent haste, they were only marked by swarms of fattened flies, living on the putrid matter oozing through the loose earth above them. They have found their freedom; such freedom as God vouchsafes to all the children of men.

In the latter part of the month of June, Gen. Taylor, in com-mand of the then small Confederate force of this District, took, by a *coup-de-main*, the opposite bank of Berwick's Bay, which gave him the command of its waters, and threw open to his occupation the country watered by the Lafourche. The planters of these Parishes immediately repaired to the captured District, in search of their lost property. Many, following the army, were present, and crossed with it; and thus had an opportunity to witness the actual condition of the slaves, the moment they passed from the Federal hands.

Seven miles from the town of Brashear, on the banks of the Bayou Ramos, they found, as we have described, the graves of the dead; the condition of the living, as they found them, we will attempt to describe. Skirting the bayou, in a thicket of undergrowth and briars, were encamped, without shelter, a wretched, death-stricken crowd of human beings, who, but a few short weeks before, had been driven from their homes full of the vigor of health, and overflowing with the exuberance of animal life, and now were dying in squalid filth, or living in abject misery. The adjacent thicket, filled with the decomposing bodies of those, who, dragging themselves thither, and falling from exhaustion, had, unable to return, died there, spread over the camps a nauseous stench, which threatened death to the survivors. Crouched to the earth, with their heads sunk between their knees, or lying with upturned faces, gazing vacantly in the air, the poor surviving negroes were moved by no sympathies for the sufferers around them. Sunk in despondency and despair, or oppressed by deadly stupor, they not only neglected the last duties to the dead, but they regarded with stupid indifference those who were falling into the jaws of death. Many were dying; and, like the living, overwhelmed and oppressed, they sought no relief; thus they passed away, uttering neither moan nor sigh, nor groan-without murmur, without complaint, without hope. Many gentlemen had come, animated, perhaps, by some vindictive feeling, against those slaves, who, in leaving, had carried off some of the movables of the plantation. Standing here in the midst of these harrowing scenes, their vindictiveness melted away in their tears. The strong man, unused to weeping, could not stifle his emotions; the less stoical, unnerved and unmanned, giving way to his natural sympathy, wept like a child. It was afterwards remarked, that even hard men, who found their slaves on neighboring plantations, softened by so many exhibitions of destitution, suffering and death, met them with the feelings of a father, and welcomed the return of the prodigal son. Whilst sadly contemplating this sorrowful spectacle, whispered tales of horrors passed among the surrounding groups, and they shudderingly drew together, as if their heaving bosoms, oppressed by horrid sensations, could only be relieved by sympathetic contact. Every eye turned instinctively to the sugar house, standing near by, as if to penetrate its mysteries. Soon the door was approached by persons whose curiosity overcame their repugnance; but most of them recoiled at the first view. Only a few entered, for the purposes of close examination. The mysteries of the sugar house, we will leave another to explain.

Dr. George Hill, a distinguished physician and surgeon of Opelousas, whose nerves had been fortified by an active professional practice for forty years, has, under the solemnity of an oath, furnished us with a statement of what he witnessed. We copy the essential portions of his communication:

"In the summer of 1863, Berwick's Bay and a portion of the Lafourche country were taken possession of by the Confederate army. I, with many others, who had lost their property by the raid which the Federal army had made, between the 20th of April and the 20th of May, of this year, visited the Bay for the purpose of recovering our property. I was among the first who crossed the Bay; and having been informed, on the night of my arrival, by a gentleman of the name of March, that I had lost several negroes at the sugar house of Dr. Saunders, and that others were there in a dying condition, in the morning, as soon as a horse could be obtained, I proceeded to the sugar house of Dr. S., and entered it by a door in the west end. The scene which then and there presented itself, can never be effaced from my memory. On the right hand side of the Purgery floor, from where I stood, lay three female corpses in a state of nudity, and also in a far advanced stage of decomposition. Many others were lying all over the floor; many speechless and in a dying condition. All appeared to have died of the same disease-bloody flux. The floor was slippery with blood, mucus and fœces. The dying, and all those unable to help themselves, were lying with their scanty garments rolled around their heads and breasts-the lower part of the body naked-and every time an involuntary discharge of blood and fœces, combined with air, would pass, making a slight noise, clouds of flies, such as I never saw before, would immediately rise and settle down again on all the exposed parts of the dying. * * In passing through the house, a cold chill shook my frame, from which I did not recover for several months, and, indeed, it came near causing my life.

"As I passed from the house I met with a negro man of my own, who informed me that he had lost his wife and two children. I asked him if his friends, the Yankees, had not furnished him with medicine. He said No, and if they had, I would not have given it to my family, as all who took their medicine died in twelve hours from the time of its being given."

This deposition having been read to Dr. Saunders, the proprietor of the sugar house in question, and now a representative of St. Mary in the State Senate, he declared, that while it was faithful in the general description, it did not exhibit all the horrors of the scene; as *before the arrival of Dr. Hill, he had caused many decomposed bodies that filled the coolers to be removed and interred.* A hundred others would, if necessary, add their testimony to that of these gentlemen.

There were other places on the island where the poor wretches were bivouacked, all presenting the same scenes of squalid misery. On the representation of the gentlemen who witnessed them, the Confederate officer in charge of the post, moved by a manly sympathy, immediately put in requisition his military transports, then pressingly needed for the military service, and had all the poor creatures removed, under proper medical superintendence, to a more salubrious place on the Teche, where they could receive proper attention, with pure water and wholesome food. Had not this been promptly done, it is the opinion of the medical men present, that every soul, amounting to many hundreds, would have perished.

Penetrating into the interior, and spreading in every direction, the planters found their negroes distributed among the plantations, through an extent of more than a hundred miles of country. Dismembered fragments of families were found recklessly scattered, without regard to affinities or family ties. One of your Commissioners found two children under ten years of age separated from their parents. He subsequently learned, that while the father had been taken for the army, the mother had been thrown upon a plantation below the city of New Orleans. He found a mother with two children, who had been separated from one, a little girl aged eleven; and he subsequently learned that she was living with a free mulatto family opposite that city. He ascertained, beyond doubt, that all the aged, all the infants, and many of the smaller children taken from his plantation had perished. Subsequently he learned the sad history of one of the families. The father and mother had lived happily together through many years of married life. They had been espoused in their youth, and lived to see grow up around them a family of six children-the eldest of whom had already attained the age of manhood. This family had been taken from the plantation with the others we have mentioned, and within the short space of three months from the time of their departure, five of the children occupied neglected graves, the father and son had been pressed into the Federal service, and the wretched mother was found living with a mulatto man at Algiers. The experience of your Commissioner has been the experience of hundreds. Every planter who lost slaves, has an analagous tale to tell. The cabins of every government plantation were found containing some of the living, while the adjacent fields were marked by the graves of many of the dead. The masters took the survivors to their homes, where they nourished and resuscitated them; and then, they too had their tales to tell! Living in the midst of this simple race, and knowing, as we do, that their habits of mind, regulated more by impulse than reason, render their evidence extremely doubtful when their feelings are enlisted, we reluctantly allude to the voluntary witness they have borne. But the Federalists, during their occupation of the country, attached the highest importance to this kind of testimony; and it is but right that they should have the benefit of all the evidence elicited on this subject. The negroes recaptured on the Lafourche and at Berwicks Bay in July, 1863, almost unanimously declare that the Yankees poisoned the aged, the infirm, and the infants! While we reject the competency of such testimony, as do our courts of judicature, we will add that we know the negroes religiously *believe* what they state.

Two thousand negroes fell victims to the perfidy of the enemy within the short space of six weeks. The flight commenced from Fort Barré on the 21st of May; on the 29th of June Gen. Taylor crossed Berwick's Bay; the planters and proprietors of slaves crossing immediately after, found, after diligent search and enquiry on comparing notes, that this number had already died. In his cruel treatment, and in his agony, ne poor negro might well have cried with the psalmist

"Bow thy Heavens, O Jehovah, and come down: touch the mountains, and they shall smoke: cast forth lightning and scatter them: "shoot out thine arrows, and destroy them: send thine hand from above: *rid me and deliver me, out of the great waters, from the hand of strange children; whose mouth speaketh vanity, and their right hand is a hand of falsehood.*"

Many of the facts enumerated in the preceding pages, though repugnant to the usages of civilized warfare, and offensive to the moral sense of mankind, have not only not been disavowed by the enemy, but have been published for the approbation of the New England public. We have before us a pamphlet published in Boston, by the officers of the 41st Massachusetts regiment, commanded by Col. Chickering, which contains the military diary of that officer, and a letter of Gen. Banks recommending him for promotion, for the very services which desolated Opelousas and Attakapas. We insert here such portions of it as seem most pertinent to the subject of our report. This regiment was claimed by the people of Boston, as a representative regiment. It was organized out of the best materials for the work before it, and was ushered upon its career of licentiousness and plunder, in the midst of the most magnificent demonstrations of the metropolis of Massachusetts. After reaching Louisiana, burning a few bridges, and attempting to destroy the salt works near New Iberia, we found it at Opelousas, where it arrived on the 20th of April. 1863. This chronicle says: "On the 20th, Col. Chickering was appointed Military Governor of Opelousas, and the regiment assigned to provost duty, AND THE COLLECTION OF THE VALUABLE PRODUCTS OF THE COUNTRY. Lieutenant Colonel Sargent was appointed Provost Marshal, and Major Vinal assumed command of the regiment. Remained in Opelousas till May 11, 1863, when Col. Chickering, with the troops at Opelousas, were ordered to Barre's Landing, there to establish a Post and Military Depot for supplies to the nineteenth Army Corps, then at Alexandria. Louisiana, and Colonel Chickering appointed commandant of the post, with a force of seven regiments of infantry, the 41st Mounted Rifles, and a section of Nim's Artillery. While at Opelousas, the 41st were converted into a regiment of mounted rifles, *providing their own horses from the surrounding country*, and drawing horse equipment's from Barre's Landing. During the term of duty of the 41st at Opelousas and Barre's Landing, they COLLECTED and sent to New Orleans, via Brashear, upwards of *six thousand bales of cotton, large quantities of sugar and molasses, and other products of the country*," hides, vehicles, silver plate, jewelry, &c. "*and at least ten thousand contrabands, men, women and children,* TO WORK THE GOVERNMENT PLANTATIONS IN THE "LAFOURCHE COUNTRY. The 41st set all the corn mills in operation, furnishing large quantities of meal to the troops and inhabitants, and feeding the contrabands. They established a free market for the benefit of the poor inhabitants, re-opened the printing office, and issued a daily paper." * * * * * "The troops at Barre's Lauding left that point on the morning of May 21st, 1863, at day-break, under command of Colonel Chickering, with a train of army wagons, contrabands,' &c., extending five miles in length," [filled up afterwards by Purlee's accessions and other contrabands so as to extend eight miles], "consisting of *fifty best army wagons, five hundred emigrant wagons, with about six thousand negroes, and a large drove of horses, mules, and beef,* guarded by the 41st Regiment Mounted Rifles in advance, with a flank and rear guard of seven regiments of infantry, and a section of artillery. The troops and train marched down the easterly bank of the Teche, via Leonville, Braux Bridge, to St. Martinsville; thence crossing the Teche, continued down the western bank via New Iberia, Franklin, Pattersonville and Centerville to Berwick-arriving at the latter city at day-break, on the 26th of May, 1863, after a march of one hundred and ten miles in five days, bringing in the whole Caravan train in safety." This diary or chronicle closes June 17th, 1863, leaving the regiment in the neighborhood of Port Hudson. It has the merit of entire faithfulness of representation. We observe in it but few errors, and only one important omission; and, as there is no attempt to conceal either motive or fact, this occurred no doubt in the rapidity of narration. The chronicle omits to mention that nearly five hundred private carriages (including every description of vehicles of luxury and convenience) were taken from the citizens of St. Landry, most of which went down with the "caravan train."

In reviewing this diary, conversant as we are with the facts, we cannot but be diverted at the vein of facetiousness which runs through it. "Bardolph, Nym, and Pistol," the Page says, "will steal anything, and call it purchase." The 41st Massachusetts only -collects! But the application of the terms "Contraband," "Emigrant wagons," and "Caravan," to the poor negro and his exodus, has a grim significance, which, under the circumstances, strikes one as did the grin of the skeleton chained bolt upright in an oubliette of Mont St. Michel. Undoubtedly this narration proved agreeable to the people of Massachusetts, who saw their peculiar notions of ethics and philanthropy, so extensively carried into practice by their representative regiment, under the supervision of the distinguished "Military Governor of Opelousas." To show that we are not disposed to judge rashly, we append a letter from the representative General of Massachusetts, which we find in the chronicle:

"HEADQUARTERS DEPARTMENT OF THE GULF,
"New Orleans, July 29, 1863.

"Honorable.........

"*Dear Sir*: I take great pleasure in commending to your favor Col. Thomas E. Chickering, of the Forty-first Massachusetts Volunteers. Colonel Chickering, in his term of command in this department, has rendered to the Government distinguished and *important* services. His regiment has been among the most faithful and efficient of the army, always *prompt* and *fearless,* appearing in full strength, *ready for any duty.* It is impossible that this should have been its invariable character except for the most thorough and honorable attentions to his duties as its commander. In addition to this, which high praise is deserved in this instance, he has well performed the very difficult and important duties which have been constantly committed to him. No city (!) in possession of our Government has been subjected *to a wiser or more just rule* than the city of Opelousas while Col. Chickering was its Military Governor. It was to his untiring energy and activity that we were enabled to *collect the products of the country,* a part of which were sent to Boston (!!) as you will remember for the benefit of the Government.

"Upon moving our small column across the Mississippi, for the reduction of Port Hudson, he was charged with the safe conduct of the train-*of nearly a thousand wagons, embracing our whole transportation,* which it was impossible to move across the river,-to New Orleans. I regarded the safety of our train as the *gauge of our success* in the campaign. It was brought in without the loss of a wagon, after a march of one hundred and fifty miles through a country occupied by the enemy's cavalry. This success reflects, as do all his other official acts, the highest credit upon Col. Chickering as an officer of fidelity, capacity and patriotism. (!) Unhesitatingly I can say that he is well qualified for higher duties and position than that he now so honorably fills."

"I am, very respectfully,
"Your obedient servant,
(Signed)   "N. P. BANKS, M. G. C."

General Nathaniel Banks

There is a material discrepancy, it will be perceived, between the statement of Gen. Banks that the train consisted of "a thousand wagons," and that of Col. Chickering in his diary, fixing his transportation at "fifty army wagons." The former doubtless intended to include what the latter denominated "emigrant wagons," and which formed the largest part of his transportation for the "caravan." It was therefore not the battles he had fought, and the armies he had conquered, that Gen. Banks regarded "as the gauge of his success;" but the safe arrival of the vehicles laden with the negroes and the rich plunder "collected" in Opelousas and Attakapas. In reference to the wise and just rule of the Military Governor of Opelousas, it may not be improper to observe that the usual population of this "city" was about 1500, but owing to the removal of many of its inhabitants the number was reduced to much less than a thousand, when its affairs were so ably administered by the distinguished commander of the 41st. Massachusetts.

We have been instructed by your Excellency to report "any special acts of kindness that may have been done to our citizens by Federal officers or soldiers, with the name, rank, &c., of those who acted thus creditably." Animated by the same feeling that prompted your Excellency to "hope for the honor of humanity that some such instances might be reported," we have made dilligent enquiries on the subject. We have found occasional instances of Federal officers evincing a disposition to protect the suffering citizen and to alleviate his condition but powerless to extend adequate relief, the disposition has only been shown in ineffectual attempts, or in words of sympathy. We have found some rare instances where Federal officers were polite and courteous, and where they have manifested a proper appreciation of the legitimate services of the army, and a desire to extend the utmost protection to non-combatants; but in these instances they requested that their names should not be mentioned, as they would be subjected to the censure of their superior officers, or quietly relieved of their commands. The fortunes of war may again bring them into the country, and our silence will best secure their future kind offices in the relief of the oppressed.

In concluding our report, we may be permitted to indulge in some brief reflections which the subject suggests. In every stage of the world's history we may undoubtedly find enacted scenes similar to those we have described: "there is nothing new under the sun." But it has been reserved to our enemies to conduct a war, professedly to restore & Union founded on compact and the consent of the governed, with all the bitterness and rancor which characterize wars undertaken to gratify the passion of conquest, the desire for booty, and the thirst for revenge; to parallel the crimes of all ages and times, without exhibiting many of the virtues which have accompanied in their warfare the most barbarous of the ancient and the most embittered of the modern nations; to shock the sensibilities of mankind by desecrating the sanctuary and disturbing the repose of the dead; and to violate the good faith practiced alike by the savage and the infidel.

If the Mohammedans, presenting the alternative of the Koran or tribute, found believing Christians to dissemble their faith for a moment; if, in the middle ages, the chivalry of Normandy and Brittany swore allegiance to every chief who alternately occupied their territory; if, in the Civil Wars, the landholders of England imitated the facility of the Vicar of Bray, and afterwards her reverend bishops risked damnation in another for their temporalities in this world; and if, in recent times, the haughty Spaniard took refuge under Junot's oaths they gave, or found the protection that the sacrifice demanded: but it is reserved to our enemies to set the first example of breaking plighted faith with those who were driven to seek their protection.

In the early part of the sixth century, Alaric sacked Rome; he plundered the nobles of their gold and silver; he carried off their precious articles of luxury and the rich furniture of their palaces; but he spared the churches and all those were sheltered by their sacred precincts. Gibbon says: "While the barbarians reamed through the city in quest of prey, the humble dwelling of an aged virgin, who had devoted her life to the service of the altar, was forced open by one of the powerful Goths. He immediately demanded, though in civil language, all the gold and silver in her possession, and was astonished at the readiness with which she conducted him to a splendid hoard of massy plate, of the richest materials and the most curious workmanship. The barbarian viewed with wonder and delight this valuable acquisition, till he was interrupted by a serious admonition in the following words: 'There,' said she, are the consecrated vessels belonging to St. Peter: if you presume to touch them the sacrilegious deed will remain on your conscience. For my part, I dare not keep what I am unable to defend." The Gothic captain, struck with reverential awe, despatched a messenger to inform the king of the treasure which he had discovered, and received a peremptory order from Alaric that all the consecrated plate and ornaments should be transported, without damage or delay, to the Church of the Apostle. From the extremity, perhaps, of the Quirinal hill to the distant quarter of the Vatican, a numerous detachment of Goths, marching in order of battle through the principal streets, protected with glittering arms the long train of their devout companions, who bore aloft in their hands the sacred vessels of gold and silver; and the martial shouts of the barbarians were mingled with the sound of religious psalmody. From all the adjacent houses a crowd of Christians hastened to join this edifying procession, and a multitude of fugitives, without distinction of age, or rank, or sex, or even sect, had the good fortune to escape to the secure and hospitable sanctuary of the Vatican."

In the seventh century the people of the Roman Empire trembled at the approach of the Saracen, who, emerging from the then almost unknown peninsula of Arabia, was carrying his conquering arms to the west, along the southern shores of the Mediterranean. The terror that then prevailed has come down to our times, embodied in history and song, investing the name of Saracen with vices revolting to society and attributes repulsive to humanity. Yet the instructions of the first Caliph, Abuleker, the companion of the Prophet, to Caleb, the Sword of God, then leading the army to its encampment amid the palm groves and by the gushing fountains of Damascus, might not be thought unworthy of an age in which it is pretended that society is regulated by maxims of benevolence, and that humanity is tempered by the influences of christianity. "Remember," said the successor of the Prophet, that you are always in the presence of God, on the verge of death, in the assurance of judgment, and the hope of paradise. Avoid injustice and oppression; consult with your brethren, and study to preserve the love and confidence of your troops. When you fight the battles of the Lord, acquit yourselves like men, without turning your backs; but let not your victory be stained with the blood of women and children. *Destroy no palm trees, nor burn any fields of corn. Cut down no fruit trees, nor do any mischief to cattle, only such as you kill to eat. When you make a covenant or article, stand to it, and be as good as your word."*

In the seventeenth century, under the direction of the French minister, Louvois, the army of Turenne entered and devastated the Palatinate. The intelligence shocked Europe, and called down upon the perpetrators of the act the animadversion of the civilized world. It exposed to infamy the character of Louvois, tarnished the laurels of Turenne, and brought upon Louis XIV the reproaches of mankind. The chivalrous French, at this day, would gladly expunge this ineffaceable blot from the lilies of France.

In the beginning of the present century England was engaged in war with France. The long continuance of this war, familiar to every reader of history, had so inflamed the passions of those at the head of the respective governments, that each party was drawn into acts of retaliation, which, in less excited moments, were found not only impracticable to accomplish the ends proposed, but contrary to the public law, and violative of the established usages of war. Among the acts of retaliation resorted to by England was the prohibition of the exportation of Peruvian bark to the countries occupied by the French— a prohibition of little consequence compared with the Federal practice of making all medicines contraband of war, and destroying them wherever found in Confederate possession. Mr. Allison, the eminent English historian, who leans always to the side of his country, expresses his views in condemnation of this act, and which, we doubt not, are now the views of all intelligent Englishmen. "There is," says the historian, "one" measure on the part of the British government connected with commercial transactions, however, on which, from the very outset, a decided opinion may be hazarded. This is the bill introduced by Mr. Percival, and which passed both houses of Parliament, for prohibiting the exportation of Peruvian bark to the countries occupied by the French troops, unless they took it with a certain quantity of British produce or manufactures. This was a stretch of hostility unworthy of the character of England, and derogatory to the noble attitude she had maintained throughout the war. No excess of intemperance or violence on the part of the enemy should have betrayed the British government into such a measure, which made war not on the French emperor, but the sick and wounded in his hospitals."

We live in an age of boasted progress, not only in the arts which add to the comforts and embellishments of life, but in that higher civilization which elevates the religion and the morals of the human race. Might we not doubt the latter, when the world views without notice or passes without censure the exhibition of vices and the perpetration of atrocities inhibited in the code of the barbarian; when licentious troops have been permitted to oppress the feeble, to make war upon the hospitals, to burn the homesteads of women and children, and to destroy the moss-grown trees which had shaded the mansions of other generations; and when, added to these, they have laid unholy hands upon the sanctuary, and wantonly ravished the homes of the dead, without the sensibility to shame of the Englishman, with less moderation even than Louvois, less good faith than the Conqueror, less reverence than the Goth, and less virtue than the Saracen? But there is a retribution; and we cannot doubt the great and universal principle which governs mankind, and which, in good time, adjusts the jarring elements set in motion by the guilty passions of men. "Every passion," says the eminent author of the History of Civilization in England, "excites its opposite. Cruelty to-day produces sympathy to-morrow. A hatred of injustice contributes more than any other principle to correct the inequalities of life, and to maintain the balance of affairs. It is this loathing of tyranny which, by stirring to the innermost depth the warmest feelings of the heart, makes it impossible that tyranny should ever finally succeed. This, in sooth, is the noble side of our nature. This is that part of us which, stamped with a God-like beauty, reveals its divine origin, and, providing for the most vital contingencies, is our surest guarantee that violence shall never ultimately triumph; that. sooner or later, despotism shall always be overthrown, and that the great and permanent interests of the human race shall never be injured by the wicked councils of unjust men."

We have the honor to be, with the highest consideration, your Excellency's obedient servants,
JOHN G. PRATT,
JOHN E. KING,
Special Commissioners.

RAPIDES PARISH.
Report of Honorable Thomas C. Manning, Associate Justice of the Supreme Court of Louisiana. Federal Atrocities-Burning and Sack of Alexandria.
ALEXANDRIA, LA., December 22nd, 1864.

To HIS EXCELLENCY,
HENRY W. ALLEN, GOVERNOR:

The devastation of this town and Parish by the enemy during the occupation of last spring was very thorough. Whether maddened by the failure of their campaign in its ultimate purposes, they determined to destroy what they could not hold-or whether they only pursued here the policy of systematic pillage and conflagration, which their Press enforces and Government approves-it is bootless to enquire. I shall attempt to give you a recital of a portion of the outrages perpetrated in this locality, premising that my narrative will not be as full as the facts will warrant. There are two reasons for this. When a man has passed through a crashing calamity, his sensibility becomes in a degree callous and hardened. Each successive blow, more severe than that which preceded it makes him oblivious of lesser suffering. When I returned to this town on its re-occupation by our forces, I found the citizens who had remained, were forgetful of minor incidents of brutality, their whole minds being absorbed in the contemplation of the last and crowning act of infamy of the enemy the conflagration of the town. Another difficulty in the way is the indisposition of the people to give information in an authentic form of the conduct of the enemy, since they fear to be again under his domination, and tremble lest his vindictiveness may subject them to new and exceptional suffering.

The gunboats appeared before the town on the 15th March, and were soon succeeded by transports conveying the 16th and 17t. corps d'armee of U. S., under command of Gen. A. J. Smith, from Fort De Russy, which he had captured a day or two before. License for unlimited pillage was either expressly given or tacitly permitted them. Roving at will through the town, entering and sacking private houses and stores, the common soldiery had but to imitate the conduct of their officers in enacting the most degrading acts of dishonorable meanness. I do not speak here of mere pillage, such as breaking and smashing the contents of drug stores, or gutting dry goods stores and such like, but I mean, low acts of theft and spoliation committed upon the property of negroes. A Capt. De West, of Mower's division, with two privates, after pilfering sundry inconsiderable articles, espied a silver watch on the person of a negro man. He was in his master's yard, watching the extraordinary spectacle of white men stealing in the open day, little dreaming that his own watch was in any danger. They relieved him of the encumberance very speedily. (Affidavit No. 9.)

Not satisfied with theft, they proceeded in some instances to the entire demolition of houses. A characteristic instance of their affectionate care for the blacks is developed in affidavit No. 4. The affiant, you will perceive, is a free negress. She owned a house, in which she had lived over twenty years, unmolested and unharmed-During that time she had accumulated the conveniencies, and enjoyed the comforts of house keeping. She speaks with feeling of the loss of her sheets, table cloths and looking glasses, her knives, forks and plates. Perhaps I shall be more graphic if I transcribe her own words. "The Yankees," says the woman, "came to my house the first day they entered town, and commenced stealing my poultry. On seeing me they asked who I was. I told them. They asked me who my master was. I said I had no master, that I was a free colored woman, They said I lied and that my master was hid. They commenced pillaging the house, taking out my knives and forks, plates, and table cloths, sheets, and looking glasses, and then pulled down my house, which was a frame house. They asked me who the house belonged to. I told them it belonged to me, at which they cursed me, and called me liar again, and said niggers could not own property in the South, and before they stopped the house was clean pulled down, and even the bricks taken out of the chimney. My own clothes, and my daughter's, a grown woman, were all taken by them among them some merinos and lawns, and my husband's gold watch, which I minded more than the clothes. My husband has been dead two years." She had several thousand feet of lumber, with which she intended to improve her homestead, but they chopped it up, and stole all her provisions, not leaving her anything whatever. "I had a great many nice things in my house, the affidavit concludes, in the house keeping way, but they did not leave me a single article."

The daughter of this free negress, (Affidavit No. 5), went on the same day to Gen. Mower, and told him his soldiers had stolen "all her clothes, bonnets and jewelry." She got no satisfaction, and made no further effort to recover them, nor did she get back anything: "The Yankees said we should not have our things back that they knew they were not ours, for colored people were not allowed to own so much property down here.*** I went to Col. Shaw and told him the Union soldiers had killed and taken away my mother's hog, and had taken all of her provisions, and wanted him to give me some. He said I could go and kill some of the rebels' hogs; that if I wanted to stay down here, I could get the rebels to feed me."

The spoliation of the negroes was in other instances even more detestable and disgraceful than that just mentioned at least in the manner in which it was effected. The negroes always hoard specie. Even in ordinary times they instinctively prefer gold or silver to the best bank note that is current. There was not one of them of ordinary industry or prudence that did not have some amount, however small, in coin, and a few could count more pieces than their masters had preserved. The Yankees had learned the peculiarities of these blacks very early in the war, and, with characteristic cunning and mendacity, turned them to their own profit. When the negro failed to disclose his hoarded earnings the soldier or officer found access to his cabin, and soon brought to light the object of his search. But in most instances the negro was seduced into an unsuspecting confidence by the assurance that the persons thus inquiring for his treasure were deputed specially by "Old Abe," or Gen. Banks, (the commander of the expedition,) to gather all such valuables, and that the negro would receive it again so soon as it and himself were transported beyond the reach of the rebels. In this way large sums in the aggregate have been transferred from the pockets of our slaves to those poverty-stricken wretches of the North, whose eyes were never gladdened by a sight of much comfort, at their own homes as they found in our negro cabins. Of course I refer here to the poorer class of whites, who compose the file of the Federal army.

I might mention numerous individual instances, the details of which would justify the general assertions I have made. Some of the despoiled negroes remained, and piteously narrated the manner in which they had been tricked to their masters. Jerry, a slave of Dr. Smith, had accumulated about five hundred dollars in coin. The rapacious spirit of the Federal soldiery, which was displayed early after their arrival, warned him of the insecurity of his money at his own house. He had often in traveling observed gentlemen deposit their valuables in the safe of the steamer, and he adopted that method of saving what otherwise could not have eluded the prying and persistent searches of the soldiers through the town. Carrying his money on either a transport or a gunboat, most likely the former, he deposited it in the iron safe. Shortly before the departure of the fleet he applied for its return. He was referred by the officer to some other officer who he said had the key, and by him to some other officer who was the one that received it, and by him to some other, and so on in endless continuity. He never obtained it, and finally went away with them, although he had been with his master through the early Virginia and Tennessee campaigns, having frequent opportunities to escape, but never availing himself of them. Doubtless his hope of regaining his money was the cause of abandoning his home. This instance is a fair example of their treatment of the slaves. *Ex uno disce omnes.*

Outrages committed, and beastly acts perpetrated by the navy, excite more surprise than when the same things are done by the army. The navy have fought as gallantly as the army. They do not steal as much. They act more in accordance with the usages of modern warfare, are more civilized, and have some regard for the opinion of the world. This arises from the circumstance that there is a greater infusion of Southern men in their navy than the army. There are more born gentlemen in it. But their volunteer navy is composed of the same materials as their volunteer army. A commissioned officer of the navy, accompanied by two marines, stole from the residence of Mrs. Caleb Taylor in this town, in broad daylight, the clock, which they took from the mantel-piece, and wrapping it up in a quilt, betook their prize to their gunboat, lying in the stream opposite. And this commissioned naval officer, (known from their badges,) with two negroes in naval dress, (doubtless marines,) were seen near the Episcopal church, while the town was in flames, rifling a pile of furniture which the owner was attempting to save. They picked up two fine paintings, a musquito bar, and some curtains, and walked off with them.--[Aff. No. 9.]

Directly the "Black Hawk" arrived, (Porter's flag boat;) her crew entered Rachal's warehouse, rolled out the cotton, all of which was private property, and marked on one end C. S., and on the other U. S. N., thus endeavoring to make it appear the cotton was captured property of the Confederate Government. Rear Admiral Porter was present, witnessed the fraud, and seemed in high glee at the adroitness with which his rascally ingenuity could outwit Banks, and appropriate the spoils of the expedition. The same thing was repeated in every yard, barn and cuthouse where they found cotton. They seemed to believe it was hidden everywhere.-[Aff. No. 9.]

The destruction of private property, and the conflagration of towns and plantation mansions are not the only acts which indicate the fiendish purposes of our enemy. Their diabolical malignity which prompts them to unparalleled atrocities, is not restrained by apprehensions of the censure of the world, by the suggestions of humanity, or the promptings of religion or civilization. They are angry that a people welcome even their inflictions of misery, if by endurance they can attest their devotion to the cause of their country's independence. They are phrenzied at the sight of so much wealth, happiness and contentment among the slaves, (I use the first term in a comparative sense,) and will not tolerate any desire in the poor creatures to remain with their masters. So well is this understood now by the slaves, that when the Federal army begins a retreat, those slaves who wish to remain, secrete themselves.

The same practice was followed here as elsewhere, of crowding them in a "contraband camp." The space between the levee and the edge of the river bank was used here for that purpose. It is of course very narrow, but large numbers were crowded into it, where the most fortunate succeeded in making a shanty, not larger than a dog kennel, in which as many crowded as could. The mortality was inevitably very great. Thence they were carried to the abandoned estates of the planters on the Teche, Lafourche and lower Mississippi, to work on what they denominate government plantations. The passionate prayer of families not to be separated was disregarded, and the men were thrust into the ranks, while the women and those of the children who survive, are put to work under the free labor system of Gen. Banks, under which they are fined for misconduct and laziness, and made to furnish their own clothes, and to beg for their own medicines-the result being that they never get either the one or the other, and the fines absorb their wages. The free negro finds to his surprise, that his labor is thus appropriated by a task-master, who, unlike his former master, furnishes him neither with sufficient food or raiment, and at the end of the year, instead of the money which as a slave he always made by the sale of his poultry and of the corn or other produce of the little patch allotted him by his master, he finds himself without a dollar with which to make a merry Christmas.

I have made a careful estimate of the number of slaves taken from this Parish by the enemy in the two expeditions of May, 1863, and March, 1864; and after comparing my own with that made by others, have no hesitation in stating the number at eight thousand. Some have been recaptured, a few returned, or rather were brought back, and all concur in representing their misery and destitution as deplorable, and the mortality as frightful. Gen. Banks in his tour through New England confesses the mortality to be one fourth, but it is believed to be at least one half.

I incorporate here, Dr. Davidson's statement, furnished at my request:

"In the progress of the barbarous and unnatural war by the North against a country guilty only of loving the laws and religion of liberty, events have transpired having no parallel in history, and whose recital will never be believed save by those who witnessed them. The truth has been studiously suppressed, and the world at large knows not what enormities have followed in the track of the Federal bands. Armies composed of the vilest material that was ever gathered to scourge mankind, inflamed by promise of gain and unfettered license, marched to the conquest of an unoffending people.

"It has become the fixed purpose of the enemy to lay waste and destroy a country they find themselves unable to conquer by the legitimate course of war. Butler in Louisiana; Hunter and Foster in the Carolinas; Rosecranz in Tennessee; Pope. Milroy and others in Virginia; and Sherman in Mississippi and Georgia, have sufficiently established the line of policy their Dictator has adopted, in the hope of subjugating a brave and unconquerable people.

"This purpose was distinctly declared in reference to the delta of Red River, by Gen. Banks, while occupying Alexandria in the spring of

1863, which he announced to a committee of citizens who waited on him, to ascertain what orders he would issue to redress any disorderly conduct of the negroes just set at large by the presence of the army, and to obtain from him assurances of protection, &c., &c., in these words: Believe it, gentlemen, as if you heard God himself speak it, I will lay waste your country, destroy your crops, stock and agricultural implements, so that you shall never organize and maintain another army in this department."

"This threat he was unable to carry into effect until his return in the month of March of the present year. In the army corps of Sherman, commanded by Gen. A. J. Smith, constituting a part of Gen. Banks' army, he found agents fresh from the sacking and burning of a large district in Mississippi meet for the work he had in hand.

"It cannot therefore excite surprise in the minds of any, that the line of march of the army under Gen. Banks can be traced like an Indian war trail, or the fire path of the prairie-by smouldering ruins of villages, dwellings, gins and sugar houses the conversion of a rich, beautiful and highly improved agricultural region into a vast wilderness. The marvel is, that attempts should have been made, on the part of the Federal press and the defenders of Gen. Banks, to prove that these acts of incendiarism and wholesale destruction were committed by the army under his immediate and personal command without his orders and sanction. As well might all the regular and legitimate operations of his army be said to have been equally conducted, without his orders or direction.

"The 16th army corps, commanded by Gen. Mower, constituted the advance of the invading army under Gen. Banks, and reached Alexandria on transports the morning of the 16th of March, 1864. Immediately on disembarking, they were permitted to rush through the streets of the town, unrestrained by the presence of their officers. They made an indiscriminate onslaught upon every private residence, appropriating to themselves everything valuable upon which they could lay their hands-and the depositories of food were at once forced open and their contents borne away. I saw officers present at Dr. French's, while his store room, meat-house, cribs, &c., were being robbed, and heard the appeal of Mrs. French to them for protection. The only reply vouch-safed was, that the army needed food and must be fed.

"Private houses were thus invaded, and the inmates subjected to the rudest insults and treatment. The defenceless females whose protectors were absent, only escaped personal violence by the determined and resolute manner in which they met the insults and gross language of the invaders of the sanctity of their homes. It would be impossible to give a detailed account of all the acts of outrage and insult inflicted throughout the town. Prominence should be given to the wanton destruction of the Public Records in the office of the Recorder and Clerk of the Court the documents from which were scattered through the streets and burnt-and to the destruction of the private letters and papers of a individuals.

"The drug stores, three in number, were among the first places taken possession of. These were at once despoiled of their contents, which were used in furnishing their hospitals in town, and one devoted to the reception of cases of small pox, two miles below town. Forty-four cases of this disease were landed from the transports on the day of their arrival. The stores of all descriptions underwent a similar spoliation pe the iron safes forced and emptied, the ledgers, promissory notes, and accounts destroyed. Private residences were entered at night; writing desks, bureaus and armoirs rifled, and the occupants insulted and abused in the grossest manner, despite the efforts of the provost marshal, Capt. Wolf, who evinced every disposition to afford protection to those applying to him for guards about their premises. I obtained from him at night, details of his guard for families whose dwellings had been disturbed by the presence of straggling soldiers, pillaging and insulting. The force at the command of the provost marshal was wholly inadequate to the protection of the town.

"Immediately on the occupation of the town by the Federal army, recruiting offices were opened for the enlistment of disaffected citizens into the service of the United States, under the title of 'Louisiana Scouts,' to whom a large bounty was offered. In a few days three o companies of these men, (commonly called jayhawkers,') were organized, and placed under the command of men notorious for their resistance to the authority of the Confederate Government, and who burned l with revenge against many of the loyal citizens of the parish. To these organizations was committed the patroling of the country adjacent; they scoured it, visiting upon individuals their vengeance and vindictiveness. This irregular force entered the residences of planters, carrying off whatever they needed or could appropriate, and in many instances offering violence and insults. In the remote parts of the parish they burnt the dwellings of those who were supposed to have been active in pointing out or aiding in arresting conscripts. In one d instance within my knowledge, an attempt was made to confine the wife of one who had been somewhat active in designating the haunts of skulking conscripts, to the house, while they committed it to the flames. After the army marched for Shreveport, something of order and quiet was enforced by Gen. Grover, the commandant of the post.

"The discomfiture and defeat of Gen. Banks' army at Mansfield and Pleasant Hill, by the forces under Gen. Taylor, brought the Federal army down upon us again, maddened by the disgraceful result of the boasted expedition, and gloating over the scenes of outrage, burning and destruction they had perpetrated on their march from Pleasant Hill to Alexandria.

"It became soon generally known throughout the town, that the enemy designed to devote the place to pillage and burning on the day they should evacuate it. Threats to this effect were publicly made by the privates as they walked the streets; and the citizens were warned by those of the army less fanatical and brutal, to provide against such a contingency. Measures were therefore taken to prevent so dire a calamity, by appealing to Gen. Banks for protection. He was waited upon repeatedly by those having access to him; and a written communication was sent by him, giving assurance that every means would be employed to prevent any attempt to fire the town. Notwithstanding this assurance on the part of the Federal commander, many persons connected with the army continued to insist that orders were issued for s the burning of the place. It was well known that friction matches were issued to the troops occupying the town two days before the evacuation, and for this purpose. Officers and men were overheard discussing the subject, and insisting that it should be carried into execution. On the morning of the evacuation I overheard a person say to Mrs. Smith, who keeps a boarding house, in a very hurried manner- As soon as you have breakfasted close your doors, for we are going to have fun this morning.' Struck with his manner, as well as his language, I asked him what do you mean by having fun ?" He replied, we are going to burn up your d--d town." On the preceding day, in the afternoon, standing at the window of the same house, I overheard three officers conversing on the side-walk, where they had just halted in their promenade one of them remarked with great emphasis The only way is to drive out the women and children and burn their dwellings! Similar remarks could be indefinitely multiplied, as the subject was constantly a theme of conversation. An army once demoralized by having been instructed in work of this kind, as was the case: with Sherman's corps, could not well omit perpetrating an act so ripe to their hands, and offering the resistless temptation of pillage. Long iv before the army marched towards Shreveport, in a conversation with a Dr. Lucas, medical director in the 16th (Mower's) army corps, I complained to him of the enormities enacted by the Federal army; to which he replied-Why, sir, this is nothing; if your town is served as were all the towns we passed through in Mississippi, nothing but the blackened chimney stacks would mark the place where your town once stood.'

"For two days and nights before the evacuation, the town was guarded by the 113th New York regiment, (Zouaves,) who faithfully and efficiently discharged the duty assigned to them. They were removed the morning of the fire, and the police of the town committed to a body of cavalry. To this circumstance is due the facility with which the burning of the town was carried out, and leads to the conviction of a premeditated design of the kind. The fire was communicated to a building on front street, in a central part of the town-a strong north wind blowing at the time-and from the drought which had prevailed for some weeks, the flames spread rapidly from building to building.

At the premises of Frozine, f. w. c., below the origin of the fire and to the rear of it, men entered the yard with a tin bucket and mop, and sprinkled the fencing and out-buildings with a mixture of turpentine and camphene, saying that they were preparing the place for Hell! At several points where the progress of the fire was arrested by the inter-position of a brick edifice, similar means were resorted to, to continue the conflagration. This was done with the Court House, the brick store houses of H. Robertson & Co., and Mr. Welsh, and the brick dwelling houses of P. O'Shee and Giles Smith. In the last named house, Mr. Smith had placed wetted blankets on the window shutters and doors, and the roof being of slate, the building, with the watching and care of the owner, would not have been consumed; but the family were ordered out, and inflammable material distributed through it, and all was consumed. At many points persons were seen, belonging to the army, in the act of setting fire to the houses. This was the case in the Court House, O'Shee's dwelling, H. Robertson's and Welsh's stores, and the railroad car depot.

During the conflagration of the buildings, they were entered by gangs of soldiers and pillaged of everything valuable-oftentimes under the pretext of aiding the occupants-while many honest and generous men devoted themselves to heroic efforts to save the buildings or the property within. Many officers were conspicuous in their exertions in behalf of the suffering citizens; and to them was due the saving of a number of dwellings from destruction -Col. Neaffie, provost marshal, Dr. Roberts and Col. De Vere, and others whose names I regret have escaped me. While the fire was raging, Gen. A. J. Smith rode through the town, sword in hand, exclaiming Hurrah, boys, this looks like war! Gen. Banks early appeared in the streets, and is said to have given orders for a detail of men to assist in putting out the fire, and to aid the citizens in rescuing their household effects.

"Many families lost a considerable part of whatever was safely taken from the reach of the fire, by the prowling stragglers who fell upon everything thus rescued by the unfortunate. Lieut. Beebe and Capt. Francis, both on the staff of Gen. Banks, exerted themselves to repress these men, and thus saved much valuable property. While thus engaged near my premises, both of these officers ascribed the fire to the men belonging to Gen. A. J. Smith's command-remarking that he gave no written orders, but that it was his custom to give them verbally, and that this was well understood by his men. It is due to this corps to say, that Capt. Slough, A. A. G, on Smith's staff, on the retreat from Alexandria, stopped at the residence of John R. Williams and said to Mrs. Williams, his sister-in-law-- All the blame of the burning of the town will fall upon our corps; but the orders to burn were issued by Gen. Banks himself. Gen. Kilby Smith and Gen. Mower, who were with the advance column on the retreat, while near the residence of Mr. Thos. K. Smith, a planter of respectability and standing, remarked, That the town of Alexandria would be burnt, and that they regretted exceedingly that the same had not been done with Natchitoches, but that the rebels pushed them so closely that they could not do it.

"In the face of all these facts, establishing clearly the purpose of the retiring army to destroy the town by fire, the apologists of General Banks, who represent him as weeping on beholding the burning town, and who attempt to ascribe the act as one of accident wholly, must be content to have their efforts in his behalf classed as a portion of the wilful suppression of the truth, and design to gloss over the enormities and barbarities of their government and its agents, in the prosecution of a war of extermination.

P. DAVIDSON.
To Hon. THOS. C. MANNING, Commissioner.

The efforts of Ger. Emory saved the upper portion of the town, says affidavit No. 9. All the guards were removed at sunrise on the day of the burning, when the apprehensions of the citizens long entertained and by this act co. firmed, impelled them to send Dr. G. W. Southwick, a refugee from the coast, to Gen. Banks, to apprise him of the fears of the citizens and the threats of the soldiers. The following reply was returned:

HEADQUARTERS, DEPARTMENT OF THE GULF,
Alexandria, May 13, 1864.

Dr. G. W. Southwick:

Sir: The General wishes me to inform you that Col. Gooding will with 500 men, guard the town, and his force will be strengthened, if possible, in order to provide against the emergency you fear.

I am, sir, yours truly,

GEO. B. DRAKE, A. A. G.

This was satisfactory, but several hours having elapsed and no guard making its appearance, suspicion began to be entertained that Gen Banks designed by this note only to disarm the citizens of their fears, and hence to diminish their precautions. As this belief strengthened, a party of citizens started to hunt up Gen. Banks, to inform him his promised guard had not arrived. He was gone. The party then found Lieut. W. S. Beebe, one of his ordnance officers, I believe his Chief of Ordnance, and shewed him Banks' note, Lieut. Beebe instantly volunteered to go with the party to Col. Gooding, whom they found at his camp, just above the last house on Second street, near the bayou Rapides. The party told him their errand, showed him Banks' note in which he officially promised, only a few hours before, that Col. Gooding, with 500 men, should guard the town to save it from conflagration. Col. Gooding was surprised, and evidently his surprise was not feigned, said "it was news to him," and then, with an oath, "this is just like old Banks."

These facts suffice to put on Gen. Banks the responsibility of the destruction of the town. He was warned repeatedly of the danger, acknowledged the necessity of precautionary measures, and admitted there were grounds for the fears of the citizens, by officially notifying them that a guard should be assigned, and designated the particular command selected. He left without ordering or intimating to that command or any other, the duty which he had promised to impose on them, and without taking any measure whatever to prevent the calamity which he knew was impending. The intended conflagration was insultingly proclaimed wherever Smith's corps were. Affiant No 7 says, "business brought me in the presence of Gen. A. J. Smith, at his headquarters on the steamboat Clara Belle, then laying at the town of Alexandria. Gen. Smith's division had just arrived from Pleasant Hill. Whilst in his presence, and that of his staff, I heard several of his officers express their determination to burn the town before they left-said they would proceed to the business at once, were it not for the sick and wounded in hospitals. They also expressed their regrets at not having burned the town of Natchitoches. Gen. A. J. Smith heard this remark-it was addressed to him."

It is not to be supposed that Gen. Banks ordered the town to be burned. Men do not usually make a record of their infamy. But my narrative substantiates that he connived at it, and intended that it should be done. His march from five miles outside of Natchitoches, had been illumined by the glare of burning homesteads. It cannot be known whether, in this, he was purposely imitating the barbarous conduct of Sherman in his Mississippi raid, or passively submitting to the headstrong will and malignant passion of his subordinate. It is most likely he was afraid to thwart A. J. Smith. The latter had unsparingly ridiculed his superior's imbecility, and denounced his cowardice. The expedition commanded by Banks ought to have been a splendid success. His army was magnificently appointed. In all the appliances of war, as in all the luxuries, indeed, of camp, it lacked nothing. -He numbered three to one of his antagonist. He was supported by the largest fleet of gunboats ever assembled. The easy capture of Fort De Rassy, the only Fort on Red River, gave them the prestige of success, and inspired their troops with martial confidence. Yet he was whipped in two battles; and driven back cowering, dismayed and panic-stricken to this place, amid the taunts of his own soldiers, and with the shouts of General Taylor's inconsiderable army ringing in his ears.

J. Smith amused the citizens here, declaring in his drunken orgies that he was only staying here to play wet nurse to Banks-that he was ordered back with his command to Vicksburg, but could not leave lest Dick Taylor should swallow Banks up. There is no doubt on my mind that Banks felt he had failed where he ought to have obtained a lasting success-that his management of the expedition had brought it to an impotent conclusion, a fact which no one appeared to appreciate with more zest than A. J. Smith, and he was afraid therefore to run counter to the latter's wishes. If the expedition could not be a military success, its fruits must be the desolation of the rich valley of Red River, which they had expected to occupy, and through which they were now forced to retreat, crest-fallen and humiliated. The power that was inadequate to the conquest was more than sufficient for the desolation of the country.

It may not be amiss to mention here, that the burning and plundering was the work of the 16th and 17th corps, composed exclusively of Northwestern men. When, on the return of peace, these men resume their commerce on the Mississippi, and attempt to foster trade relations by professions of a common hatred of New Englanders, the recollection of wanton cruelties and brutal outrages voluntarily inflicted by them, may serve to keep alive our indignation, and perpetuate a hatred which it were more than human not to feel. The 19th corps was composed entirely of New England regiments. Besides being more orderly and disciplined, they did not have the savage thirst for devastation, which distinguished both officers and men of the 16th and 17th corps. They stole, but with the sly cunning which forms one of the peculiarities of the Yankee pure and proper, and when caught in the act, substituted to the truculent defiance of the hoosier, the sanctimonious placidity of the self-justified puritan.

The town was fired between 8 and 9 o'clock, A. M., of the 13th May. The first building fired was a store on Front street, in the block next below the hotel. A fence in the rear of this house had previously been smeared with turpentine, which quickly caught. This fact is stated by a lady who lived on the block, and who saw the soldiers applying the turpentine, but whose affidavit is not made for excess of prudence. Affiant No. 1 was standing on the levee in front of the store when it was fired by the soldiers, who first plundered it, and then ascending to the second story applied the torch.

A considerable portion of the houses on Front and Second streets were brick. On the lower corner of the block first fired, there was a fire-proof brick building, which effectually stayed the progress of the flames. To insure a successful incendiarism, it was necessary to apply the torch again, and below this fire-proof building. When the flames reached the Court House square, they would again have been stayed, had they not been renewed. The Court House was the only building on the square. It fronted the river, the three other sides facing blocks of buildings, all of which had been consumed, and had fallen down in smouldering ruins, and yet the Court House stood uninjured. It was fired in the interior, and was consumed, with every record of the Parish. The Episcopal and Methodist churches were burned, and every building upon twenty-two blocks.

One of the most disgraceful stratagems adopted by them to facilitate the plundering, was that of alarming the residents in the neighborhood of the Episcopal Church, by telling them the Church was about to be blown up with powder, in order to stay the progress of the fire. The inhabitants fled from their houses in dismay, and the soldiers who had told the tale entered and rifled them of their contents. Two doors below the Church was a house, "built," says its owner, (Affidavit No. 3,) "entirely of brick, with slate roof and parapets. Hynson's house, (between his and the Church,) had burned to the ground. It was of wood, distant about ninety feet from mine. My house had not caught fire; I had wet blankets on the side next to Hynson, and took out the window sash, which were of wood. Four or five officers came into the lower apartments, and ordered my wife and family out, when I observed the cavalrymen go up stairs, whom I immediately followed. One of them went into the rooms on one side of the passage, and the other into the other side. There was a mattrass in one room, and the Yankee who went into that room walked up to it, and drawing his hand across it with a wide swoop, the mattrass instantly caught fire, and the room was in a blaze. I did not see anything in his hand, and do not know what it was he had, but suppose it was turpentine that he threw upon the mattrass, which was ignited by a lucifer match. I seized the mattrass, got it down stairs, and in the street where it burned up. After this, a Lieutenant and two privates, (cavalry,) came to my house, and asked me roughly what I was doing there. On my answering it was my house, they ordered me away, but I would not go, and they went in. Soon after they came out, an explosion was heard in the house, and the whole fabric tumbled down. It was blown up by the last party, doubtless by a torpedo, since it did not catch fire from the neighboring buildings, and that seemed the only means of destroying it. -The torpedo was exploded by means of a galvanic battery. I have now from the ruins a part of the battery, and jars, which I picked up, which are of course broken. I saw an officer set on fire the car-house of the Railroad. He sat on his horse and ejected from some sort of instrument in his hand, a liquid upon the roof, which immediately ignited and burned with great rapidity."

I conclude my narrative of the destruction of the town, by giving Gen. Banks the benefit of a disclaimer, made by one of his officers. -The atrocity of the conflagration, was so great, that those officers who deserved the name were solicitous to relieves themselves and their commander of its odium. "I heard Capt. Francis," says a citizen, "whom I understood to be on Gen. Bank's staff, say to the daughters of Dr. Davidson, one of our citizens, that Gen. A. J. Smith gave verbal orders to his troops to burn and destroy, and that he would be court-martialed for it." At the time he said this, the young ladies were near the lot, upon which their residence had stood in the morning, and Capt. Francis and Lieut. Beebe, another Yankee officer, were offering assistance to the ladies. The former had before offered to such citizens as had been burned out free passage to New Orleans, as he said, by orders of Gen. Banks. He denied that Gen. Banks approved or countenanced the burning that had been accomplished, and was, as I understood, repelling the natural suspicion of the citizens, that his Chief, who was the Commander of the army, was the cause of the disaster."-Aff. No. 2.

The army was then evacuating the town. The evacuation was complete that night, or before daylight on the 14th.

The wanton destruction of property on plantations is circumstantially related in affidavit No 6. The mansion houses were first robbed, and the valuable furniture in some instances broken, in others removed. The piano, in that particular instance, was carried on board A J. Smith's boat, the "Clara Belle," the family portraits defaced, and the quarters, gin-house, etc., totally demolished. Every building on the plantations of Ex-Gov. Moore, and Lieut. Chambers, was raised. The residence of Mrs. Winn was burned to conceal its robbery. Gen. Dwight, whose command was encamped near, advised that lady to go into town, (it was but two miles distant,) to obtain a protection for her place. On returning, she met soldiers carrying different pieces of her silver plate, and on approaching her residence discovered it in flames, notwithstanding that officer had assured her nothing should be touched during her absence.

But it were needless to specify these individual instances of outrages on plantations. Each homestead has some story to tell of mingled perfidy and ruin. A desolate waste marks the path of Gen. Banks' retreating army a track of ruin, embracing alike their property of men in public service, of women, and orphan children. Nor did these latter escape without personal indignity. A child of Capt. Kelso, a little boy of four years, boasted that he was a rebel in the presence of a knot of Yankee officers and soldiers. One of them applied a cord to his neck and suspended him as if he intended to inflict death. When gasping for breath he was taken down, and asked if he were still a rebel. The stout hearted little patriot reaffirmed his rebellious sentiments, when he was again suspended, and so remained until a returning sense of humanity of some of the bystanders compelled his release. The child bore for some days the mark on his neck of this partial strangulation.

Besides the entire destruction of the Records of this Parish, consumed in the conflagration of the Court House, many valuable libraries were destroyed. In the mansion house of Mrs. Seip was a very considerable collection of rare and costly works, selected through a series of years by a deceased lawyer. A skirmish was had near it (seven miles from this place) and one of their wounded comrades was carried to the piazza by the enemy. They retreated through the plantation, hard pressed by our cavalry, but halted long enough to set fire to the house with the aid of their matches and turpentine. Their wounded companion, unable to move himself, frantically implored them not to devote him to a sure and horrible death, but his cries were unheeded, and his ashes now mingle with the cinders of the house and its contents.

I have approached with disgust, and shall leave with satisfaction, the narrative of brutalities which shock the common sensibilities of mankind. I turn to the more pleasing office of recording the acts of humanity performed by a few of the officers, and regret that in so large an army and fleet as formed this formidable expedition, the number of those who exhibited the feelings and principles of christian people and native gentlemen were so small that their names can be remembered without omission, and their acts specified without tediousness.

Col. Neafic and Lieut. Vernum, who were quartered respectively at Dr. Smith's and Mr. Elgee's, were considerate in their attention to these families during the occupation, and untiring in their efforts to assist in saving a portion of the furniture and provisions, when the near approach of the fire made the loss of the house certain; Gen. Emory never disgraced his sword and his manhood by encouraging or permitting the rapine of his soldiers, and Lieut. Beebe's effort to assist the citizens in procuring the guard which might have saved the town, has already been mentioned. Gen. Grover remained as Commandant of the Post, while the army advanced to receive their chastisement at Mansfield, and while performing his duty to his Government, remembered that he was ruling a heroic and gallant people whose temporary reverses were only due to their disproportion of the resources of war. Col. Sharp displayed the consideration which humanity claims of all who feel its instincts. Major Von Heovnan, a foreigner, and an officer of Gen. Banks' staff, who was quartered in my own house, energetically stigmatized the conduct of the army as degrading to the national character, and Dr. Cleaver bore himself with a refined and gentlemanly delicacy that was the more conspicuous from its rarity. Dr. Roberts, an elderly surgeon of the Marine Brigade I believe, was an inmate of my house during the whole occupation, and has entitled himself to my respect and gratitude for his paternal protection to my family. When the fire approached my dwelling, he considerately bore to a place of safety, on his own shoulders, my family portraits, and took under his charge y silver. After the cornice and front steps of my house had caught fire, he labored with generous assiduity to extinguish the flames, and with a faithful slave, aided by some of the citizens, finally succeeded.

It were strange indeed, in a nation which has grown up under the influences of the present century, and which can justly lay claim to extraordinary progress, to a rapid improvement in literature, and to the sudden attainment of respectable national importance, if some instances were not found, where brutish passion had not degraded manhood, and obliterated the effects of civilization from the human heart. But they are rare in their army and navy. The present war exhibits to the world the people of the United States in no doubtful or uncertain light. The Eastern troops are needy adventurers, whose poverty at home is exhibited by their careful theft of the commonest articles of ornament or use in the parlors of our planters and the cabins of our slaves. Following the examples of their New England Generals, (Butler and Banks,) whose houses are adorned by the furniture stolen in Louisiana, they content themselves with appropriating luxuries never before within their reach. The Western troops destroy what they cannot plunder. Ferocious in their brutality, scorning the restraints of humanity which they do not feel, and the instincts of civilization of which they are ignorant, they revel in a fiendish saturnalia of ruin, which spares neither age nor sex, homestead nor barn, the vessels of the sanctuary, the vestments of the priest, nor the sacred house itself-- nay, their infernal malignity penetrates the recesses of the tomb, and rudely disturbs the bones of its inmates.

Political or social affiliation with such a people would be to us more degrading than any human vassalage yet known on earth, more to be dreaded than death, and more intolerable than exile, penury or other earthly calamity. Providence, and the heroism of our army and the endurance of our people, will take care that no such fate is reserved for the people of the Confederate States.

Respectfully submitted,
THOS. C. MANNING.

[No. 1.]

STATE OF LOUISIANA,
Parish of Rapides.

I have resided in this town (Alexandria) twenty-four years, and am a native of Germany-am fifty years old. This town was fired on the morning of Friday, May 13th, between 8 and 9 o'clock, A. M. Several Yankee soldiers broke into the store on Front street next to mine, and pilfered the tobacco, sugar and lard, which were the sole contents. While the party were below, another set went into the second story, and immediately afterwards the house commenced burning. The fire was applied in the second story. While this was going on, I was standing on the levee, which runs along one side of the street, immediately opposite the store, and about eighty feet from it. This was the commencement of the conflagration. The store and those on either side adjoining were wooden buildings.

1. WALKER.

Sworn to and subscribed before me, June 27th, 1864.
THOS. C. MANNING,
Associate Justice Supreme Court La.

I was in the town of Alexandria during the conflagration, and for many days previous. On the morning of the day the town was burned I heard Capt. Francis, whom I understood to be on Gen. Banks' staff, say to the daughters of Dr. Davidson, one of the citizens, that Gen. A. J. Smith gave verbal orders to his troops to burn and destroy, and that he would be court-martialed for it. At the time he said this the young ladies were near the lot upon which their residence had stood in the morning, and Capt. Francis and Lieut. Beebe, another Yankee officer, were offering assistance to the ladies. The former had before offered to such citizens as had been burned out, free passage to New Orleans, as he said by orders from Gen. Banks. He denied that Gen. Banks approved or countenanced the burning that had been accomplished, and was, as I understand, repelling the natural suspicion of the citizens that his chief, who was the commander of the army, was the cause of the disaster.

LEWIS TEXADA.
Sworn to and subscribed before me, June 28th, 1864.
THOS. C. MANNING,
Judge Supreme Court.

STATE OF LOUISIANA,
Parish of Rapides.

I have resided in this town eighteen years. My residence was on Second street, with one house (R. C. Hynson's) intervening between it and the Episcopal Church. It was new, built entirely of brick, with slate roof and parapets. Hynson's house had burned to the ground; it was of wood, distant about ninety feet from mine. My house had not caught fire. I had wet blankets on the side next to Hynson, and took out the window sash, which were of wood. Four or five officers came into the lower apartments and ordered my wife and family out, when I observed two cavalrymen go up stairs, whom I immediately followed. One of them went into the rooms on one side of the passage, and the other into the other side. There was a mattrass in ones room, and the Yankee went into that room, walked up to it, and drawing his hand across it with a wide swoop, the mattrass instantly caught fire, and the room was in a blaze. I did not see anything in his hand, and do not know what it was he had, but suppose it was turpentine that he threw upon the mattrass, which was ignited by a lucifer match. I seized the mattrass, got it down stairs and in the street, where it burned up. After this, a lieutenant and two privates (cavalry) came to my house and asked me roughly what I was doing there. On my answering it was my house, they ordered me away, but I would not go and they went in. Soon after they came out, an explosion was heard in the house, and the whole fabric tumbled down. It was blown up by this last party, doubtless by a torpedo, since it did not catch fire from the neighboring buildings, and that seemed the only means of destroying it. This was about noon. The torpedo was exploded by means of a galvanic battery. I have now from the ruins a part of the battery and jars, which I picked up, which were of course broken. I saw an officer set on fire the car house of the little railroad, about 150 feet from Denis Sullivan's house. He sat on his horse and ejected from some sort of instrument in his hand a liquid upon the roof, which immediately ignited and burned with great rapidity.

GILES O, SMITH.
Sworn to and subscribed before me, July 11th, 1864.
THOS. C. MANNING,
Associate Justice Supreme Court.

STATE OF LOUISIANA,
Parish of Rapides.

I am a free black woman, and have lived in this town (Alexandria) over twenty years. I was a slave of Mr. Henry Patterson, and was freed by him about twenty years ago. The Yankees came to my house the first day they entered town, which is in the suburbs, and commenced stealing my poultry. On seeing me they asked who I was. I told them. They asked who my master was. I said I had no master, that I was a free colored woman. They said I lied, and that my master was hid. They commenced pillaging the house, taking out my knives and forks, plates and table cloths and sheets and looking glasses, and then pulled down my house, which was a frame house. I begged them to stop, to leave me my house. They then asked me whom the house belonged to. I told them it belonged to me, at which they cursed me and called me liar again, and said niggers could not own property in the State; and before they stopped the house was clean pulled down, and even the bricks taken out of the he chimney. My own clothes and my daughter's, a grown woman, were all taken by them, among them some merinos and lawns, and my husband's gold watch, which I minded more than the clothes. My husband has been dead ten years. The clothes were given by them to one of their colored women and a white woman who came off one of the gunboats in the river just in front of the town. I had a great many nice things in my house in the housekeeping way, but they did not leave me a single article. The clothes I had on my back were all that I had when they got through. They even chopped up my lumber, of which I had several thousand feet, and stole all my provisions.

her

FANNY **X** CARR.

mark

Sworn and subscribed before me, July 11th, 1864.

THOS. C. MANNING,
Associate Justice Supreme Court.

STATE OF LOUISIANA,
Parish of Rapides.

I am a free black woman, am the daughter of Fanny Carr, and live with my mother. 1 was not at home when the Yankees came there and robbed the house, being at that time in service to Mrs. Manning; but went down next day, when I found they had stolen all my clothes and bonnets and jewelry. I went on the same day to Gen. Mower, but got no satisfaction; but made no further effort to recover my effects!! I never got back anything. The Yankees said we should not have our things back; that they knew they were not ours, for colored people were not allowed to own so much property down here. I told them they did belong to us, but I never recovered anything. They wanted me to go away with them. I went to Col. Shaw and told him the Union soldiers had killed and taken away my mother's hog, and had taken all of her provisions, and wanted him to give me some. He said I could go and kill some of the rebels' hogs, that if I wanted to stay down here I could get the rebels to feed me. I told him the rebels would feed me, and I should not go away from them. Since my mother's house was destroyed, she has been staying with my sister, and I have stayed chiefly at Mrs. Manning's.

CATHERINE CARR.
Sworn to and subscribed before me, August 2d, 1864.
THOS. C. MANNING,
Associate Justice.

The two negroes-mother and daughter-whose affidavits I have taken above, are well known to me. They are truthful and industrious people.

THOS. C. MANNING.

COTILE, LA, December 4, 1864.

Dear Sir: In conformity with your request I send you a statement of
the Yankee outrages done in Cotile vicinity. The house of E. Blanchard
& Brother's plantation was completely sacked, on their advance, having
made their encampment on the opposite side of the bayou for ten days,
giving them full time for the damages sustained, viz: All the furniture
was broken to pieces, bedding torn up, scattering all the feathers
over the yard, and mattrasses carried away, together with the bedding
paraphernalia, such as sheets, blankets, &c. Carpets were torn from
the floors and carried to their damping ground, horse coverings being
made Tout of them, which I saw my self, upon their backs, on a visit
over there. They also carried away all the kitchen utensils, and stole all
the meat, molasses and sugar contained in the smoke house and store
rooms. A good deal of furniture, such as chairs, were carried on board
their boats, leaving the house completely riddled, save the bedsteads
and broken looking glasses. They even cut into ribbons the portraits of
the Colonel's two wives, and defaced his own and that of his mother.
My own library and that of Col. B. were stolen away, as well as all my
clothes, leaving me only the suit which covered my body at the time.
The crockery ware was taken off; in a word, the whole house was
robbed of its contents.

On their retreat they burned the dwelling house, gin, stables, and
every house in the quarter yard, leaving nothing but a few chicken
houses. They put themselves to the trouble of going into the different
parts of the field and burned some weather sheds. The gin and the
houses around contained between 400 and 450 bales of cotton in seed,
which Mr. Labat is demanding taxes on, and which I refused to pay
as I saw a law published in the Democrat and other papers, passed
by Congress, February 17th, 1863, remitting such taxes, and I would
like to learn from you whether I am responsible for such payment. I

peremptorily refused to pay them, and what I can gather from others, who met the same losses on their cotton, they have done the same. The estate has no money to pay, as its only revenue from which taxes could be gathered was destroyed by the Yankees and Confederates. The latter burnt 250 packed bales. Such as I have described is the condition of the plantation and its resources.

There is now remaining of what was once a beautiful plantation the naked land, and only fifteen negroes out of ninety-nine which were on the place prior to the last raid of the Yankees. What a sad picture I have portrayed of what was once beautiful to behold, but now its wretched remains are heart-rending to the eye.

I have given a lengthy detail of the destruction *complete* of one plantation. Of my neighbors' losses, I shall be brief: -Mrs. Dark lost only her gin house and three cabins, burnt by the Yankees; Judge Boyce's place, adjoining Dr. Sullivan's, was entirely burnt, only a few chicken houses standing; Mrs. Manning's gin destroyed also, and Mrs. Jones'; Ben Hunter's gin, and nearly all his cabins; Daniel Roberts' gin house and at the hands of the same vandals.

I believe I have given you, as you, as far as I am able, a narrative of the Yankee outrages in my vicinity. Most of my neighbors suffered more or less in negro property: Mr. Bowles lost twenty-three; Mrs. Jones lost all but seven or eight, out of forty or fifty on the place. The property of Mr. Roberts' sons and buildings contained thereon all destroyed.

Hoping my narrative will meet the demand in your note, I will conclude, giving all the information I have, relative to the vicinity in which I reside, of the outrages committed by the Yankee scoundrels. I however must inform you that Gen. A. J. Smith sent a party of men and took the piano from the Blanchard house, which I saw landed on board of his flag boat, the Clara Belle. What a dog he is; the English language hardly affords epithets too vile, with which to stigmatize him. Enough for the present, as the mention of such a man makes my blood boil. God grant he may meet with his deserts; but according to the old adage, nought is never in danger.

In haste, yours respectfully,
J. N. TAYLOR.

Judge T. C. MANNING,
Alexandria, La.

I have resided in the parish of Rapides, State of Louisiana, upwards of twenty years. My residence is on Red River, nine miles below Alexandria Business brought me into the presence of Gen. A. J. Smith, at his head quarters on the steamboat Clara Belle, then lying at the town of Alexandria. Gen. Smith's division had just arrived from Pleasant Hill Whilst in his presence, and that of his staff, I heard several of his regimental officers express their determination to burn the town before they left; said they would proceed to the business at once, were it not for the sick and wounded in the hospitals. They also expressed their regrets for not having burnt the town of Natchitoches when they passed through it. Gen. A. J. Smith heard this remark-it was addressed to him.

THOS. K. SMITH.
Alexandria, Nov. 30th, 1864.-Sworn and subscribed before me,
THOS. C. MANNING,
Associate Justice Supreme Court of La.

ALEXANDRIA, LA, Dec. 5, 1864.

HON. T. C. MANNING,
Commissioner, &c.:

Sir-I remained here during the occupation of this place by the Federals, from the 15th of March to the 14th of May, 1864, and had good opportunities of being an eye witness to their outrages.

So soon as the men of Gen. A. J. Smith landed from the boats, for full twenty-four hours they were left free to do as they pleased, and well did they employ their time. Every store in the town was at once forcibly entered and robbed of every article, and the cases, windows, iron chests, shelves, etc., broken to a thousand fragments. I was on front street and saw these scenes: officers of all grades were present, and took a part in it, and did their share of the plundering. Private houses were entered in like manner, and robbed and desecrated in the most infamous manner. A Captain De West, of Gen. Mower's division, walked in my premises with two privates, and acted well their part. The Captain stole my gun and a small piece of carpeting; his two men all the eggs they could find, and a silver watch from my servant boy George.

Nearly all the poultry of the place was taken by the marines, and nearly in every instance an officer with sword belted on was present, and gave the orders. I saw several trips &c., on board the Black Hawk, the flag made with loads of chickens, ship of Admiral Porter.

In less than *fifteen* minutes after the arrival and landing at the wharf, at Rachal's warehouse, of the Black Hawk, the entire crew marched to the warehouse, broke down the doors, and rolled out the cotton in the streets, and *at once* marked it C. S. on one end, and U. S. N. on the other!! Admiral F. Porter I saw present, and looking on with apparent glee, in thus getting the start of Banks. They overhauled every yard, back house, barn, etc., in the town, in search of cotton and sugar, and without ceremony had it taken aboard their gunboats and their tenders. I saw a commissioned officer of the navy with two marines in broad daylight walk into the private residence of Mrs. Caleb

Taylor, on second street, take the clock down from the mantel-piece, wrap it up in a quilt on the bed, and then take both off aboard their gunboat, lying anchored out in the river opposite the street where the pontoon bridge is. These men started expressly on this thieving raid, and seemed to be perfectly at ease in the business. I also witnessed a regular commissioned naval officer, with two negro marines, near the Episcopal church, while the town was in flames, go to a pile of furniture, &c., saved from the fire, and pick out two fine paintings, a fine musquito bar, and two curtains, and walk off with them. I am almost certain these articles were from the residence of the late J. K. Elgee, as I recognized the portrait of Bishop Polk. Three infantry Captains and a detective entered my house and rudely searched it for three hours, and took off all my title deeds, a copy of which I had made out-all my private papers, and a large lot of stationery.

As regards the firing of the town, nothing else was spoken of for weeks before they left. It was the work of design and premeditation. The efforts of Gen. Emory alone saved what is left of it. All the guards were removed at sunrise the morning of the burning. We expected the fire, and as a matter of safety we desired Dr. G. W. Southwick, who knew Banks, to write him a note and tell him of the fears of the people, and the threats of the soldiers. I enclose you his reply. It is useless to tell you that Gen. Banks falsified his word, and never sent the guard; nor did he ever order Col. Goodwin to guard the town. After waiting several hours for the guard to come, several of us hunted for Banks and found he had left. We then called on his chief of ordnance, Lt. W. S. Beebe, showed him the note of Gen. Banks, on which he volunteered to go with us and see Col. Goodwin, whose head quarters were just above Ryan's house. We found him in his tent, told him our errand, and showed him the note of Gen. Banks. He was perfectly surprised, and stated it was news to him and with an oath remarked, "it is just like old Banks." In a word, his written and official promise was a cheat and a fraud, designed to cover up his real design.

Respectfully, &c.,

R. BIOSSAT

THE BURNING OF ALEXANDRIA.
YANKEE TESTIMONY,

The Richmond Enquirer of August 11, 1864, republished from the St. Louis "Republican," a long extract from the letter of a correspondent who wrote from Cairo, Illinois, giving an account of the burning of Alexandria. It appears to be from an eye-witness, and although inaccurate in some of its details, it corroborates the foregoing report.

The correspondent says:

When the gunboats were all over the falls, and the order to evacuate was promulgated, and the army nearly all on the march, some of our soldiers, both white and black, as if by general understanding, set fire to the city in nearly every part, almost simultaneously. The flames spread rapidly, increased by a heavy wind. Most of the houses were of wooden structure, and were soon devoured by the flames. Alexandria was a town of between four and five thousand inhabitants. All that part of the city north of the railroad was swept from the face of the earth in a few hours, not a building being left. About nine-tenths of the town was consumed, comprising all the business part and all the fine residences, the Ice House Hotel, the Court House, all the churches except the Catholic, a number of livery stables, and the entire front row of large and splendid business houses. The "Ice House" was a large brick hotel, which must have cost one hundred thousand dollars, which was owned by Judge Ariail, a member of the late Constitutional Convention, who voted for immediate and unconditional emancipation in Louisiana; which convention also sent delegates to the Baltimore Convention. While Judge A. was thus serving the administration, the Federal torch was applied to his houses, his law office, his private and law library, and all his household goods and effects. All this property, be it remembered, has been protected for three years by the Confederates, who all the time knew the Judge's Union proclivities. Hundreds of other instances might be cited of Union men who suffered in like manner. *Ex uno judice omne.*

The scenes attending the burning of the city are appalling. Women gathering their helpless babes in their arms, rushing frantically through the streets with screams and cries that would have melted the hardest hearts to tears. Little boys and girls were running hither and thither crying for their mothers and fathers; old men leaning on a staff for support to their trembling limbs, were hurrying away from the suffocating heat of their burning dwellings and homes. The fair and beautiful daughters of the South, whose fathers and brothers were in one army or the other the frail and helpless wives and children of absent husbands and fathers were, almost in the twinkling of an eye, driven from their burning homes into the streets, leaving everything behind but the clothes they then wore. Owing to the simultaneous burning in every part of the city, the people found no security in the streets, where the heat was so intense as almost to create suffocation. Everybody rushed to the river's edge, being protected there from the heat by the high bank of the river. The steamboats lying at the landing were subjected to great annoyance, the heat being so great that the decks had to be flooded with water to prevent the boats from taking fire. Among those who thus crowded the river bank were the wives, daughters and children, helpless and now all homeless, of the Union men who had joined the Federal army since the occupation of Alexandria. Their husbands had already been marched off in the front towards Simmsport, leaving their families in their old homes, but to the tender mercies of the Confederates.

The Federal torch had now destroyed their dwellings, their household goods and apparel, the last morsel of provisions, and left them starving and destitute. As might be expected, they desired to go along with the Federal army, where their husbands had gone. They applied to Gen. Banks with tears and entreaties to be allowed to go aboard the transports. They were refused. They became frantic with excitement and rage. Their screams and piteous cries were heart-rending. With tears streaming down their cheeks, women and children begged and implored the boats to take them on board. The officers of the boats were desirous of doing so, but there was the peremptory order from Gen. Banks, not to allow any white citizens to go on board. A rush would have been made upon the boats, but there stood the guard with fixed bayonet, and none could mount the stage plank, except they bore the special permit of the Commanding General. Could anything be more inhuman and cruel? But this is not all. General Banks found room on his transports for six or seven thousand negroes, that had been gathered from the surrounding country.

Cotton that had been loaded on transports to be shipped through the Quartermaster to New Orléans, under Banks' order, was thrown overboard to make room for negroes. But no room could be found for white women and children, whose husbands and brothers were in the Federal army, and whose houses and all had been burned by the Federal torch. I challenge the records of all wars for acts of such perfidy and cruelty.

But there is still another chapter in this perfidious military and political campaign Banks, on arriving at Alexandria, told the people that his occupation of the country was permanent. That he intended to protect all those who would come forward and take the oath of allegiance while those who would not were threatened with banishment and confiscation of property. An election was and were sent to the Constitutional Convention then in session at New Orleans. A recruiting officer was appointed, and over a thousand white men were mustered into the United States service. Quite a number of permanent citizens of Alexandria took the oath, and were promised protection. Their houses and other property have now all been reduced to ashes, and they turned out into the world with nothing absolutely nothing- save the amnesty oath! They could not now go to the Confederates and apply for charity. They, too, applied to General Banks to: be allowed to go aboard the transports and go to New Orleans. They were refused in every instance! Among those who applied was a Mr. Parker, a lawyer of feeble health, who had been quite prominent making speeches since the Union occupation, in favor of emancipation, unconditional Union, and the suppression of the rebellion. Permission to go on a transport was refused him. He could not stay, and hence, feeble as he was, he went on afoot with the army. Among the prominent citizens who took the oath was Judge John K. Elgee, of Alexandria.

Before the return of the army from Grand Ecore, Judge Elgee went to New Orleans, leaving his family behind expecting to return. He was not able to do so before the evacuation of Alexandria. Judge Elgee is one of the most accomplished and able men of the South. A lawyer by profession, he occupied a prominent position, both politically and social, and had immense influence. So great stress was placed upon his taking the oath, that one of our bands serenaded him at his residence, and Gen. Grover and Gen. Banks honored him in every possible way. During my stay in Alexandria, I had occasion to call upon the Judge at his residence, and at his office, (which were both in the same building,) on business. His law and literary library, occupied three large rooms- being as fine a collection of books as I ever saw. His residence was richly and tastefully furnished; a single painting cost! twelve hundred dollars. In his absence, the Government he had sworn to support, and which had promised him protection, allowed its soldiers to apply the torch to his dwelling, and turn his family into the streets. His fine residence, with all its costly furniture, his books, papers, and his fine paintings, were burned up. It may be that many of the last named articles will yet find their way to the North, having been rescued from the flames by pilferers and thieves; for where arson is resorted to, it is generally to cover theft.

Madison Wells, the Lieutenant Governor of Louisiana, selected with Hahn, by General Black's orders, was not spared. He had been a Union man from the beginning. He had a splendid residence in Alexandria, well and richly furnished, at which his own and his son's family resided. His son was absent in New Orleans, attending the Constitutional Convention, of which he was a member, and in which he voted for abolition and all the ultra measures. But that did not secure his family the protection of the Government. All was burned. Thousands of people men women and children, were, in a few short hours, driven from comfortable homes, into the street. Their shelter, their provisions, their beds, were all consumed. In their extremity, which our own culpability had brought about, the Commanding General turned his back upon them. The General, perhaps, did not laugh at their calamity, nor mock when their fear came, but doubtless regarded it as the dawn of a political millenium. The march of the army from Alexandria to Fort De Russy was lighted up with the flames of burning dwellings. Thus has General Banks become the "Liberator of Louisiana."

When the army arrived at Simmsport the feeling against Banks was perfectly uncontrollable. He was absolutely afraid to appear in the midst of the men, lest he might be assassinated.. He took refuge in an iron-clad gunboat. As the boat lay in the Atchafalaya river, the soldiers on the banks would cry out aloud for Banks to put his head above the decks, declaring, with curses, that they would put a ball through it. He kept his head inside. When General Canby arrived, he made a speech to the men, and told them that no more fatal expeditions should be gotten up. A long cry arose from the men: "We want to see Gen. Banks punished; we want to see him hung;" and many such expressions. Gen. Canby said that he had reported Banks to the authorities at Washington, and had no doubt he would be dealt with as his conduct deserved. The soldiers were furious, and would have mobbed Banks, if he had made his appearance. Many declared that they would do no more service until Banks was punished. Gen. Canby told them that hereafter they were under his command, and appealed to the men to return to duty and obey all his orders. Thus ended the Red River expedition-a fine sequel to a scheme conceived in politics and brought forth in iniquity.

2

Inaugural Address of Governor Allen

DELIVERED AT SHREVEPORT JAN. 25, 1864.

Gentlemen of the General Assembly, and Fellow Citizens—Having been called to the Executive chair by the almost unanimous voice of the State, I now enter upon the duties of that office with the proud satisfaction that I have the confidence of the citizens of Louisiana. That confidence, I trust, has not been misplaced, for it shall be the sole object of my life to serve the State faithfully, honestly, and zealously.

Without any solicitation whatever on my part, I have been elected to the highest honor within the gift of the people. If I were ambitious, the measure of my ambition is full. To be called to the helm in these stormy times, to pilot the Ship of State, (I trust to a port of safety,) is indeed honor enough for any man. I would, therefore be recreant to every principle of honor, of manliness and of patriotism, if I permitted anything but a high sense of conscientious duty to govern me in the administration of the affairs of State. I shall not falter in the discharge of the duties assigned me by the constitution, but whenever the good of the people require it, and I have the power, I shall take all responsibilities, and trust to you and your constituents to support me.

My distinguished predecessor this day leaves the Executive chair, and returns to private life I fully appreciate the trials and troubles through which he has been called to pass. I honor his spotless integrity and his patriotic heart. May' long life and happiness attend ' him, for he has been to the State a faithful servant The people having called me from the camp to assume the robes of civil office—come weal, come woe—I am prepared to do my duty. For nearly three years we have battled with a cruel and vindictive foe. We have suffered many losses, and gained many victories. The spirit of our people is still unbroken. The fires of patriotism still blaze as brightly on hill-top and on mountain, as when this great revolution began. Many portions of our fair State have been overrun by the enemy, many houses and homes have been burned and destroyed—many brave men have died in defense of our soil. Age and innocence have alike been murdered, and the widow and orphan have been brought to the door of starvation. The enemy, glutted with murder, rapine and plunder, seem to have sickened at their own outrages, and are now offering terms of peace; a species of mock pardon. But what terms of peace does the bloody Moloch at Washington suggest to his Congress?

1st. You must give up all your negroes and make them your equals.

The constitution of the United States guarantees property in your slaves—for Washington and Madison, and Jefferson, were all slaveholders under that constitution. But Lincoln's proclamation overrides all constitutional and judicial barriers, and aims a death blow at your - dearest rights.

2d. You must swear not only to support the Federal constitution, but all the nefarious acts of the Black Republican party, and these 2 unconstitutional proclamations of Abraham Lincoln.

3d. You must, if required, hunt down your brother and your neighbor, bind them hand and foot, and deliver them up to death. The father who has sons in the Confederate army, is ordered to forswear the land of his birth or adoption, and aid in the assassination of his own offspring.

The fiend of hell in all his malice never conceived such unnatural and infernal wickedness!

Great God! Peace to whom? Peace to you whose brothers have been slain—whose lands have been despoiled—whose homes have been burned—whose wives and whose daughters have been basely insulted! "tis the voice of the murderer with bloody hands reeking from his assassination, who now proposes terms of amity to the brother of his bleeding victim! 'Tis the incendiary outlaw who returns from burning our houses and despoiling your lands! 'Tis the black hearted villain who has insulted your wives and daughters, and who now asks you to take a seat around his loathsome fireside and bask in the smiles of his own licentiousness! Forbid it, Almighty God! Let there be no peace between us until we are free forever from this accursed race! Is peace so sweet as to be purchased at the price of reconstruction? Oh, think not of reconstruction. Reconstruction means subjugation, ruin and death. -The martyrs of our holy cause—those heroic men who shed their blood for us at Manassas, at Shiloh, at Sharpsburg, and a hundred other battle fields, would rise in solemn procession from the chambers of the dead and rebuke this unholy alliance. A gallant young Louisianian was dying on the field of Shiloh; as I passed him, he called me to his side, said he: " My Colonel, I um dying. If you should live to get back to Louisiana, tell my aged father that I died for my country, and oh, tell him to fight this battle out—to lose negroes and lands and life itself, but never, never go back to the old Union."

Those words are still ringing in my ears, and I tell them to you today: " Lose negroes, lose lands, lose everything, lose life itself," but never think of reconstruction, there is a sea of blood between us, we cannot pass that sea. Let us rather add thereto a wall of living fire, and a gulf, deep and dark of eternal hate. I speak to-day by authority, I speak as the Governor of the State of Louisiana, and I wish it known at Washington and elsewhere, that rather than reconstruct this government and go back to the Union, on any terms whatever, the people of Louisiana will, in convention assembled. without a dissenting voice, cede the State to any European power. Give us the guillotine or Botany

Bay, the knout, or Siberia, the bow-string or the Bosphorus, rat her than suffer the brutal outrages of Yankee subjugation. I speak to day nut only for the loyal citizens of Louisiana who have stood by the state in all her trials, but in behalf of the misguided individuals who have been compelled to take the oath of allegiance to the federal government. In their hearts they are true to us, and are praying daily for the triumph of our arms. They have felt the very Iron in their souls, and know full well the curse of reconstruction. I speak by authority, for they write me daily, that they would rather, by ten thousand tittles, be the subjects of the Emperor of France, than the slaves of Abraham Lincoln. If God in His inscrutable Providence, should permit the enemy to overwhelm us, then let us retire to our mountains and our caves, and there let us swear by the blood of our murdered fathers and brothers—by the sufferings and the insults of our mothers, wives, and sisters, that we will issue forth and hunt the enemy, as we hunt the wild beast of the forest. Oh! give us honorable graves by far, in preference to base servitude; to chains and slavery, "Aye! better be Where the ensanguined Spartans still are free, In their proud charnel of Thermopylae."

The despot who now site upon the Federal throne, is doubtless dreaming of the axe and halter—of the rack and dungeon--wherewithal to wreak his vengeance on his supposed rebellious subjects. So - once,

"At midnight. in his guarded tent,

The Turk was dreaming of the hour When Greece, her knee in suppliance bent,

Should tremble at his power."

Morning came—Marco Bozarris was there. The Turk it was that died, and Greece was free. Our Bozarris will yet live to see the proud oppressor humbled in the dust. The history of the world does not show a solitary instance wherein six million of brave people. determined to be free, were ever conquered. The wars of Scotland began by Sir William Wallace and the Bruce, were carried on for a century against the power of England, and would have been continued to this day by the brave Scots, but Scotland's King became Sovereign of the Realm. The history of the Netherlands and the Low Countries is full of interest—full of encouragement to every patriot's heart. The militia, a mere mob, badly officered, and poorly armed and equipped, fought the armies of Spain, then the " harnessed chivalry " of Europe, for years and years, one generation taking up the war where the other had left it, until the Dutch Republic finally triumphed but the history of the American Revolution claims our attention more than any other. We have as yet fought but three; our fathers fought for seven long years. At one time all their ports were more closely blockaded: than ours—Boston and New York and Philadelphia—Baltimore, Norfolk, Charleston and Savannah, were all in the hands of the British, and remained in their possession for years. After a most disastrous campaign, Gen. Washington crossed the Delaware with only three thousand weary-worn soldiers. He had no army stores, no parks of artillery, no arsenals, no foundries—still he did not despair. He trusted in God and fought the British, and at Yorktown gained our independence. Should you be despondent when you have an army of three hundred thousand men in the field, commanded by such generals as Lee, Beauregard and Johnston? After all our wars and sieges and battles—after disease and death have done their work, we still have in this Confederacy, between the ages of fifteen and fitty, 700,000 men. The two States of Georgia and Alabama alone can easily furnish the entire Confederacy, east of the Mississippi River, with corn. South. Carolina furnishes the rice and Florida the beef. Who talks then of despair? who is desponding? Let the croaker go to his wife, if he has one, and tie himself to her apron strings, and nurse the children the rest of his days! Providence has smiled upon the land everywhere, and blessed us with bread in abundance. Gen. Marion lived upon hard fare —Gen. Lee does the same. he lives on the same fare with the 'humblest soldier. But they all have enough. The heart must be ungrateful indeed, that murmurs now, when we have carried on this. great struggle for three years and still there is plenty in the land.

Our people, it is true, have suffered much, but they bear their losses with patriotic fortitude. Yes, our people have suffered—how much, the Almighty Ruler of the Universe only knows. The world will ever know. In the country parishes, black desolation is found in the trail of the despoiler..., Farm houses have been stripped of every article of furniture—barns and fences destroyed, the implements of husbandry have been burnt, and the very cloth of the poor widow has been cut from the loom by the order of Yankee Generals. In our cities it has been worse. The Beast Butler came to New Orleans a poor New England bankrupt, with empty pockets and a lie upon his coward lips. He left that devoted city with the maledictions of all, for he basely insulted the women and robbed the men. The untold millions of wealth that this Beast stole in New Orleans are only known to himself and his robber brother.

General Benjamin Butler

Benjamin F. Butler, of Massachusetts, I arraign you to-day at the bar of the civilized world. You told the people of New Orleans, upon your arrival there, that none should be compelled to take the oath of allegiance to the Federal Government, but that it was a privilege to be sought after by the citizens. But just so soon as you had them in your power, you required every man and woman in the city to come forward and take that oath. Many lefts, and many stayed and registered themselves as enemies. Then began by your orders the most outrageous promiscuous plundering that was ever witnessed on this continent. It was indeed the saturnalia of thieves All were robbed who came under the ban of your displeasure. A very respectable merchant of that city, a non-combatant, finding that he, like all his friends and neighbors, would be robbed, sold his silver plate, a large and valuable set, to a widow lady to whom he was indebted. This lady put the plate on board a Danish ship, and took bills of lading for same. You heard of it. sent armed soldiers, took the ship, broke open the hatches, and seized the plate. Not satisfied with that, you sent this merchant to Ship Island, and kept him there, in hard labor for months, until Gen. Banks released him. You arrested another merchant, and demanded his plate—he informed you he had sent it off. Your reply was, " the plate or Ship Wand." Finding that you could net get the plate, you released him upon his paying you a large amount of money, which money you pocketed. These are facts sworn to and subscribed in my office, and I record them here to show to the civilized world how the people of Louisiana have been treated by one of the Satraps of Abraham Lincoln. Every Sabbath morning, the thieves met at the den of the Beast, and the stealing of the past week were divided out. To the jackals he gave the spoons and trinkets, but reserved to himself the lion's share, the coin, the plate and the jewels. A large portion of the moveable wealth of the city of New Orleans and lower Louisiana, has been transferred to the pockets of this blear-eyed, incarnate devil—a great part of which he put into foreign exchange and sent to Europe; and now he is by far the richest man on the continent. He can loan money to the Rothchild's, and buy out the wealthiest citizen of Now York. Cicero has given the name of Verres immortal infamy, and that of Butler is now known throughout the civilized world as a synonym for crime, cowardice and brutality. When the Southern student shall in future ages study the classics, as he reads that beautiful oration of Cicero against Verres, he will involuntary pause, and for the Sicilian robber, will read, Butler, the Beast! "I ask now, Verres, what hast thou to say against this charge?" I ask now, Butler the Beast, what host thou to say against thy dark and damning crimes? At the dead hour of night, upon the false accusation of a negro woman, you dragged from a sick bed, an aged man, one of the most respectable citizens of New Orleans, and thrust hint into a cold and miserable cell. He died of your treatment. His wife, an amiable, well-bred and lovely woman, went to you, and upon her knees begged for her husband. Yon held a loaded pistol to the weeping face of that lady, and drove her from your bloated presence with the most vulgar and obscene oaths. With the fiendish heart of the hyena you tore open the tomb of Gen. Albert Sidney Johnson, and robbed the grave of that gallant soldier. Yon may never feel the halter draw in this world. You may live to old age, and possibly die in your bed, with your stolen property around you. But a day will come, the "dies iroe" will come, when you shall meet face to face the women you have brutally insulted, and the men you have robbed and murdered, at the bar of an avenging God! Beware the fate of Verres, he died a felon's death. Mark Anthony demanded a portion of his ill-gotten gains, he refused and was slain. When lead to death he begged for that mercy he had so often denied to others. The spirits of your murdered victims say, beware! the living friends of the dead say, beware! " The patient search and vigil long" will find you out, and drag you from your hiding place. Your coat of mail will not save you, for your hour will come at last.

There is in the Vatican at Rome, an extraordinary painting, by one of the old masters. It is called the "Devil reproving Sin." The great artist has by prophetic pencil, portrayed the exact, features of Benjamin F. Butler. As statues will. no doubt, be erected to him in all the Federal cities, I suggest that the holy Father. Pius the Ninth, be urgently solicited to send this painting to the city of New Orleans, for the present and all future ages to behold with horror and disgust.

In the small city of Baton Rouge, the enemy took special delight in destroying not only public, but private property. Not, satisfied with burning the State House, with its valuable library, they took a malicious pleasure in robbing nearly every private residence in the place. They carried away as part of their "warlike trophies," fifty private pianos. The wardrobes of ladies were broken open and searched by Yankee commissioned officers, and their silk dresses were taken by these same officers and sent to their own families in Yankee land.

The Provost Marshal at Baton Rouge, an officer thought by some of our people to be a gentleman, and treated as such, was the foremost man, the leader, in this paltry theft. When an officer under orders from his general drives off a gang of negroes, he can perhaps be excused, for he 's obeying orders. But when a federal officer with a commission in his pocket, robs defenseless widows of their pianos, and steals their silk dresses, what can you think of such a nation. They are robbers all. In Point Coupee, they deliberately fired their cannon upon the Parish church while the people were engaged in worship; and in Florida they tore the sacred emblems of the Savior front the altar of the Living God, and with unholy hands prostituted them in their filthy camps. If all the rich household furniture, and jewels, and plate, and coin, that Federal officers have stolen from the people of this Confederacy were heaped into one vast pile, it would form a huge monument of shame at, which the civilized and Christian world would stand aghast! Yet, no Federal officer has ever been punished for these robberies; on the contra's, all have been promoted The Beast, and Neal Dow, and Milroy, and Hunter, with a host of lesser scoundrels, like Dudley and Killborn, still go un-whipped of justice. The jewels which they have torn from the persons of the most respectable ladies in the country, they now offer for sale in the public markets. The army and the navy rob—commanding Generals and Commodores steal. Some Farley a likely negro girl, others prefer a cordage and horses, while a third will take your piano or your wife's ilk dresses. There is a wild hunt for plunder a mania for stealing, from the

Major General down to the humblest private in the ranks and all this is done in the nineteenth century, and countenanced, yea, applauded, by the people who read the Bible and claim to be Christian! •When Warren Hastings returned to England, with his skirts dripping with Indian blood, and his pockets filled with Indian gold, he was met by the eloquent rebuke of Burke and Sheridan, and a host of noble Britons. Ho was arraigned at the of his country, and impeached for high crime and misdemeanors. In eloquent, burning, and indignant language, he was denounced as the enemy of mankind. There is no Burke, no Sheridan in the Federal Congress. But the robber who returns from the South with a hundred cold blooded murders upon his soul, and millions of stolen properties in his possession, is honored and promoted and feted, and bespattered with fulsome praise.

But let us turn from these disgusting scenes to more pleasant topics.

In a recent tour through most of the parishes of the State, I found the great wants of the country to be cotton cards and medicines. Our fair country-women have been the truest patriots of the laud. The main object of their lives seems to be to clothe their sons and brothers. It is a pleasing sight to visit the farm-houses of the State in these warlike times. You will find the mother and her daughters seated around the fire side, plying the loom, the spindle and the needle—all busily engaged in making clothing for their soldier boys. Heaven will smile upon these noble women, and a grateful country will ever hold them the dearest treasure on earth. I shall in due time recommend to you, that you enact a law, placing in the hands of each female of this State, above the age of eighteen, a pair of cotton cards, free of cost and charges.

I shall further recommend to you the passage of a bill for the purpose of supplying the people of the State with medicines. In many portions of the country, calomel, opium, and quinine cannot be had. The people must have them; and I shall recommend that the Executive be empowered to send competent and trustworthy agents to purchase a supply of these necessary articles for the people of the State. I propose, when purchased, that they be distributed among the practicing physicians at cost and charges, requiring them by bond, to administer the medicines to their patients at the same prices. With a plenty of cot on cards we can clothe our soldiers in the field, and with a plenty of medicines, we can heal our sick at house—and backed by a patriotic people, we will fight the enemy for forty years to come. When was there ever seen, since the world began, so much patriotism exhibited as you find among the ladies of New Orleans. They have been imprisoned, robbed and insulted. Like the chosen people of God who sat by the rivers of Babylon, they are now weeping in their captivity, and looking with anxious hearts for the coming of our armies, and the triumph of our cause. Many of our noble women, hearing of the sufferings and insults of their sisters in the city, have fled the approach of the enemy, and now with their tender children are living in wretched hovels, battling the discomforts of life and the hardships of war with hearts of Spartan mothers. They shall see their homes again,

"The baby that's sleeping While its mother is weeping,"

shall live to be the joy of its mother's heart. Oh, Mothers of Louisiana, God Almighty bless you in this your hour of trial! Kiss your gentle babes and send your sons to battle. Your prayers have pierced the clouds—they have ascended to the skies, and our Heavenly Father will, in his own good time, answer your petitions. We are told in the Sacred Scriptures that Miriam once stood upon the Red Sea banks and clapped her hands for joy, for the hosts of Pharaoh were destroyed—" the horse and the rider were thrown into the sea." Yes, ladies of Louisiana, you too shall clap your hands for joy, for we will triumph. The vandal hosts of the destroyer will be hurled back to their homes, and peace, gentle peace, with healing in his wings, will come and bind up the broken hearts, and bless our distracted land.

And now, Gentlemen of the General Assembly, I cannot close this address without touching upon a very important, subject—by far the most important that will come before you. You are the auditory nerve of this State. What is spoken here is, or will be, heard in every portion of the land. I therefore address the people of Louisiana through you to-day. Would to God that all my fellow citizens were here on this occasion. If a soldier deserts his flag, leaves the army without permission, and comes home to look after his wife and children, do not you and I, and all the people, point the finger of scorn at him?

A hue and cry is raised —the cavalry is sent out—he is arrested, court-martialed, and punished as a deserter. Why? Because there is an obligation resting upon him, to obey his commanding officer, stand by his colors and fight the battles of his country. There is an obligation equally as strong resting upon those who stay at home and enjoy the comfort of life, to support the soldier's wife and children. You men of wealth whom God has blessed in " basket and in store," open your corn cribs and your meat houses, and send for the soldier's wife and children. Bid them come freely, without money and without price, and consider it not only a duty, but a privilege to aid them. Oh, you have a fearful responsibility resting upon you. You have it now in your power to do much good to your country, for by feeding the soldier's wives at home, you will keep the soldiers themselves in the field. _Most of the desertions that take place are caused by news from home that the soldier's family is starving

Our wealthy men, generally have nobly done their duty. They have given their sons cheerfully, and their substance freely, to the Confederacy. They have opened their barns and store-houses to the poor and the needy, and are now, with generous hearts, doing all in their power for our sacred cause. Noble Louisianians, be not weary in well doing. You will be embalmed in the affections of your countrymen, and the recipients of your kindness will ever bless you.

There are however, I am sorry to say it, a few men in our midst, who seem to take no interest whatever in this war. They send their negroes to labor on the public works through compulsion, and pay their taxes grudgingly. They stay at home and hoard up their riches with miserly care, and leave the soldiers to fight their battles in the field.

Their barns and their store houses are shut up to all except the monied man, the speculator, who buys in large quantities, and then grows fat upon the necessities of the poor. To these men I would say, the talent which you have received, and digged and hid in the earth shall be taken from you." If we fail, the robber will lay his rough and heavy hands upon your lands and your slaves, and neither you nor your children will ever enjoy them again. What are your broad acres and your hundreds of slaves compared to the issues of the great struggle now going on in this country. The lurid fires of war are now blazing around you. The enemy is at your door, and you sit still hugging to your bosoms the delusive hope that you will make some terms with him, and save your property. If the enemy spared not the slaves of good Union men, do you think he will spare yours? If we fail your negroes will be driven off at the point of the bayonet, and your lands will be parceled out amongst the hireling soldiery of Abraham Lincoln.

I, therefore, urgently appeal to every man in the State, not to speculate in order that he may make more money, but to do all he can for the wives and children of those who are fighting his battles. I earnestly appeal to every man rich or poor, to aid in every possible way he can, the wife of the gallant soldier, who cannot remain at home to take care of his property, or minister to the wants of his family. It may well be asked in these troublous times, what will become of the negro?

The status, of the negro race has been fixed by the immutable laws of God, and the Yankee at home does not wish to change it even if he could. That race has ever been, is now, and ever will be " the hewers of wood and drawers of water." Go to New England, New York, or Illinois, and you will find them everywhere performing the menial offices of life. if when this war is ended there should be found alive any negroes in the hands of the enemy, they will have a hard time indeed. They will not be permitted to labor on the railroads, the canals, or the public works of any kind, for the Irish and the Dutch will rise in mobs and drive them off. Yankee society will not educate them for the bar, the bench, or the pulpit. Yankee pride will not tolerate their inter-marriage with the whites. Driven from the social circle and all the industrial pursuits of life, what will become of the poor negro? As a drivelling out-cast, he will become a mendicant wanderer. His doom will be the prison and the work-house.

There are two kinds of abolitionists in the United States—the political and the religious. The religious steal the negroes, and the political kill them. From reliable informant on in my possession, two-thirds of all the negroes that have gone to the enemy, are now in their graves. Many are daily deserting and returning to their old masters. sick and sore and emaciated, and begging that they may be permitted to die at home in peace. There was once in the river parishes and the lower portion of this State, the most contented and happy race of laborers ever seen on this earth. Music and the merry laugh were nightly heard from their comfortable quarters, for peace and plenty and quite blessed both master and servants. But now desolation, want, disease fill the cabins of these once happy and contented laborers. In an evil hour the destroyer cane. Ile poisoned the ears and corrupted the hearts of these people They have either been enticed away from their comfortable homes or driven off by force of arms, and now upon hard fare and harder work they can only dream of the blessings of the old plantation, where the meat house and corn crib were always full and at their command.

The white inhabitants of our State have suffered much in this war, but the blacks have suffered far more. I have seen many of these unfortunate creatures who, at the risk of their lives, have run off from the enemy's encampments. They all give the most heart-rendering account of their sufferings. Men, women and children are crowded together in miserable huts. No attention is paid to the sick, but little medicine, and ho nurses. Mothers die on the cold ground, with their little helpless children around them. In their own language, " the Doctor was seldom sent for, and when he did come the sick ones always died," nail when they died they were buried more like dogs than human being! What a commentary on Yankee philanthropy! They first killed the negro to make him free, and then refuse him a christian burial

We will carry the institution of domestic slavery with us triumphantly through this war, and then it will rest on a firmer bask than ever, and be administered better and more wisely. This institution will triumph with us, because it is right and just in the sight. of Almighty God. That best of all books, the Bible, which is so much despised by the Abolitionists, from the beginning to the end thereof, sanctions slavery. The patriarchs were all slave-holders, and bought and sold their slaves then as we do now. The same inspired men to whom the Ten Commandments were delivered, and who stood in the presence of the Great Jehovah, gave laws for the government of slaves. President Lincoln and his followers say that it is an awful sin to own a slave, but that it is not only right but highly commendable to burn a church, rob the widow and the orphan, and shoot down unoffending citizens!! It is no harm to break open a Masonic Lodge, and with sacrilegious hands steal and desecrate its regalia! It is all right and proper to devastate whole parishes, burn villages and barns and store-houses, bombard cities without notice, and hang non-combatants; but oh! it is a terrible crime to buy a negro, treat him well, and let him work for you! Shame, eternal burning shame upon such loathsome hypocrisy! There ever has been, and there is now, the kindest feeling existing between the master and his servants. Notwithstanding a brutal and vindictive enemy has advised the negro to murder their masters, there have been no evidence of insurrection in our midst—on the contrary there are hundreds of instances where the master has gone to the war and left his wife and children in the hands of his negroes, and well have they served, and guarded, and protected them.

When the children of Israel went up out of Egypt to the promised land, they took their servants with them. Master and servant hand in hand together crossed the Red Sea, and when safely over, they both alike rejoiced at the destruction of their pursuer. The faithful historian who shall in after times write the history of this war, will doubtless record many instances wherein the negro slave has been unfaithful to his owner—but he will, on the other hand, devote many a bright page to the deep fidelity and noble heroism of the servant in defense of the rights and interests of his master, and that historian may close his volume by recording this important fact—that " at the close of the great struggle between the North and the South, master and servant were found in the ranks, side by side, .fighting bravely, shoulder to shoulder, for the independence which they have FO gloriously achieved, and for the liberties which they now enjoy."

I shall take occasion to call the attention of the General Assembly to the passage of such laws as I think the time demand and the exigencies of the country require. Especially shall I call your attention to the unauthorized and illegal manner in which the " Impressment Act" has been executed in this State. Officers, those claiming to be officers of the Confederacy, in making their illegal impressments, have added insult to injury. This must be stopped, and I shall look to you for the passage of a law making such offences a felony, and punishable by imprisonment in the State Penitentiary. The people must and shall be protected in all their civil rights. In this connection, I am happy to express my hearty approbation of the conduct of Lt. Gen. E. Kirby Smith, the Commanding Officer of this Department, and of Major Gen. Taylor. These commanding officers have not only done their duty most nobly, as gallant soldiers, but whenever there has been a conflict between the civil and military authorities, they have most cheerfully submitted to the decisions of the Courts of the State. Happy are we indeed, in these days of despotic power, to have such patriotic Generals. May they long live to receive the plaudits of a grateful country!

You, gentlemen, are assembled together on no ordinary occasion. You have much to do. Your constituents expect much at your hands. My hearty co-operation will cheerfully he given to every measure that may tend to guard the citizen in his rights, and secure the liberties of the people While I urge upon you the strictest economy in all your acts, still I would say, spare no expense. Stand not upon dollars and cents, when the safety of your country required your action. Let every man who owes service to his country go to the army. Let every man who stays at home do his duty—frown down extortion and vice in every shape and every form. Be true to yourselves, and leave the rest to God. Be true to yourselves, and the country is safe.

3

Annual Message of Governor Allen

EXECUTIVE OFFICE,

SHREVEPORT, LA., Jan. 16th, 1865.

GENTLEMEN OF THE SENATE

AND OF THE HOUSE OF REPRESENTATIVES:

You have assembled again, in regular session, for the purpose of transacting the business of the Commonwealth. During the year that has elapsed since I had the pleasure of meeting you, very important events have transpired. Many bloody battles have been fought with varied success—many valuable lives have been offered up on the altar of our common country. The war has raged with unabated fury, yet our troops, with a few recent exceptions, have been everywhere triumphant; and the armies of the Confederacy are to-day well organized and are still formidable. Divine Providence has blessed the land with plenty, while that terrible scourge, which often in our climate decimates whole cities, has been but partially felt. Our own queenly metropolis, though cursed with the presence of an insolent, thieving, vandal foe, has yet been spared the visitation of pestilence; and Louisiana has perhaps lost fewer lives in a year of battles than she has often lost in a summer of the fever. In this department, although our people have suffered much from the wicked raids of the enemy, we have no reason to complain. We should not murmur, for our arms have been victorious in an eminent degree. The enemy have been driven out of the Attakapas parishes, and are not now seen on the right bank of the Atchafalaya. Although many of our farmers have suffered from drouth, and from the late planting caused by invasion, we still have corn enough in Louisiana for two years' subsistence. With grateful hearts we should thank Him, who rules the destinies of the universe, for this plenty in the land.

Since your last session we have been called to mourn the loss of many of our best citizens. HENRY JOHNSON, once Governor of Louisiana, a contemporary of Clay, and Webster, and Calhoun, died at his home in Pointe Coupee, full of years and full of honors. PIERRE EMILE BONFORD, Associate Justice of the Supreme Court, after a brief illness, died at Alexandria, exiled by war from home and family. He was a finished scholar, a thorough and very learned lawyer and jurist, and a devoted patriot. His singularly pure, candid, genial and generous nature won the love of all who knew him. I took him from the army and placed him on the bench. In his death the State has suffered irreparable loss. HENRY MARSHALL and BENJAMIN L. HODGE, the one succeeding the other in Congress, have also departed this life. Both were distinguished for their sterling integrity and great patriotism. Your own body has also lost one of its brightest ornaments, in the death of PRESTON POND, Jr., Senator from East Feliciana. On the battle field death has stricken many a shining mark. Generals POLK, MOUTON, and STAFFORD Have fallen fighting gloriously for their country. Their memories are embalmed in the hearts of all Louisianians—a nation's tears will flow for them—their graves will be hallowed ground. ARMAND, and BEARD, and CLACK, and CANFIELD, and SHIELDS, and BELL, and WINANS, and WALKER, and TAYLOR— all fell as fall the brave. I would recommend that a few acres of the battlefield of Mansfield be bought by the State. and that a monument be erected to the gallant Mouton and his brave comrades, who fell there in defense of their country.

General Alfred Mouton

FINANCES

I respectfully refer you to the report of the Hon. B. L. Defreese, State Treasurer for much valuable information. At your last session you appropriated the sum of 11,042,630 dollars. I have drawn from the Treasury 6,247,979 dollars, leaving a balance of appropriations unexpended of 4,794,651 dollars. You will see that there is in the Treasury, of all funds, 3,227,369 dollars.

I would also invite your attention to the report of Col. James C. Wise, Quarter-Master General, by which you will perceive that a very large proportion of the above expenditure is represented by valuable stores, advancing in market price, and more available than Treasury Notes to meet the future wants of the State. Accompanying this Report will be found a tabular statement of all the property now on hand acquired for the State during the past year. It consists of cotton, sugar, subsistence stores, drugs and medicines—all of which have been paid for—amounting in the aggregate to $5,510,000.

As authorized by your Act of last session, the Treasurer has prepared and issued three hundred thousand dollars in Treasury notes of one dollar and fractions of a dollar. This well-timed supply of change has proved a great relief to the public, at small expense. The object of the law has been accomplished most admirably, since all local and corporation small notes have been withdrawn from circulation.

For a statement in detail of the Finances of the State, I refer you to the report of the Hon. H. Peralta, Auditor of Public Accounts. You will perceive that the State of Louisiana owes, in round numbers, nineteen millions of dollars. Under your recent Act authorizing the sale of six per cent. bonds, I have had occasion to sell only to the amount of 571,940 dollars, all at a premium of ten per centum. The proceeds of these bonds have been applied to draw in State Treasury Notes. The Confederate Government owes the State about four millions of dollars, expended for Military purposes. I have had the accounts and vouchers properly arranged and -Classified, and have placed them before the Hon. Thos. C. Kennedy, Comptroller-of the C.S. Treasury at Marshall. As soon as they are examined and adjusted, they will be forwarded to Richmond for payment.

STATE GUARD.

You authorized and instructed me at your last session to raise four companies of mounted men, which, joined to the six companies already in State service, were to form two -battalions of State troops, whose duty was plainly prescribed. I raised, armed and equipped the companies, organized the battalions, and placed them at once in the field. At that time the enemy had arrived at Natchitoches, in their 'advance up Red River valley. I ordered the battalions, commanded by Lien' tenant Colonels H. M. Favrot and Ben. W. Clark, to report to General Taylor instanter. Promptly obeying, they shared in the hard-fought battles of Mansfield and Pleasant Hill, and acquitted themselves gallantly as good and efficient troops.

Although State forces, I kept them in C. S. service, doing constant and heavy duty in Lower Louisiana until the 26th day of July last, when they were regularly mustered into the C. S. Army, and turned over to the General commanding this Department. The two battalions have since been consolidated, and now form the eighth regiment of Louisiana Cavalry, numbering eight hundred officers and men. Composed of excellent material, I doubt not that this corps will prove very useful to the Department, and much more efficient by being thus transferred. As the -State had no depots of corn and provisions. no forage, and inadequate transportation, it was incurring very heavy expense. I cannot speak too highly of the bravery and good conduct of the "Guard;" they have performed their duty nobly wherever assigned. For the military organizations and, operations of the State troops, and all the details incident thereto, I respectfully refer you to the concise and able report of Brig. Gen. T. G. Hunt, A. & I. G.

STATE DISPENSARY.

The sum of five hundred thousand dollars was appropriated by you for the purchase of medicines for the families of soldiers. To obtain enough to make the distribution contemplated by the Act was found impracticable. I therefore established a Dispensary at this place, from which every portion of the State has been supplied' as far as possible. Every parish has, I believe, derived benefit from this Dispensary. To none has medicine been denied. To the poor and destitute it has,' been given "without money' and without price:" For a statement of the affairs of this establishment, I respectfully refer you to the report of Surgeon General Amzi Martin. You will see that he has furnished to citizens of the State medicines; at about one-third of the market price. here, to the value of $274,972; that he has distributed for charitable purposes $13,790 worth; and that the net profits for five months amount to about $50,000, all of which has been paid into the State Treasury. Although my agents have been very active, they have succeeded, at great personal risk and labor, in keeping the Dispensary only partially supplied. I have found it exceedingly difficult to procure medicines for the people, as the enemy took a malignant pleasure in destroying all drug-stores in their march through the lower portion of the State, and by a refinement of cruelty, have declared all medicines contraband of war. Notwithstanding all these difficulties, I am happy to inform you that I have received a large supply from Mexico—amply sufficient for many months to come. Every citizen of Louisiana can now be abundantly supplied with medicines of all kinds.

IRON AND LEAD ORES.

In obedience to the instructions of the General Assembly, practical men were employed to examine thoroughly all portions of the State where lead and iron ores were thought to exist Traces only of lead ore were found in several places, but not in sufficient quantities to justify any outlay whatever for the necessary machinery to work and smelt the same. The parishes of DeSoto, Sabine, Bossier, Claiborne and Bienville have iron in large quantities. Upon subjecting specimens of ore from these parishes to the proper test, they were found to be so refractory, that it was not deemed advisable to prosecute the matter further. I thought it more prudent, too, in the unsettled condition of affairs, to establish a furnace. (which is a great undertaking,) at a more retired and secure place. I therefore sent Lieut.Col. E. Miltenberger, A. D. C., to Texas; and, after thorough examination, purchased one-fourth of the "Sulphur Forks Iron Works," in Davis County, of that State, for fifty thousand dollars. This furnace was erected but a few months since, and is now going into successful operation. It will abundantly supply the

State with all the iron needed. - It is situated about ninety miles from Shreveport, and within a few miles of water transportation. I consider this purchase very fortunate. Already the stock is worth double the money stipulated. The Company owns a valuable tract of land covered with inexhaustible beds of rich iron ore. The buildings and machinery are of the most substantial kind. The "Works" are managed by a Board of five Directors, two of whom are appointed by the State of Louisiana. I refer you to the accompanying. papers for full particulars respecting these valuable works.

STATE STORE.

When entering upon the duties of my office, I found the currency of the State very much depreciated. Farmers, merchants, butchers, bakers, mechanics, all refused to take it. Notwithstanding it was well known that the State was amply able to redeem her circulation, still her paper was in had repute, and its exchangeable value daily declining. Much concerned at this, I earnestly sought a remedy. After mature reflection, I determined to establish a State Store, to sell cheap goods to the public, and to take payment in our depreciated currency. This has served a double purpose. It has drawn in from circulation a large amount of State notes, thus increasing the exchangeable value of the remainder, and has supplied our fellow-citizens with articles of necessity, at prices comparatively moderate. For details of the transactions in this purchase and sale of merchandize, I respectfully refer you to the report of C. H Ardis, Military Store-keeper. You will perceive that he has paid into the Treasury, from proceeds of sales, $425,249.61, besides giving to destitute wounded soldiers, to orphans and to widows, goods to the value of $22,159.50. In addition to this, you will see that goods to the value of $87,326.19 have been transferred to the several State departments, and that army supplies, ordnance stores, &c., to the value of $627,816.60 have been turned over to the Confederate Government, making the transactions of the State Store since its inauguration on the 30th of June last, amount to the gross sum of $1,162,551.90. These goods were imported from Mexico, and paid for in cotton, as will appear from documents annexed to the report above mentioned. All of which are submitted for your inspection.

I am happy to inform you that the Treasury notes of the State are now much in demand, not only in Louisiana, but in this entire department. It is my intention, unless otherwise instructed by the General Assembly, to keep up the "State Store," to continue the importation of goods, and to sell them to the public at prices within a fraction of their cost. Many a wounded and destitute soldier has been clothed, free of charge, from this store, while the widow and the orphan have also been supplied. In dispensing these charities, I have made no distinction. Wounded and disabled soldiers from Texas, Arkansas and Missouri have all been relieved—and, none have been refused. To extend the two-fold benefits of this purchase and sale of merchandise, it is my purpose, your honorable body approving, to locate three or more branch stores, in different towns of Louisiana. The insufficient receipt of goods, the want of transportation, my unwillingness to take men from the army to act as store-keepers, and the difficulty of giving such orders for the sale of goods at a distance as would secure their just, equitable and judicious disposition, are among the reasons which have prevented me hitherto from sending them to remote sections for sale and distribution. I hope, however, to prove to the people of all portions of the State, by the potent logic of facts, that the very exorbitant prices of imported necessities are to be accounted for by the greed of traders more than by the actual cost of importation. Should I thus incur the ill-will of venal, grasping, insatiable peddlers and speculators, I shall be abundantly consoled by the approbation of all honorable and patriotic merchants.

MANUFACTORIES.

At the last session of the General Assembly, you made large and liberal appropriations for the establishment of manufactories; and the Executive was invested with almost unlimited powers. I trust that your confidence has not been misplaced. Having found the State destitute of manufactories of all kinds, I am pleased to inform you that there are now in successful operation, the following works:

Two Turpentine Distilleries.

One Castor Oil Factory.

One Cotton Card Factory.

One Establishment for making Carbonate of Soda.

Two Distilleries for pure medicinal Alcohol.

One Rope-Walk, for Cotton Cordage.

One Foundry, for cooking utensils, machinery and agricultural implements. Two Cotton Cloth Manufactories.

Two Laboratories, for indigenous medicines.

These works have been constructed under very unfavorable auspices. and have succeeded, although, in many instances, we did not have skillful mechanics, nor proper tools. I invite to them your attention, with pride. They will soon supply the people with all necessary articles. Much credit is due to Col. John M. Sandidge, Chief of Ordnance, for their success. The State has been fortunate in having the benefit of his untiring energy and indomitable perseverance. He has acted as my general agent and superintendent, while performing the proper duties of his office.

For information as to the amount of clothing made and distributed to Louisiana troops, and the operations of the Cotton Card Manufactory and Rope Walk, I respectfully refer you to the report of Clinton H. Ardis, Esq., Chief of the Clothing Bureau and Military Store-keeper. The business of his department has been methodically and successfully conducted.

I respectfully refer you to the report of Dr. B. Egan, Superintendent of State Laboratory at Mt. Lebanon. Although he has labored under great difficulties, he has established an institution of which we may well be proud. His success is due to his zeal and energy. You will observe that the value of property acquired greatly exceeds the amount of the outlay. No further appropriation is required, as "the Laboratory will soon be self-sustaining.

The press has been amply supplied with printing paper.

COTTON CARDS AND WOOL CARDS.

I have imported and distributed in the State, fifteen thousand pairs of Cotton Cards—selling them to the soldiers' families at ten dollars per pair. To accomplish this, I have had agents in every part of the country. One was sent to His Excellency, Governor Joseph E. Brown, of Georgia, for a machine with which to manufacture cotton-cards. He very kindly and promptly furnished it, together with sufficient wire to make a small number of cards. For this generous act, the State of Louisiana will be under lasting obligations to him. The machine was put in successful operation at Minden, and made superior cards until the little stock of wire was exhausted. I found it very difficult to obtain wire, and have sent to Europe for it.

Through the indefatigable exertions of my agent, D. A. Blacksher, I have received from Virginia two more machines, with six hundred pounds of wire—enough to make a large number of cards and now at the factory in Minden there are three machines, which will soon be in successful operation, with the capacity for making one thousand pairs of cards per month. As these machines cannot supply the demand, I shall continue to import cotton and wool cards.

I promised every lady in Louisiana a pair of cotton cards. This promise is nearly fulfilled. The cards will soon be delivered. There are to-day no fair hands in the State idle. All are busily engaged in making cloth, first for the soldiers in the field, then for themselves. The music of the spinning-wheel and loom is to be heard in every farm-house from early morn till dewy eve. It is a glorious sight and cheering to the patriot's heart, when the aged mother, with silvered locks, sits by the fire-side, lighted by the brightly blazing native pine, (candles being no longer in use,) her fair daughters assembled around her, some carding, some knitting, while others are engaged in that truly graceful task of spinning; all cheerful and all happy; though a tear may steal from the mother's eye, as she thinks of her dear boy far away, fighting the battles of his country on the banks of the James or the Tennessee. God bless the noble mothers of Louisiana! I was called on by an aged matron, who said to me with tearful eyes: "Governor, I have eight sons in the army; I have but one more, my darling little Benjamin. He is just seventeen, and now the Captain of the Reserve Corps has sent for him. He wants to go, Governor, but I want him to stay and take care of me in my old age. But God's will be done! I love my children much, but I love my country more. He shall go! He is young and tender—my last hope—but he shall go! he shall go!" Gentlemen, with such mothers as these, we must, we will triumph.

INTOXICATING LIQUORS.

The laws forbidding the distillation of alcoholic liquors flora grain and the produce of sugar cane, have been strictly executed by me. It is believed that not one gallon of intoxicating liquor is illegally produced in the State. I trust this law will not be repealed during the war. All bread-stuffs, sugar and molasses, are required for the army and for destitute families of soldiers. In many portions of Louisiana, grain is already scarce. I daily receive appeals for assistance, and every surplus barrel will be needed during this and the coming year.

I would again respectfully urge upon you to prohibit the sale of intoxicating liquors in the State, during the war, except for family use and medicinal purposes. Put a stop to the retail traffic in whisky and rum. The only man whose death-warrant I have had to sign since I have been Governor, was brought to execution for murder when drunk. Every criminal now in jail here is suffering the penalty of intoxication. You must pardon me, gentlemen, if I press this subject with seeming pertinacity. I know that it is considered by some unpopular to advocate such measures, and that by others it is thought puritanic; but he who blenches at a sickly public sentiment, or wishes to evade responsibilities, in times like these, is not worthy the confidence of an intelligent and patriotic people. While I shall dispense public charities with a liberal hand, clothe our gallant men in the field, relieve the sick and destitute, take care of our wounded soldiers, and support the widow and the orphan, I also feel it to be my conscientious duty to strike at vice in every shape and form, and to do all in my power, as Governor of this Commonwealth, to sustain the morals of the land. The General commanding this department cannot suppress the sale of alcoholic liquors unless authorized by you. He and his District Commanders have often appealed to me. Good order and discipline cannot be kept among troops when whisky shops are near them. I, therefore, again most respectfully but urgently request that you will give this matter your serious consideration. Pass the law, and it shall be executed to the very letter. The large capital employed in this traffic, will find other and better investments; drunkenness, that scourge of every land, will disappear; crime will be greatly diminished; good order and discipline will be preserved, while the women, our truest and best patriots, will bless you for the act.

KIDNAPPING SLAVES.

At the commencement of my term of office, the country was full of lawless bands of evil-doers of every character. In order to suppress them, I issued the following proclamation:

TO THE SHERIFFS AND MAGISTRATES OF THE SEVERAL PARISHES OF LOUISIANA.

I am informed upon reliable authority, that many negro slaves, taken from plantations on or near the Mississippi river and its tributaries, which are under the control of the Federals, or which are abandoned by their owners, are brought into our lines and there sold by the captors or their agents. This fraud on the rights of the owners must be promptly checked and punished. I desire you to arrest every man having in his possession a negro thus brought into your parishes in violation of law, and to permit no negro bought or hired from such captors or their agents to leave your respective parishes. You will hold the offenders in custody for trial and punishment, and retain the slaves subject to the demand of their owners.

Violations of the rights of property are becoming so common, that it is incumbent upon all officers and law-abiding citizens to unite for the protection of society. Our State swarms with marauders of all descriptions. Horse-thieves, negro-thieves, swindlers and robbers pursue their wicked purposes with impunity.

As soon as the active operations of the campaign will permit, the civil authorities will be aided by the military in arresting and punishing all offenders. Until that time, I earnestly entreat you to call to your assistance all good citizens to suppress and restrain these violations of law and outrages upon private property.

HENRY W. ALLEN, Governor of Louisiana.
Executive Office, Shreveport, La., May 20, 1864.

It has had the desired effect. I sent two active and responsible officers through the State with proper orders. Under these orders about five hundred negroes have been recovered, and many have already been returned to their masters. "While this has put a stop to negro stealing., it has at the same time restored to many soldiers, widows and orphans, their lost property. I have appointed a commissioner to take charge of these recovered slaves, to hire them for the benefit of their owners, and to see that they are well provided for and kindly treated. His office is self-sustaining, not taking one dollar from the Treasury. In connection with this matter, I have sent the Hon. F. H. Farrar, as commissioner, to confer with His Excellency, P. Murrah, Governor of Texas, in order to devise some means by which all persons taking slaves into Texas shall be required to exhibit their titles, and have the same duly recorded; and, also, to aid our citizens in recovering their lost property when found in Texas. I respectfully refer you to the report of the Commissioner, and to the very satisfactory correspondence of His Excellency, Governor Murrah, on this vital and important subject.

MISSOURI SOLDIERS.
I am glad to state that our patriotic people, and especially the ladies, have taken_ a deep interest in the Missouri soldiers. Our country-women have labored unceasingly for the relief of these brave and veteran troops. I have thought it to be my duty to give liberally to

these "orphans of the army," without homes, without friends, but who always fight on every field with distinguished valor. I deemed it proper to issue a circular letter in their behalf. It was promptly responded. to, and the monies and clothing collected have been forwarded to these gallant patriots.

God bless them! The Citizens of Louisiana have adopted them. They shall share alike with our own soldiers.

LOUISIANA SOLDIERS.

It fills the heart of every Louisianian with pleasure and pride to see how well our troops have acted. In Virginia, in Georgia, in Tennessee, in Mississippi, in East Louisiana, in this Department, everywhere they have nobly done their duty, and won fresh laurels upon many a bloody battle-field. The early regiments that went to the armies of Virginia and Tennessee have been most terribly decimated, leaving but a few small brigades of that gallant host, who went forth with strong arms and stout hearts, to battle for their country's cause. The regiments in this department have suffered nearly as much in battle and by disease, but have been more fortunate in recruiting.

I have appointed as agents, Moses Greenwood and Geo. W. Ward, to act in con-junction with Dr. E. D. Fenner and Mr. T. O. Sully, in visiting the armies of Virginia and Tennessee. Ample means have been furnished them for the relief of every sick and destitute soldier from Louisiana, in these armies. Through my agent, W. D. Winter, Esq., $5,000 was given to our returning prisoners at Savannah, and $5,000 to the Louisiana Relief Committee, at Columbus, Ga. I also gave to the Richmond Association for furnishing artificial limbs the sum of $10,000. The Soldiers' Home and Louisiana Hospital, at Richmond, have been furnished with funds, and the destitute sick and wounded soldiers at Mobile have not been forgotten.

I have appointed Col. H.M. Favrot, Keeper of the Military Records of the State. and have sent him to the armies of Virginia and Tennessee to enter upon the responsible duties of his office. I trust that this appointment will meet with your approbation. I deemed it my duty to anticipate the action of the General Assembly, in order that no time should be lost in bringing up the military records of those gallant men, who have fought and are still fighting the battles of their country.

John Bunyan has portrayed, in language that will never die, the troubles, trials and tribulations of "Christian," while journeying to the New Jerusalem. This soldier of the Cross passed the Slough of Despond, through the valley of Humiliation, up the Hill of Difficulty, and fought the Dragon Apollyon, shouting with a loud voice and saying; "Rejoice not against me, oh! mine enemy; when I fall, I shall rise!" By incessant toil and hard fighting he gained the victory at last, and crossing the river, entered into the gates of the Celestial City.

Citizen soldiers of Louisiana! emulate the example of this heroic warrior. Halt not at the Slough of Despond. With quick time, march straight on. Listen not to the delusive promises of the enemy—they are as hollow and as false as hell. Oh! remember the widow and the orphan, whose cries daily ascend to heaven. Think of the women of Louisiana who have suffered crucifixion of the soul. Think of the torrents of Southern blood shed by Yankee hands—think of the acres of bleaching bones—think of the thousands of mutilated forms—think of the burning cities, of the devastated lands, of the broken hearts. Think of all these, and let the memory nerve your hearts to do or die.

When the armies of France returned from the late Italian campaign, all Paris received them with that pomp and circumstance which can only be displayed in that brilliant capital. All that wealth, and taste, and art could do, was brought into requisition. Wit, and beauty, and fashion were there, for this was the proudest day that France ever saw. The triumphal procession of returning columns, was headed in person by the emperor, the most sagacious and successful monarch that ever reigned over any people. Soldiers of Louisiana! when this war shall end and you shall return to your homes, a greater triumph awaits you than that of Paris. Each man, the humblest private in the ranks, will be a hero. The garland and the wreath shall he prepared_, Sowers shall strew your paths and lovely women shall shed tears for you of joy. Soldiers! my heart warms to you all. I have had the proud privilege of sharing your privations and hardships in camp, and your dangers on the battle-field. Yon shall never, never be forgotten.

PROVISIONS FOR THE DESTITUTE.

I respectfully refer you to the report of Col. J. C. Wise, Q. M. General, for a detailed statement of provisions furnished to the suffering citizens of the State. You will see that there has been distributed 30,792 bushels of corn, 20,182 pounds of bacon, 59,965 pounds of flour, 62,195 pounds of sugar, and 700 beeves. My agents were instructed to sell to those who were able to pay, and to give freely to the destitute, who had no means of paying. Upon the withdrawal of the Federal army, desolation and ruin were left behind them. All were stripped of everything valuable. Every ear of corn, every pound • of meat, every living thing in the shape of stock, was taken off. This left the parishes of Natchitoches, Winn, Rapides, Avoyelles and St. Landry to be supplied—a duty which I have performed to the extent of my available means. In them much distress has been relieved, and many helpless families have been saved from starvation. I have made sufficient arrangement to furnish corn and other provisions, in case of need, in these and other paint es. It affords me pleasure to relieve, when in my power, the suffering. Their tribulations have been great, but their patriotism has been greater. Some have gone astray, and have taken the oath of allegiance to the enemy. Many did so under duress. They deeply regret it, and are now showing by their daily walk that they are more firmly than ever attached to our cause. They are a good and brave people. They have been crushed to the earth. They are of us—with us—for us. Let them not be alienated and driven off. I respectfully ask your attention to their present political status and recommend them to your favorable consideration.

The sum of two hundred thousand dollars, appropriated for the poor and destitute, was placed in the hands of L. V. Reeves and N. D. Coleman. They have impartially and judiciously distributed it, and accomplished much good. This timely aid has gladdened the hearts of many a suffering family. I respectfully refer you to their accompanying reports.

CIVIL RIGHTS.

Immediately after the expulsion of the enemy last spring, many citizens were arrested by the military authorities and imprisoned, without the benefit of that speedy trial guaranteed by the Constitution and laws. It seemed that a reign of terror bad begun, and that the bayonet was about to rule the land. Taking prompt issue with the military authorities, I issued the following proclamation.

TO THE CITIZENS OF THE STATE OF LOUISIANA.

As the Chief Magistrate of the State, sworn to maintain the integrity of her laws, I deem it appropriate to renew to her people the assurance that I shall keep that oath, and fulfil that duty While doing this I have thought proper to add such suggestions as the occasion demands.

The presence of armies in our midst, raised by the Confederate Government, commanded by officers of its appointment, governed by the rules and regulations it has adopted, and amenable solely to it in a military capacity, produces inconveniences which are inevitable, and of which, when necessary, a patriotic people will not complain. These inconveniences form a part of the price you must pay for your country's independence, and for the liberties you will hereafter enjoy.

But that Government is of your creation, and has no legal power beyond that which you have conferred upon it. Its duties are strictly defined. and its authority limited by the constitutional charter which your representatives have aided in forming, and which you. through your convention, have ratified the armies of the Confederate States have no authority or power, except what the laws of Congress give them, and that body cannot go be) and the grant emanating from Sovereign States. The authority of military officers is. therefore, the creation of constitutional laws. They can rightfully do nothing but what Congress has authorized them to du. Properly viewed, an army is only a police force on a large scale, whose sole function is to maintain the laws of the land, and to protect the rights of the nation. Hence the machinery by which it acts ought never to come in collision with the civil laws, or the machinery of local or State governments. Over the citizen, or his property, no military officer has any other authority than what is given him by law. It is the glory of every really great military commander, that the civilian is never made to feel the presence of an army as a burden, a nuisance, or a terror. Over his troops his authority as given by law, is necessarily very great. This is right; but beyond the circle of his army the humblest citizen in the land is his equal.

I therefore earnestly admonish every one whose rights may be violated under pretense of military authority, to appeal promptly to the courts of justice. Let every citizen having just cause of complaint against military officers, report the same at once to the grand jury of his parish. If arrested and deprived of your liberty, it is your right to have the cause of your Arrest judicially inquired into at once, and to be discharged unless found to be legally detained.

This writ of Habeas Corpus is always open to every citizen; to invoke it is his hallowed rights and I earnestly request all judges to issue it whenever legally demanded.

Extended authority has been conferred on the Commanding General of this department. He has never used that power against a citizen, and is entirely free from any disposition so to use it. I know it to be his earnest wish, that every abuse of authority by any subordinate officer shall be resisted by citizens under all circumstances, and promptly reported. If there are acts of petty tyranny, annoyance and proscription committed in this department, they will be repro-bated by him. being. as contrary to his will as they are in contrast with his character. All such acts brought to his knowledge, I doubt not, either have been, or will be punished promptly. Thus far but one citizen of this State has been illegally and wrongfully exiled, and he shall be returned to his home and his family. While I am Governor of the State of Louisiana. the bayonet shall not rule her citizens, but they shall be protected at every hazard in all their legal and constitutional rights.

HENRY W. ALLEN, Governor of Louisiana.
Executive Office, Shreveport, La., July 5th, 1864.

When the Commanding General of this Department was appealed to, the prisons were thrown open, and all not subject to military tribunals were turned over to the civil authorities. He has forborne to suspend the writ of Habeas Corpus, though such suspension was authorized by Congress. He has carefully avoided contacts with civil functionaries and encroachments on civil rights. His profound respect for the laws of the land, and his eminent love of equity and justice, as manifested in his course towards the citizens of Louisiana, are among the traits that distinguish him as a safe depositary of power.

BANKS' LAST RAID.

In the month of March last, Maj. Gen. N. P. Banks, of the Federal army, arrived at Alexandria with a force estimated at forty thousand men, and a co-operating navy of sixty gunboats and transports, with a legion of camp-followers and speculators in their train. He pushed his columns up the valley of red river, meeting with no obstacles until within a few miles of Mansfield, where he found what he did not look for--a fight. The gallant Taylor was there, surrounded by the elite of Texas, Arkansas, Missouri, and Louisiana. The battle was fought, and such a battle! History will record it as one of the most brilliant conflicts of the war. Banks & Co. were routed, horse, foot and dragoons. They were pursued to Pleasant Hill, where another severe engagement ensued, and the "grand army" fled in wild confusion to Grand Ecore. Here was the most disgraceful retreat of modern times. Every transportable article of value was carried off, and the rest destroyed. I saw feather beds ripped up—windows smashed in—looms and spinning wheels broken in pieces—the rich and poor faring alike. Gen. Banks slept at the residence of a highly respectable lady at Pleasant Hill, during his hegira. Upon leaving the house of this gentlewoman, his body-guard stole all the furniture, bedding, etc., from the room which this gallant General occupied! From Mansfield to the Mississippi the track of the spoiler is one scene of utter desolation. The fine estates on Cane and Red rivers, on bayous Rapides, Robert, and DeGlaize, were all devastated. Houses, gins, mills, barns, and fences were burned—the negroes, old and young, were carried off—horses, cattle, hogs, and every living thing driven away or killed. When they left, the beautiful town of Alexandria, it was fired in many places by order of commanding officers. While it was in flames, and the women and children flying, in terror from their burning houses, the drunken and redoubtable Gen. A. J. Smith rode amidst his infuriated myrmidons, and exclaimed with fiendish delight: "Boys, this looks like war!"

It is a sad commentary on human nature, and sickening to the hearts of all honorable men, to see to what extent the Yankees have carried their thieving propensities, and how low they have descended in the scale of common decency. Yankee preachers boastfully exhibit on their shelves rare and costly books stolen from the 'libraries of Southern gentlemen. Yankee women are daily seen in the streets of Yankee cities and towns, bedecked in stolen silks and bespangled with jewels of which their husbands and paramours have robbed the persons of our country-women. Yankee boys drink from stolen silver cups, while Yankee babies cut their teeth on stolen silver spoons! As a steamer descends the Mississippi, a Yankee school-mistress calls to the commander from the bank to capture her a piano. Those are facts--notorious, well authenticated and undeniable. Such are the Christian men, who are fighting us! Such the Christian women who receive the fruits of all these robberies.

In order that the world may know, in part, what Louisiana has suffered, and that future generations of her sons may recur to these sufferings as a perpetual incentive to hate the Yankee race, I have caused reports of Yankee outrages in the several parishes to be prepared, supported by affidavits, made under the supervision of men of great respectability and integrity. These reports when published will comprise a mass of information of a reliable and documentary character, interesting to all civilized people.

In perusing this volume of crime and infamy, the very blood will boil in your veins. The evidence taken is under oath, carefully weighed and strictly scrutinized; my instructions having been to learn and record the truth; without coloring of any kind.

One occurrence has come to my knowledge not mentioned in these papers. On the retreat of Banks last spring, one of his Generals rode to a lady's house and asked for a drink of water. She gave him with her own hands a silver goblet full of cold water. After satisfying his thirst, the unblushing scoundrel examined the cup with the eye of a foot-pad, deliberately put it in his pocket and rode off! Can any age, clime or nation show in the dark and bloody annals of war, an act of meanness to exceed this theft by a Federal General dressed in full Yankee uniform

Orders were issued by their Commanding Generals to take all personal property and to destroy what could not be carried off, No christian or even civilized people have heretofore pursued this brutal policy. It was reserved alone for the Yankee race to sanction and applaud in this nineteenth century, that which shocks the moral sense of the Christian world. Even when the Czar of all the Russia's confiscates whole Polish villages, seizes the lands, blots out the very name of the department, and exiles the victims of his wrath to Siberia, he respects their personal property and allows them to carry it with them; but the Federals rejoice in destroying all they cannot steal.

A traveler visiting the field of Solferino a few months after the collision of the hostile armies there, would scarcely have known that a great battle had occurred. A few fallen mulberry trees, a few rifle pits, and the long trenches that held the silent dead, were all the marks of the terrible conflict where forty thousand brave men fell. No farm houses were burned, no villages sacked, no blackened ruins were-seen. Two Christian nations were contending for the mastery, and their campaign& were conducted by the rules of civilized warfare. Here, how different! To the Christian stranger I would say Come and see our blackened walls—our smoking ruins—our desolated homes— our demolished villages. Come, oh! come and see the widow and the orphan, robbed by a Yankee General, begging bread from door to door.

Come and see tender women with their little children flying from the too rich of the incendiary and the brutal touch of Yankee officers. See the venerable mother, seventy years of age, hung by the neck and stripped of her clothing to make her disclose where she had placed her own treasure. [This was done by Col. McCaleb, of the U. S. Army, now stationed at Natchez, in his raid upon "Sicily Island," who at the same time robbed many young ladies of their jewelry, tearing open their dresses and exposing their persons.] Think of all this, ye Christian strangers, and tell us are we wrong or are we right in fighting these fiends of hell to the last extremity? Tell us would it not be right in the eyes of God and man, to arm the whole population—to arm every man, woman and child—every free negro and slave—and fight these devils with burning hate and holy revenge? We are told that this world and all that in it is, will one day be destroyed by fire, and that matter itself will return to the God who made it. Yet one thing will remain: it is Eternal Justice. To the justice of the Great Ruler, we appeal, and with His blessing we mean to triumph.

Gen. Banks had emblazoned upon his banners, "Shreveport or Hell." He did not reach Shreveport. His legs saved him from hell. It is believed, however, that he will reach the latter place-for it is prepared for those who have shed their brothers' blood—for the "Devil and his angels."-

If the "dark and sulphureous pit" was paved with cotton bales, I verily believe that N. Y. Banks with his co-partners in trade, Messrs. Mansfield & Co., of New Orleans, would get up- an expedition with government transportation, in order to beg, buy or steal from the devil the aforesaid cotton. The disgraceful overtures which they have made, and which they are now making, for cotton, are disgusting to every honorable man.

And now the country presents the appearance of the Carnatic as de-scribed by Edmund Burke, after the terrible raid of Hyder Ali upon its plains. You can travel for miles in many portions of Louisiana, through a once thickly settled country, and not see a man nor a woman, nor a child, nor a four-footed beast. The farm houses have been burned—

the plantations deserted—the once smiling fields are now grown up in briars and brakes, in parasites and poisonous vines—a painful melancholy broods over the land and desolation reigns supreme.

WOUNDED AND DISABLED SOLDIERS.

At your last session you provided ample means for the relief of the wounded and disabled soldiers of Louisiana. Learning that there were many in the State in a destitute condition, I published the following notice:

TO DISABLED LOVISIANA SOLDIERS.

Louisiana soldiers, disabled by wounds, or by sickness incurred in actual service, and without means of support. are requested to apply to me for relief and assistance. Such applications must be accompanied with certificates as to disability, service rendered, and present circumstances. They will all be promptly relieved.

HENRY W. ALLEN, Governor of Louisiana.
Shreveport, La., August 4th, 1864.

Thus invited, these unfortunate children of Louisiana came forward and it has been a labor of love to supply them with money and clothing. No one has ever applied in vain, and there are now none of this class in want of funds, food or clothing.

Having seen in the Texas papers that the friends of the late Maj. Gen. Tom Green were raising a fund for the widow and children of that lamented officer, I subscribed in the name of the State, five thousand dollars, and sent it to the bereaved widow as a small tribute to the memory of her gallant and heroic husband.

General Tom Green

COMMISSIONER OF CLAIMS.

Finding that very many citizens living a long distance from Shreveport, had claims against the C. S. Government for property impressed, purchased, taken or destroyed, I appointed Hon. A. R. Hynes. of Madison parish, Commissioner of Claims. His office has become important, with a large business to transact, requiring an assistant at Monroe and at Opelousas. This Bureau is self-sustaining and requires no appropriation—a small fee being charged for collections. I respectfully refer you ' to the accompanying report of the Commissioner.

EAST LOUISIANA.

In consequence of the great difficulty of communication, I have not been able to- do all I wished for the parishes of East Louisiana. I deeply sympathize with our fellow-citizens who reside in that portion of the State, and have sent two of my Aids, Lt. Cols. D. S. Cage and T. G. Sparks, to learn their wants and redress their grievances. They have been partially supplied with cotton cards and medicines through my agents, Messrs. Winter, Walsh and Neafus, whose report is herewith submitted. They have shipped and sold one hundred and thirty-three bales of cotton—the net proceeds of which have beers expended in medicines and cottons cards—all of which have been distributed gratuitously, as they cost the State nothing. These agents have simply been reimbursed for their outlays, without acquiring-. one dollar's profit.

Dr. Edward Delony was appointed agent to supply that section of the State with indigenous medicines. His arrangements have been seriously interfered with by the raids of the enemy. His report is herewith submitted.

As empowered by the Act, approved Feb, 10th, 1864, I appointed Mr. Hugh H. Connell, collector of taxes, to be voluntarily paid, by persons living East of the Mississippi river, and I now submit his report.

Under the Act, approved Feb 9th, 1864, the machinery of the penitentiary, at Clinton, has been placed in charge of Mr. Wm. F. Lockwood, to whose report your attention is directed.

I respectfully refer you to the report of the Administrators of the Insane Asylum at Jackson; As this institution had become very much pressed for provisions, I gave the Administrators a permit to ship one hundred bales of cotton, with which to procure the actual necessities of life. I earnestly recommend that you authorize the Governor to take such steps as lie may from time to time deem requisite to supply this Asylum with articles of prime necessity. At present it is a sacred duty which we owe to God and our country, to take care of the poor inmates of this institution. It is in a deplorable condition.

By an act of your last session, the Governor was authorized and instructed to raise one hundred and fifty mounted men in East Louisiana, for purposes well defined in said Act. I appointed Maj. J. B. Corkern to the command of this force, together with the other necessary commissioned officers. He immediately entered upon the duties assigned to him, and notwithstanding every obstacle was thrown in his way, succeeded in collecting, mounting and equipping eighty men. By my orders he reported at once to Col. John S. Scott, then commanding in East Louisiana, and performed most efficient service under that gallant, meritorious and well-tried soldier—For reasons which will be communicated to your proper committee, I ordered this battalion to this department, and it is now actively engaged in the front, under orders temporarily of Lt. Gen. S. B. Buckner. For further information on this subject, I respectfully refer you to the report of my Adj't. Gen. T. G. Hunt, and to the accompanying correspondence with the Secretary of War.

ADVICE TO PLANTERS.

I would most respectfully recommend through you, that the planters continue to husband all their resources—pay strict attention to their plantations—keep up and repair their enclosures and apply themselves to the increase of their stock of all kinds. Let their cotton gins be kept in order, and a small quantity of cotton be planted, enough with which to pay their taxes and support their families. If not interrupted, I will promise to supply them with iron, farming utensils, &c- Let them cultivate the Chinese sugar cane extensively-, and also the plants that can be used for indigenous medicines—castor oil bean, poppy, mustard, red pepper, et cetera—all of which are wanted in large quantities at the State Laboratory. We must endeavor to be as far as possible, a self-sustaining people. A beginning has been made. I promise them if they will adopt these suggestions, and give me their hearty support, their wants shall all be supplied. I am now causing to be constructed a very simple machine, which will, I think, in a large measure take the place of cotton cards—the great desideratum of the country. This machine is simple in construction and cheap in price, and will be put at the disposition of all who may wish it.

Although Louisiana has been invaded by the enemy and most terribly devastated —let peace once more visit us, and in a few years our people will be prosperous and happy.

The historian, Dupin, informs us that the wars waged by France against herself and the rest of Europe, continued through twenty-three years. One million, five hundred thousand men had perished—property of untold value was destroyed. The nation was thought by all to be utterly ruined, her people to be crushed, her exchequer totally bankrupt. Yet within nine years after peace the profound and terrible wounds inflicted on France were all healed, and their scars entirely obliterated. Thus, it will be with us. Within less than nine years after peace is declared, a stranger passing through the State would not perceive that the iron heel of war had pressed her soil. Commerce and the arts will flourish. Smiling fields of cotton, sugar cane, corn and rice, will greet the eye in every direction, and wealth and plenty will crown the labors of the husbandman. Think of all this, planters of Louisiana, and bear your burdens cheer fully. I know that your taxes are heavy—that you are annoyed with the collectors and impressing officers—but remember this is the price of liberty. The soldiers are fighting your battles— you must do your duty at home, and in due season we will all reap the rich reward together. Our recuperative energies will rise triumphantly in the end. Our flag high advanced will be respected and beloved by all who revere morality and religion—who honor manhood, or respect patriotic women.

YANKEE TREATMENT OF SLAVES.

To the English philanthropist who professes to feel so much for the African slave, I would say, come and see the sad and cruel workings of your favorite scheme. — Come and see the negro as he is now in the hands of his Yankee liberators. See the utter degradation—the ragged want—the squalid poverty. These false, pretended friends who have taken him away from a kind master and comfortable home, now treat him with criminal neglect, and permit him to die without pity. I give you good Yankee authority--one William H. Wilder, a convict in the penitentiary at Baton Rouge, pardoned by the President of the United States, and made the agent for Yankee plantations. He says the negroes on these estates have died like sheep with the rot. On one in the Parish of Iberville, out of six hundred and ten slaves, three hundred and ten have perished. Tiger Island, at Berwicks Bay, is one solid grave yard. At New Orleans, Thibodaux, Donaldsonville, Plaquemine, Baton Rouge, Port Hudson, Morganza, Vidalia, Young's Point and Good-rich's Landing, the acres of the silent dead will ever be the monuments of Yankee cruelty to these unhappy wretches. Under published orders from General Banks, the greatest farce was perpetrated on the negroes. The laboring men on plantations were to be paid from six to eight dollars per month, and the women from two to four dollars. In these orders the poor creatures after being promised this miserable pittance, were bound by every catch and saving clause that a New England lawyer could invent. For every disobedience their wages were docked. For every short absence from labor, they were again docked. In the hands of the shrewd grasping Yankee overseer, the oppressed slave, without a friend or guardian, has been forced to toil free of cost to his new master. I saw a half-starved slave who had escaped from one of the Yankee plantations. In his own language he said "that he had worked hard for the Yankees for six long months—that they had 'dockered' him all the time, and had never paid him one cent!" This is the sad history of them all. The negro has only changed masters, and very much for the worse! And now, without present reward or hope for the future, he is dying in misery and want. Look at this picture ye negro worshippers, and weep, if you have tears to shed over the poor down-trodden murdered children of Africa.

UNITED STATES NO LONGER A HOME FOR THE OPPRESSED.

There is in the City of Pisa, Italy, a master-piece of statuary, called the "Exiles," sculptured from pure Carrara marble, by one of the best living artists. - It represents the exiles flying from the despotism of Italy to America. The husband and wife, with a beautiful child in her arms, are represented in the most graphic manner. One foot of each rest upon a rock marked "Italia," the other foot is placed upon a rock marked "America." While pressing the rock of America, the exiles turn their saddened faces to Heaven, but wish confidence beaming in their features, expressive of hope and joy and future happiness. Oh! how changed! America was once indeed the asylum of the oppressed, the home of all who loved liberty, and fled despotism. But now she is driving from her bosom all who dare to use freedom of thought, of speech, or the press— Canada, England, France, Cuba, Mexico, all are filled with exiles from the United States—refugees from their homes—

from Yankee land. Seward has touched the wires and they have had to fly—without a charge against them—without a writ of habeas corpus—without any legal redress whatever, they have had to hasten to a land of strangers and beg for a place to rest their weary heads. The days of Washington have sadly changed, and now instead of that pure and good man who was the President of a free and happy people, a satyr sits upon the throne, drunk with the blood of martyrs. The future sculptor will mould with classic art, and fix in dull cold marble, not the glory, but the shame of America.

PRISONERS OF WAR.

The castle of Chillon still stands on Lake Leman's shore. The curious traveler is still shown the foot prints of Bonnivard. The very chains which bound this wretched man are still to be seen. All have read his melancholy story in beautiful verse or elegant prose. When the true 'history of this war is written, the sufferings of our poor prisoners at Johnson's Island, Camp Chase, Camp Morton, Alton, Cairo, St. Louis, Forts Delaware, Warren, Lafayette, Pickens, Jack. son and Ship Island, will shock the age in which we live, and make all good men shudder at "man's inhumanity to man." The sufferings of the prisoner of Chillon will pale before the terrors of Yankee cruelty, and the story of Bonnivard will almost be forgotten. When at last released, see our brave men returning home! as they pass through the Yankee towns and villages, they are pelted with stones, and subjected to the rude jeers of a heartless mob. Sick, sore and emaciated, at last they reach their homes, and are often consigned to an early grave.

"Their hair is grey—but not with years,
Nor grew it white
In a single night,
As men's have grown from sudden fears,"
but from long confinement within the walls of a cold and damp dungeon, 'debarred from the free air of Heaven, and tormented by all that a wicked, cruel and vindictive foe could invent. The all-seeing eye of the Eternal God alone has penetrated the dark recesses of those

Yankee bastilles. Officers are literally packed into the narrow casemates of the forts, and there, upon short allowance of miserable food and bad water, are suffered to die without pity. Out of a number of prisoners captured by the enemy from the "State Guard," near Trinity, only two have returned. They report to me that nearly all are dead. They died as martyrs to our holy cause, and victims of Yankee cruelty.

THE WOMEN OF LOUISIANA.

Gentlemen, when our trials and troubles are ended, —when all our battles shall have been "lost and won "—when the soldier shall lay down his arms, and with his wife and children return to his now desolated home—when gentle peace shall come to bless this torn, bleeding, and distracted land—the highest honors will be due to those who have deserved the most. The private soldiers in the ranks will be the first in the affections of the country—the ladies next. I appeal to history to tell us where was there ever such self-sacrificing patriotism as manifested by the women of Louisiana. See the high-born aid once wealthy lady, educated and refined, and raised in the very lap of luxury, now reduced to penury, rather than dwell within the lines of the enemy! See the aged mother, once the mistress of a hundred slaves, now sewing for the support of herself and children! See the only daughter of a once wealthy planter, or princely merchant, now giving lessons to maintain her aged parents! See the families of the thrifty merchant, and of the honest and intelligent mechanic, driven from their comfortable homes into exile, battling with poverty- and want, while their protectors, their husbands and SODS, are in the army! See all these noble women bearing up most cheerfully under every new misfortune, praying daily for our sacred cause, and urging their fathers, husbands and brothers to be true to their country, to fight on, fight ever, never to despair, never to submit to northern despotism—but, if such be the will of God, to die like freemen.

In other lands there may be women equal to those of Louisiana, but I cannot believe it. Throughout the State, the ladies have not only clothed our own troops, but have given great assistance to other

Confederate soldiers. Sewing societies, concerts, tableaux and banquets have all been brought into requisition; and many a brave soldier has reaped the fruits of these patriotic exertions. One venerable lady, seventy-seven years old, in the parish of DeSoto, has knit with her own hands, one hundred and twenty pairs of socks for Missouri soldiers. Good men tell us, and I believe it, that it is highly pleasing in the sight of the All-wise and ever just God, to see lovely woman strengthening the arms and ministering to the wants of brave men who are engaged in such a sacred cause as ours.

MINISTERS OF THE GOSPEL.

It is a grateful duty to notice the course pursued by the Ministers of Religion of all denominations in the State and Confederacy. From the beginning of the war, they have been, as a profession, with few or no exceptions, steady, consistent, calm and resolute supporters of our cause. Before secession, they were unknown to political discussions, for they were singularly exempt from that baneful propensity of northern preachers, to intermeddle with public affairs, out of which grew that fanatical crusade against us, our institutions and our rights; but when the blast of war blew in our ears, the clergymen of our States began to manifest and illustrate that

love of political freedom eminently characteristic of those whom the truth makes free." A goodly and sufficient number of them have joined the army as Chaplains, and have done most faithful service, teaching holy precepts, doing most pious deeds of charity, rebuking the heedless, restraining the vicious, awakening and vivifying in all a sense of moral obligation—giving comfort to the afflicted, consolation to the dying, and here to all., Of that piety which adorns physical, and heightens moral courage, they have been the industrious teachers. The seed they have sown, has produced a harvest of good and wholesome fruits. Many have taken the field as officers, or privates in the ranks. They have done their duty most nobly, and in many instances have sealed with their blood their devotion to their country.

At home, the clergy have been equally distinguished for their labors, charity and beneficence. Many of the comforts, attainable formerly by even those of limited incomes, are denied to them, for their salaries are now paid in a depreciated currency; but none are heard to murmur. They go from their scanty boards in thread-bare garments to their respective churches with greater _zeal than ever. The sufferings incident to war have opened a wider field of labor to them, and they are performing their duties with commendable fortitude. In sections overrun by the enemy, the courage and steadfastness of our pastors have been especially conspicuous. Though compelled to see their churches polluted and robbed by a brutal and ribald soldiery or given to flames, they have been true to their trust, and rendered efficient help to their flocks. At Alexandria the truly patriotic and heroic priest stood at the door of his church, with sword in hand, ready to offer up his life to save the sacred edifice. This is an act of Christian heroism unsurpassed in any land.

THE EMPLOYMENT OF NEGROES IN THE ARMY.

While looking for an early close of the war, it behooves us none the less to prepare for its duration for years. It is indeed wisest for us to act as though war were to be the permanent condition of our tenure of independence. Preparation for the worst is the best means of warding it off; for, if we can convince our enemies of the steadiness of our purpose, and of our resolve to use all our resources, we take from them a moral element of strength—the hope of success—thus hastening peace. It is therefore our duty to inquire diligently into all our means of making war, not only for the campaign of this year, but for a series of years. Our antagonists, with a population of twenty million, have annually about one hundred thousand youths reaching the age for military service, besides an influx from Europe, of men capable of bearing arms, nearly equal in number. To a government become despotic, with great armies to execute its decrees, these recruits are available. Our resources for replenishing our armies are strictly limited to our own population, numbering half that of the enemy. Of fighting immigrants, we have

none. Of our youths, many thousands have nobly anticipated the con-
script age by volunteering. After the campaign of 1865, therefore, we
have reason to apprehend that a scarcity of recruits will become a serious embarrassment. While this is a powerful motive with our generals
to spare the lives of our soldiers by shunning indecisive battles, it is
also an incentive to earnest inquiry on our part, as to any means we
have left untried to add to the virtual strength of our armies.

I have long been convinced that we have in our negro slaves the
means of increasing the number of available fighting men. They are already, by the wise dispensation which placed them under our tutelage,
disciplined to labor. They are peculiarly adapted to the endurance of
our climate. Many of them are skilled in the ruder portions of mechan-
ical work. The most of them are good drivers of teams, and all know
the use of intrenching implements. In active military operations, immense manual labor must be done; and where white soldiers are scarce,
and good black laborers are plenty, it seems wise to employ the latter
whenever practicable. Whenever a negro laborer can be substituted
for a white soldier; a musket is added to some depleted regiment. With
hundreds of thousands of laborers thus available, it is rank injustice to
our chivalric defenders to exact from them that labor which ought to
be done by negroes.

It cannot be urged that our slaves are all needed to raise food for our
people and supplies for troops. Before the war, our southern population was greater than it is now, including the army. We then produced
a surplus of food, and three or four million of bales of cotton, together
with large quantities of sugar, rice and tobacco. We now need no more
food than then, and raise no cotton, and but little rice or sugar. All
having been mainly the product of slave labor, it is evident that there
are now more negro laborers than we actually need for agricultural
purposes, and that the surplus can well be spared for army use, after
making due allowance for those taken away by the enemy.

In view, also, of the possible calamities of a protracted war, it
will be wise to have many thousands of negroes thus attached to our
armies, mobilized, used to military discipline, habituated by army labor

to action in concert, and thus made ready and ripe for that important step which the exhaustion of our armies may necessitate—the arming of negroes. It is the deliberate purpose of the ruling majority of our enemies to prosecute the war on such a scale, and so long, as to exhaust our fighting men. In this Satanic game they seem willing to play three or four lives of their soldiers against every one of our own, as is shown by the last campaign; for they know they cannot rule over the living white men and soldiers of our country. This horrid policy of butchery must be met by the employment of all our resources. Our willingness to fight armed negroes against them, when made necessary by their own diabolical and persistent malignity, may be taken by them as the sign and measure of our inextinguishable hatred, while it will prove conclusively to the nations of the world that we intend to maintain our independence at any and every possible cost. If a master may, with the help of his faithful slaves, drive thieves from his corn-crib, incendiaries from his cotton-gin, and marauders from his house, why may not many masters, helped by their many slaves, act in concert to drive away armies of thieves, incendiaries, and assassins?

There may now be differences of opinion as to the exigency which shall call for this measure; but if we are driven to the wall, there will be none. Each section of the country should be the judge of the necessity. While in this department our army is still comparatively full, east of the Mississippi they want of troops has turned the thoughts of very many able statesmen, soldiers and journalists to the subject of putting negroes into the field. I hope the public mind in this State will be prepared for any action of the Confederate States Congress, and that our people will be ready for the emergency contemplated. Securing to the army a large number of organized negro laborers, appears to be the best possible preparation for this contingency. Should you concur in this opinion, I leave it to your wisdom to suggest such legislation as you may deem appropriate.

In the multiplicity of topics necessary to be called to your notice, I should have treated the subject of employing negroes in the army with more brevity, but for the capture and publication by the enemy of a letter to the Secretary of War, in the concluding paragraph of which I expressed the conviction that the time had come for putting negroes in the field. An expression of my views on this topic was naturally expected; and having no desire to withhold my opinion, in order to give it, I was obliged to state in part the 'reasons 'and facts on which it was based. I am indebted to the peripatetic Yankee general, who never fought a battle, for damaging his bad cause, by publishing my letter, and making it the subject of a special (order. This redoubtable general seems to have been much exercised; for the letter of the "Rebel Governor" has had the desired effect: it has put a stop to conscripting negroes by 'the enemy its ads department. Gen, Canby tells them if they will run to him for protection, they shall not be sent to the slaughter-pens and butchered anymore! One fact is certain and cannot be concealed—the enemy fear, above all things, the arming of our negroes.

In every battle with the enemy, we have been compelled to meet him one to our one. We have triumphed over him always, and will continue to do so, when the numbers are anything like equal. In one respect, however, he has the advantage. He can and does out-working. His soldiers are generally laborers or mechanics, of strong limb and muscle, accustomed from infancy to hard work. Ours are different; they cannot perform The Herculean tasks done by 'the enemy. Place two hundred thousand able-bodied negroes in the army, and this difficulty is removed. They will make the fortifications and garrison them, while our White troops fight the battles in the field.

I speak by authority; I speak the sentiments of the army, of every officer and private, of every man and woman in Louisiana, and stow sum up the argument on this question: If necessary, if the worst should come, perish slavery—perish the institution for ever—but give us independence; give us freedom now, henceforth and forever, from the accursed Yankee nation. If we are subjugated, the negroes are lost to their -owners. If we triumph, we can well afford to give freedom to every slave who fights the battles of his country.

This has now become a War of endurance, of heavy blows, and long, stout and determined resistance. Peace can never be made with

Abraham Lincoln except by armed intervention. This blood-hound, like the "dark Madonna," has deceived his people -will still deceive them until the terrible day of retribution comes. The time may come-- is perhaps fast approaching--- when we will have to give up the institution of domestic slavery in order to secure our independence as a nation. The civilized world is opposed to the name of slavery--it prefers bondage under some other name. In Mexico they have Peons— in Russia Serfs-in England, France and Spain, Cooleys. The position of the slave in Louisiana is far superior to any of these; he is better clothed, better fed, better treated and cared for; and in every respect a much happier being. Still, we cannot convince the world that they are wrong and that we are right. The public mind must be prepared for the --change. Shall we continue to fight on, in a long-protracted war with slavery, or shall we give it up and have peace and independence! Louisiana will rise in masse and say without hesitation, "We will abolish the institution—we will part with slavery without regret— if necessary to gain our independence,"

THE PROSPECT

In nay inaugural address I informed you that I. believed peace would he declared at no very distant day. I am still of that opinion. I believe the war will not last much longer. All revolutions must end, and become more bloody as they approach their close. Peace will come when we least expect it. It will come by intervention, and that no remote period, that we are tired of the war, none will pretend to deny, all acknowledge the fact; but we are resolved to fight on- to fight it out until we are recognized as a separate, free, and independent nation.

If there is any man in this state who for one moment thinks- of reconstruction on any terms whatever, let me beg him, for God's sake, for his country's sake-, for his own sake, to ask himself these few plain questions: Can I trust the Yankees, swayed as they are by a fanatical mob? Can I trust men who have committed every crime in the decalogue can I shake hands with murderers and robbers? Can I sit down with thieves, and house-burners, and assassins, and break bread with those who have insulted my wife, my mother, my sister? No, never never! never !!!

If the sainted spirits of those brave men, whose. bodies have been. butchered- in this unholy war, take an interest in earthly -affairs, I implore them to visit the pillows of those misguided persons if there be any—who in this trying hour would sacrifice the independence of their country, and shriek their protest in their unpatriotic ears. What! oh! what would be gained by reconstruction If the Yankees violated the Constitution for a series of years before 1861, will they not do it again But, it is suggested We will call for a convention of the States an ask for guaranties! Great God.! Imagine a convention of all the States! They must of course be admitted as equals. Every northern. State except three has voted for Lincoln and his policy.

We all-know what that policy is: it is as dark as Erebus as black as Hell It is-subjugation or death! We once had a constitution. It was, thought by all good men to be a sufficient guaranty; it has been over-thrown, and now a despotism is inaugurated. What, then, would be gained by reconstruction? Nothing but political annihilation--nothing but utter degradation and loss of all your property. Once lay down your arm and then farewell, a long farewell to all your liberties. Your ne-groes. will be. made your equals, your lands will be declared confiscate, and you will become the Slaves of those very hirelings who are now waging War upon you, abolitionism, agrarianism., and miscegenation, with all their horrid brood, will rule the "court and the camp."

Black men—our own, slaves, are now in the Yankee army and navy; they will soon be their congress, in the cabinet, in the pulpit, and. on the bench. Are you willing to live under such a government in any manner, in any way, in any position whatever? If I, were asked are there any terms on which you would consent to reconstruction and return to the old Union, my answer is emphatically none! Better fight for four years longer-aye, better fight for forty years to come, than -contemplate anything short of independence.   .

If there be any who have thought of a convention of the States, to the end that peace-propositions might be submitted, I would say, this is not, only unconstitutional and impolitic, but utterly impossible. By the recent elections at the north, the democratic -peace party has been, crushed. Lincoln & Co. are, now in blood stept in so far, that should they wade no more, returning were as tedious as go o'er. If it were possible to assemble a convention of delegates from all the States, it would be a Babel of passion and, confusion—of crimination and recrimination., Peace proposition would. not for one moment be entertained except on the terms: already offered, which -is an insult to every honorable man. But peace will come—it will come by intervention. The great-powers of Europe are pledged to the integrity of the Mexican Empire. If the South, should he subjugated, the victorious armies of the North will march over its ruins to the conquest of Mexico. This the Yankee congress -has declared—this the Yankee press has published—this -Mr. Lincoln has openly said—this his people applaud but this the European powers will not permit.

The recent misfortunes which our army have sustained in Georgia and Tennessee, are comparatively of a trivial character; if Richmond even should fall, our cause would not by any means be desperate. One thing is certain-we can never be conquered. We may be harassed for years by war but we will never be conquered—never!

I Must gentlemen through you bid my Country men be of good cheer. We all have 'steadily hoped that this War would end that this revolution would abate that the mountain top might be viewed, and the dove of Peace would at last go forth to return no more. I am firmly convinced that this is near at hand, in the meantime, let us do our duty under all circumstances.

The Ruler of the universe who spoke peace to the troubled waters of Galilee, will not forsake us

but in his own good time will speak peace to us. When Israel warred With Amalik, Joshua, 'was sent out to give battle. Moses stood hard by and held up his hands, As long as. they Were up, Joshua prevailed but in course of time they became tired, -and fell to his side- Then Amalik prevailed Upon seeing this, Aaron and Hur came to the assistance of Moses, and stayed up his hands till the going down of the sun. Joshua prevailed and Israel was free. Let us all then rally around the Chief Magistrate of the Confederacy. He is our President, and this is our fight. He is a pure patriot. Let us hold up not only his hands, but these of-all' others in authority. We will prevail--we will win the -fight—we will be free!

RECOMMENDATIONS.

I respectfully recommend that you pass an act resuming the collection Of all State taxes; that. you continue your appropriations for the relief of the families of soldiers, and the indigent of the State; that you enact a law authorizing the convicts to be sent to the-Penitentiary of Texas for confinement and labor—the Legislature of-that State having consented thereto; that you pass -stringent laws, punishing with severe penalties all persons who may kidnap; or illegally take away slaves from their Owners, and all who may aid or abet those so offending, or 'who may buy or sell negroes -knowing them to have been unlawfully taken from their owners, or from the agents or overseers of such owners, or from their plantations during their absence. Many of our soldiers, who are mow in the field doing their duty nobly, as well as many refugees, widows and orphans, have suffered heavily from these robberies; that the Governor be authorized to purchase one or more sea-going steamers, with which to run the blockade, and that he be empowered to buy and ship such-quantities of cotton, or other produce, as will suffice to supply the people of the State with all such staple articles as are now so much needed ; that the Governor have full power to call out every able bodied free male --capable of bearing arms, not already in the C. S. service, at any time he may deem such call necessary for the defense of the -State, under such regulations as lie may think proper, and that none shall be exempt from such duty ; that the sum of one. Hundred thousand dollars, or so much thereof as may be, required, be 'appropriated for the. purchase or; publication of, School -Books, to be -distributed amongst the several parishes, as -in: your wisdom. you shall direct. I have now a series of such school-books in course of publication, but cannot-Supply the Wants of the public in full. The youth of the -State must be educated. While the War taxes our energies to the utmost, we must not forget the sacred duty parents owe to their children. Finally, I recommend that you pass no private bills.

This is no time for special legislation. Let-all claimants be placed on the same footing. Of even general legislation, we need but little- let that be short. The country is at war the whole State is an immense camp.

Since my accession to office, I have had no-recreation. My duties as Governor have been very arduous. Many a weary day and sleepless night have I spent in. the service of the State. I -could have done otherwise and lived inactive, and at my ease; but I chose a different course. In these troublous times I have taken many responsibilities. I have dispensed to the destitute. to the widow, and-to the orphan, to the wounded soldier and his family large sums of money. This money has-not, however, been wrung from the people.by taxation, but has been put into the Treasury in due course of honorable traffic, giving great benefits to all. The people have paid no State taxes. They have been supplied with medicines and cotton cards, with clothes and 'stationery, with provisions and farming utensils, and with school books for their children—all 'without one dollar from the Treasury; for the profits on by investments for the State have paid all outlays and expenses.

If it is your desire that I should continue my administration as I have begun it, I wish your expressed approbation. If you do not 'approve it, I will in future adhere to the strict letter of the law, and spare myself a vast deal of toil, trouble and responsibility. I have no ambition but to serve the commonwealth of Louisiana. I do assure you, from the bottom of my heart, that I shall be the happiest man in this Republic, if during my term I can welcome back to their homes every son and daughter of Louisiana. Then, but not till then, will I ask to be relieved from duty, in order to repair my broken fortunes; for, having suffered along with many of ray fellow citizens, and lost all, I must begin life anew.

I cannot close this message without saying a word in behalf of our fellow-citizens of New Orleans; outraged daily by a brutal soldiery, insulted and annoyed by a traitor police, far worse than that of Austria—

robbed by officers in high station, and swindled by every petty official. Under all changes—under every new misfortune, the people of that unhappy city have exhibited the most unswerving patriotism. To our soldiers and citizens who have been confined in Yankee dungeons, the ladies have been more than kind. God bless these noble women! The heart expands, and the tear of gratitude flows in thinking of the ladies of New Orleans. Be of good cheer my fair constituents. I hear from you often. Your ardent devotion to the cause of the South, challenges the admiration even of the enemy. Go on in your good work. Relieve the sick, bind up the broken hearts, minister to the wants of those who still languish in the "Captive's lonely cell." Visit the tombs of the gallant dead who have died from Yankee cruelty, and place love's last offering of fresh flowers upon their hallowed graves; and then and there renew your vows of eternal hostility against their murderers. For these acts of patriotism and devotion, you will be thrice repaid. You will receive the blessings of all the good and brave in every land. The ways of divine Providence are inscrutable. None can find them out. I commit you. to His hands. He will not forsake you. We are told in the book of Ezra, that when the chosen people of God returned from their captivity, they erected an altar, and assembling around it, "wept with a loud voice, and many shouted aloud for joy." You shall meet your friends again. They shall assemble around your sacred altars. Your temples which have been made the "den of thieves" shall be purified, and on bended knees before the throne of the Great Jehovah, we will mingle together our tears of gratitude, and then with heads erect, and in the conscious pride of freemen, we will shout for joy!

HENRY WATKINS ALLEN.

4

Selected Correspondence and Proclamations

TO DISABLED LOUISIANA SOLDIERS.

Louisiana soldiers, disabled by wounds, or by sickness incurred in actual service, and without means of support, are requested to apply to me for relief and assistance. Such applications must be accompanied with certificates of disability, service rendered, and present circumstances. They will all be promptly relieved.

Henry W. Allen,
Governor Louisiana.

Shreveport, August 4th, 1864.

To the Citizens of the State of Louisiana;

As the Chief Magistrate of the State, sworn to maintain the integrity of her laws, I deem it appropriate to renew to her people the assurance that I shall keep that oath and fulfil that duty. While doing this, I have thought proper to add such suggestions as the occasion demands.

The presence of armies in our midst raised by the Confederate Government, commanded by officers of its appointment, governed by the rules and regulations it has adopted, and amenable solely to it in a military capacity, produces inconveniences, which are inevitable, and of which, when necessary, a patriotic people will not complain. These inconveniences form a part of the price you must pay for your country's independence, and for the liberties you will hereafter enjoy.

But that Government is of your creation, and has no legal power beyond that which you have conferred upon it. Its duties are strictly defined, and its authority limited by the constitutional charter which your representatives have aided in forming, and which you, through your convention, have ratified. The armies of the Confederate States have no authority or power, except what the laws of Congress give them, and that body cannot go beyond the grant emanating from sovereign States. The authority of military officers is therefore the creation of constitutional laws. They can rightfully do nothing but what Congress has authorized them to do. Properly viewed, an army is only a police force on a large scale, whose sole function is to maintain the laws of the land, and to protect the rights of the nation. Hence the machinery by which it acts ought never to come in collision with the civil laws or the machinery of local or State governments. Over the citizen or his property no military officer has any other authority than what is given him by law. It is the glory of every really great military commander that the civilian is never made to feel the presence of an army as a burden, a nuisance, or a terror. Over his troops, his authority, as given by law, is necessarily very great. This is right; but beyond the circle of his army, the humblest citizen in the land is his equal.

I therefore earnestly admonish every one whose rights may be violated under pretence of military authority, to appeal promptly to the courts of justice. Let every citizen having just cause of complaint against military officers, report the same at once to the grand-jury of his parish. If arrested and deprived of your liberty, it is your right to have the cause of your arrest judicially inquired into at once, and to be discharged unless found to be legally detained. This writ of habeas corpus is always open to every citizen ; to invoke it is his hallowed right; and I earnestly request all judges to issue it whenever legally demanded.

Extended authority has been conferred on the commanding general of this department. He has never used that power against a citizen, and is entirely free from any disposition so to use it. I know it to be his earnest wish that every abuse of authority by any subordinate officer shall be resisted by citizens under all circumstances, and promptly reported. If there are acts of petty tyranny, annoyance, and proscription committed in this Department, they will be reprobated by him, being as contrary to his will as they are in contrast with his character. All such acts brought to his knowledge, I doubt not, either have been or will be punished promptly.
Thus far but one citizen of this State has been illegally and wrongfully exiled, and he shall be returned to his home and his family. While I am Governor of the State of Louisiana the bayonet shall not rule her citizens, but they shall be protected at every hazard in all their legal and constitutional rights.

Henry W. Allen,
Governor of Louisiana.

Executive Office, Shreveport, La., July 5th, 1864.

SHREVEPORT, La., December 21, 1864.

General E. Kirby Smith, Commanding Trans- Mississippi Department :

General — It becomes my official duty to communicate to you my very respectful, but earnest and emphatic protest and remonstrance against the proposed destruction of all cotton on the Ouachita, and in other sections of this State, liable to the incursions of the enemy.

While doing this, I do not ignore the requirements of that military necessity which sometimes renders imperative, acts which work great hardship to the few for the benefit of the many ; but knowing you to be especially averse to the commission of arbitrary acts of power on any pretext, or for any object, and fully aware of your extreme reluctance to do what can be justified only by the plea of necessity, so often alleged as an excuse for wholesale spoliation and robbery, I feel assured that you will accept my remonstrance in the spirit which dictates it, and heed the reasons which constrain me to make it.

1. A government has the right to destroy its own property, to prevent its being possessed and used by the enemy ; but this right is strictly limited to government property. If it is necessary to keep private property out of the hands of the enemy, government should buy and pay for it, thus placing its right to destroy it beyond question.

2. If it is right to destroy a citizen's cotton to keep it out of the hands of the enemy, it is equally right to destroy any and all other property of the citizen which the enemy can steal and use. But the Federals have generally stolen and used the bread, meat, stock, furniture, and clothing, of our citizens, and found the theft more profitable to them individually, and more serviceable in a military way, than stealing cotton. If, therefore, you burn the cotton to keep it out of their hands, why should you not burn their corn-cribs, their barns, their stacks of grain and fodder, their houses and their household goods?

3. No apparent benefit has resulted from the destruction of cotton after the first year of the war, and there is much room to doubt its benefit at any time. If the Federals only wanted cotton, they know they could get a hundred times as much by peace as they can expect to get by raids, the war continuing.

4. If to procure cotton, it is supposed the enemy -will organize largo corps, with a numerous attendant fleet to ascend our rivers and invade our Western Territory, the Cotton might be judiciously left as a bait for them. Cotton is supposed to have influenced General Banks to invade this State in March and April last — a diversion of the Federal forces which contributed immensely to our great success in the now closing campaign of 1864. A similar Federal diversion in 1865, would be cheaply bought at the cost of every bale of cotton West of the Mississippi.

5. The cotton which it is proposed to burn, is mainly the property of the producers, and is owned in small quantities by those whose grain, meat, cattle, mules, horses, and all other means of subsistence have been lost, impressed, captured, or destroyed. The inhabitants cannot move, for want of transportation. If their cotton, their only remaining resource, is destroyed by you, they must, in the event of invasion, starve or beg

from the enemy, and receive Yankee rations at the cost of the oath of allegiance to Lincoln. Will you reduce them to this extremity ? Is it not better that a few speculators should make money, than that thousands of widows, orphans, and destitute citizens should suffer?

6. The fact that large quantities of cotton in the Ouachita Valley have been acquired by the Confederate States Government, and sold to Yankee agents, is well known. This cotton was bought mainly from large owners, whether producers or traders, who are enjoying the results of their sales. It will, therefore, be all the more odious and oppressive to destroy the cotton of small proprietors, who have little else to exchange for their current necessities. If the procuring of army supplies justified the sale of cotton to Federals (as I believe), it cannot surely be criminal for the poor people who own a few bales of cotton, to sell it for food, when they have no other resource.

If disloyal men, or speculators of doubtful loyalty to our cause, have accumulated cotton on the Ouachita, and held it in anticipation of the invasion of the Federals, it would be right to take it, pay for it, and when necessary destroy it. There would be different opinions about the policy of this course, but not about its justice.

I have the honor to be, General, with great respect, your most obedient servant,

Henry W. Allen,
Governor State of Louisiana.

General Kirby Smith

Marshall, Texas, May 13, 1865.

Memorandum:

We advise General E. Kirby Smith, commanding the Trans-Mississippi Department, to accept the following terms, in order that peace may be restored to the country.

1. On or about the ----- day of ------, that the Commanding General will disband his armies in this Department. Officers and men to return immediately to their former homes, or such as they may select, within the now existing lines of the Confederate States or the United States; and there to remain as good citizens, free from all disabilities and restored to all the rights of citizenship. The United States troops and authorities not to advance within the Confederate lines till after that day.

2. Guarantees to be given that no officer, non-commissioned officer, private, or citizen, shall be prosecuted in any courts for offences committed against the United States during this war.

3. That permission be granted to all persons (officers civil and military), soldiers and citizens, to leave this Department within days, through its ports or boundaries, with their arms and effects, unmolested, and go to any place, State, or country, beyond the limits of the United States.

4. That the present State Governments in this Department now in arms against the United States authority, be recognized until Conventions can be called with the view of finally settling any and all conflicts between the people of the respective States.

5. That on or before the day of , all military authority shall be surrendered to the several States, and that each State shall keep and retain number of men to act as a guard to preserve good order, and to protect the lives and other property of the people. That a safeguard, to extend for days, be granted the officers of state and others, to leave the country, in case they should wish to do so.

The above terms will be acceptable to the people of Louisiana.

Henry W. Allen,
Governor of Louisiana.

Shreveport, May 17th, 1865.
* * * * * * * * *
The Federal Commissioners have left to-day. The Convention of Governors, as I wrote you from Mar-

shall, agreed to appoint me as their agent to settle all difficulties. General Smith has also delegated me to arrange terms of peace. I shall await here the invitation of the Federal authorities, and proceed to General Grant's headquarters in a week or ten days. In the mean time there will he a cessation of all hostilities. I would advise all who intend to live under Federal rule to return to their homes with their property of all kinds, for *the war is over.* * * * *

I shall stay at the helm of state just as long as I am needed by my people; and then I shall seek a home as an exile in a strange land.

* * * * * * * * * *

It is probable we will never meet again; for within the next sixty days I shall in all probability be on my way to Mexico. But wherever I may be, you shall always have the high esteem, warm affection, and devoted friendship of

Henry W. Allen.

EXECUTIVE MANSION
SHREVEPORT, June 1st, 1865
My Dearest Friend :

I send you this by my friend and private secretary, Mr. Halsey, "who leaves to-day for Crockett, to spend some time with Governor Moore's family. He will tell you all. I shall wait till the very last moment. It is truly melancholy to think of our sad fate. I am just beginning to realize it. Oh my country! if my life could save thee, how cheerfully would I yield it up ! I want to see you so much — you feel to me like a most dearly-beloved sister, to whom I can open my whole heart, and speak freely, while I know that you fully appreciate my warm affection. 1 wrote you to-day by mail, shall continue to write, as usual, every day, till I leave this. Hope to see you within a week, as I expect to leave here on Sunday next.

Adieu, my dearest friend, and believe me ever yours,

Henry W. Allen

TO THE PEOPLE OF LOUISIANA

Executive Office,
Shreveport, La., June 2nd, 1865
Fellow Citizens, — I have thought it my duty to address you a few words in parting from you, perhaps forever. My administration as Governor of Louisiana closes this day. The war is over, the contest is ended, the soldiers are disbanded and gone to their homes, and now there is in Louisiana no opposition whatever to the Constitution and the laws of the United States. Until order shall he established, and society with all its safeguards fully restored, I would advise that you form yourselves into companies and squads for the purpose of protecting your families from outrage and insult, and your property from spoliation. A few bad men can do much mischief and destroy much property. Within a short while the United States authorities will no doubt send you an armed force, to any part of the State where you may require it for your protection.

My countrymen, we have for four long years waged a war, which we deemed to be just in the sight of high heaven. We have not been the best, the wisest, nor the bravest people in the world, but we have suffered more and borne our sufferings with greater fortitude

than any people on the face of God's green earth.
Now let us show to the world, that as we have fought
like men — like men we can make peace. Let there be
no acts of violence, no heart burnings, no intemper-
ate language, but with manly dignity submit to the
inevitable course of events. Neither let there be any
repinings after lost property — let there be no crimination or recrimination — no murmurs. It will do no
good, but may do much harm. You who, like myself,
have lost all (and oh, how many there are !) must
begin life anew. Let us not talk of despair, nor whine
about our misfortunes, but with strong arms and
stout hearts adapt ourselves to the circumstances
which surround us.

It now rests with the United States authorities to
make you once more a contented, prosperous, and
happy people. They can within five years restore
Louisiana to its original wealth and prosperity, and
heal the terrible wounds that have been inflicted
upon her — so great are our recuperative energies —
so rich is our soil — so great are the resources of the
State! Our rulers have it in their power to dry the
mourners' tears — to make glad the hearts of the
poor widow and the orphan — to cause the past in a
great measure to be forgotten, and to make your
devastated lands "to blossom as the rose." If my voice
could be heard and heeded at Washington, I would
say, " Spare this distracted land — oh, spare this
afflicted people. In the name of bleeding humanity,
they have suffered enough!" But, my countrymen, this
cannot be. I am one of the proscribed— I must go into
exile — I Lave stood by you, fought for you, and
stayed with you, up to the very last moment, and now
leave you with a heavy heart. The high trust with
which you have honored me, is this day returned. I
leave the office of Governor with clean hands, and
with the conscious pride of having done my duty. All
the officers of State, and all employees in its various
departments, have rendered their final accounts,

made full and complete statements. I thank them for their uniform kindness to me, and their patriotic devotion to the several duties assigned them. These accounts are in the hands of Colonel John M. Sandidge. I invite the closest scrutiny, not only of these papers, but to all my acts as Governor of Louisiana. My State Stores, and Dispensaries, and Manufactories, have all been conducted, in the most successful manner. None can tell the vast amount of good they have done, not only to you, but to the people of Texas, Arkansas, and Missouri.

Fellow citizens, in this the darkest hour of my life, I do not come before you as an old man, broke down by storms of state, nor do I come to plead for mercy, at the hands of those whom I have fought for four long years. No, no, I come in the pride and vigor of manhood, unconquered, unsubdued, I have nothing to regret ; I look back with mournful pleasure at my public career, now about to close. As a citizen, as a soldier, as a statesman, I have done my duty. The soldier's family, the widow and the orphan, the sick and the wounded, the poor and needy, have all had my especial care, while the wants of the soldier and the citizen have not been forgotten. I have protected the people from the encroachments of military power, and have never permitted a bale of cotton in the State to bi seized or impressed. It is partially in remembrance of these acts, that you have always given me your entire confidence. But few in authority have ever had so many evidences of affection and regard as you have so often shown me.

Refugees, return to your homes ! Repair, improve, and plant. Go to work, with a hearty good-will, and let your actions show that you are able and willing to adapt yourselves to the new order of things. We want no Venice here, where the denizens of an unhappy State shall ever meditate with moody brow, and plot the overthrow of the government, and where all shall be dark and dreary — cold and suspicious. But rather let confidence be restored. If required, let each and every one go forward cheerfully, and take the oath of allegiance to the country in which they expect in future to live, and there pursue their respective avocations with redoubled energy, as good, true, and substantial citizens.

I go into exile not as did the ancient Roman, to lead back foreign armies against my native land — but rather to avoid persecution, and the crown of martyrdom. I go to seek repose for my shattered limbs. It is my prayer to God, that this country may be blessed with permanent peace, and that real prosperity, general happiness, and lasting contentment may unite all who have elected to live under the flag of a common country. If possible, forget the past. Look forward to the future. Act with candor and discretion, and you will live to bless him who in parting gives you this last advice.

And now, what shall I say in parting, to my fair countrywomen! Ladies of Louisiana, I bow to you with tears of grateful affection. You have always responded most promptly and cheerfully to the calls of patriotism and duty. You clothed the soldiers, nursed the sick and wounded, cheered up the faint-hearted, and smoothed the dying-pillow of the warrior patriot. God bless you! God bless you! I can never forget you. In the land of the exile, I shall remember you with feelings of gratitude too deep for utterance. Sometimes think of him who has sacrificed all for you. Perhaps, in better days, when the storm of passion and prejudice shall have passed away, we may meet again; I may then be permitted to return — to mingle with my friends — to take them by the hand, and " forget my own griefs, to be happy with you." If this should be denied me, I humbly trust we may all meet in Heaven, at last, to part no more.

Henry Watkins Allen,

Governor of Louisiana.

San Antonio, Texas, June 15, 1865.
Colonel John Sandidge:

My dear Sir — We arrived safe here last evening, having had quite a pleasant trip, all things considered. The people everywhere were more than kind. I actually feel proud that I have been the Governor of Louisiana, for even the women and children had heard of me, and all vied with each other to do me honor. This is a city full of goods and strangers — full of refugees going further west. General Shelby will arrive to-day, with his command: we will all go together. If you are intimate with the Federal commander, give him my compliments, and say to him, that I have to ask of him but "one favor" — that he will rule our poor people mildly, and not let them feel the horrors of subjugation. If he will do this, all my feelings of hatred and antipathy will cease, and I will never again raise my hand against the United States authorities. I ask nothing for myself. I am perfectly willing to remain in exile the rest of my life. D---- sends his regards. Please remember me kindly to Mrs. Sandidge and your gallant boys, and ever believe me, very truly.

Your sincere and devoted friend,

Henry W. Allen.

San Luis Potosi, Mexico,
July 18th, 1865.

My dear Colonel — This will inform you that we have arrived safe at this place, after a long, tiresome trip. Governors Moore and Denis are with me. We are all very well. Will remain here a few days, and then go on to the city of Mexico, about 300 miles. It is my intention to settle permanently in that place, as I have no idea that I will ever he permitted to return. My means are nearly exhausted, but I do not despair. I shall go to work, with a hearty good-will, at any thing by which I can turn an honest penny. I often think of you, my dear friend, as one of the best and truest men I ever knew. It is highly probable that we shall never meet again, as I see by the United States newspapers that all who are excepted from the proclamation of amnesty will be brought to trial. It is a hard fate to be cut off from home and all we hold dear on earth; but, my dear Colonel, I think I am equal to the emergency. I shall not whine over my misfortunes; but with cool head and firm purpose, endeavor to rise above all my troubles. I sincerely trust, my dear friend, that the United States authorities are governing our people with kindness, and that their lot may be made as easy and pleasant as possible. God grant that Louisiana may be wisely governed, and that her people may never be made to feel the horrors which many anticipate. The citizens of Mexico have everywhere and on all occasions treated us with great kindness. I was invited to an elegant party, last evening, at Signor G 's, where were assembled many ladies and gentlemen to do us honor. This is a delightful place. In latitude twenty-four — still the climate is as cool to-day as our fall weather. Present my kindest regards to Mrs. Sandidge, and say to her that I have not yet seen a pretty woman in Mexico! Even in the most elegant society, all smoke the cigarrita. They sing, and play, and dance very well. Wear no bonnets, but go bare-headed. Denis sends his regards. And now, my dear and noble friend, good-bye. God bless you. Write me often, to the city of Mexico.
Ever your friend,
Henry W. Allen.

Courtyard of the Iturbide Hotel

Iturbide Hotel, City of Mexico. August 7th, 1865.

My dear Mrs. ------: I arrived in this great city some ten days ago, and have been well received by the civil and military authorities. I wrote you from Monterey and San Luis Potosi, and also, frequently, on the road from Crockett to Monterey. Governor Moore, and Generals Preston, and Smith, and Walker have all gone to Havana. Generals Magruder and Wilcox are here. I left Generals Price, and Hindman, and Hardeman in Monterey. This, I believe, disposes of all our distinguished exiles.

My dear friend, I am delighted with Mexico, so far. It is certainly the garden-spot of this Continent, and in the hands of the Americans or the French, will make a most delightful country in which to live. This is the climate for all who are suffering with pulmonary diseases. Here are no consumptions. We are 8,000 feet above the level of the sea, and to-day, the Vth of

August, is as pleasant as the month of October with us. On last Sunday, I went to military mass, at the grand cathedral. The Marshal and his staff, brilliantly dressed, were present. The old church was crowded, a full band of music played, and during the ceremony, the soldiers, who were around the altar, with their muskets in hand, knelt and saluted, *a la militaire*. The band played beautiful pieces from the Trovatore and Norma. This is life in Mexico! Here is great display of fine carriages and elegant equipages. -The houses of the wealthy are most luxuriously furnished. In fact, every thing is in barbaric splendor. The city has a population of 250,000, of which only 50,000 are gentlemen or merchants. The rest are Indians or Leperos, who throng the streets as fruit-sellers, or venders of small-wares, water and Pueke carriers, &c., &c.

I have been kindly received by the Marshal and others in high position. Many persons have called upon me, and made my stay, thus far, in Mexico, very agreeable. The ladies here are truly very handsome. At the opera, the other evening, I saw a great many very pretty women. They dress very elegantly, with a profusion of jewelry. They wear no bonnets. An elegant mantilla is thrown over the head. Notwithstanding the Mexican ladies are pretty and splendid, I prefer the beauty of those of Louisiana. I could never lose my heart with women who seem to lack intelligence, and whose love for show and expensive dress and jewelry, seem to be their ruling passion. To me, intellect and gentle goodness alone are divine in your sex! I wish you were here, to join me in my daily rides and excursions. Your knowledge of Spanish, and all languages (how many is it ?) would be of such great assistance. I went to-day to the celebrated cypress tree, known as the tree of Cortes. It is near the city, on the Paseo, and it really looks very old indeed! It was here that Cortes sat down and wept. It was here he spent the "triste noche." Everywhere around this great city, you see places full of historic interest. In

the museum stands the huge sacrificial stone,
covered with hieroglyphics. I regret so much, dear
friend, that I cannot, in the short space of this letter,
give you an account of many things I have seen here.
I have taken a Spanish master, and am now daily engaged busily in
learning the beautiful language. I am preparing myself to teach school, by giving English lessons in a few
good families. I find I can make a support, which is all
I want, thank God. I, at least, breathe free air, and,
although I am poor and penniless, yet I am a free
man; not shut up in a dreary prison. *Poor Mr. Davis!*
An invitation has just been handed me to the palace,
to be presented to the Emperor and Empress, to-
morrow, at 1 1/2 o'clock. I shall go, and write you
again an account of my interview. Commodore Maury
is here. He is in high favor at court. He is with me in
this hotel. He is in fine health, and has become a
citizen of Mexico. One can get the finest coffee and
sugar lands at $1 per acre, payable in five years.
Write me immediately. Regards to Mr. -----.
Ever your friend,

Henry W. Allen.
P. S. I left San Antonio on the 17th of June last. I have
not received a line nor had a word from the United
States since. You promised to write! Please write by
every opportunity. We get no mails here, regularly, of
any kind. Adios, mi cara querida senora.

Admiral Matthew Fontaine Maury,

"Pathfinder of the Seas"

City op Mexico, August 10th. My dear Madam :

Since writing you, I have been presented to their Majesties. They received us very graciously. The Empress is an elegant woman, highly cultivated, and speaks the English language very well. She assured us that we poor Confederate exiles had her heartfelt sympathy, and that we were welcome in Mexico. I am much pleased with both of them, and shall make this city my home, while an exile. It is hard to be exiled from home and friends, and all we hold dear on earth; but I suppose it cannot be helped ! Generals Price and Polk, of Missouri, and Judge Perkins, arrived to-day. They are all well. Thank God ! we are all, at least, beyond the power of persecution, prisons and chains. Judge Perkins looks in fine health. He sends

his Warmest regards to you and Mr. . He says he will
write you soon. No letters yet from anybody! Not a
line from you! It is strange! But your letters may be
at Matamoras. I know, I told you to write there. I have
no doubt, I blame you unjustly, in my impatience; but
we don't even get - newspapers from the States. It
makes it seem so far, far off! I think sometimes you
have forgotten me. " Les absens ont toujoiirs tort." I
am reading a Spanish paper every morning. The
carriage containing the Host is just passing my windows. All are on their knees. Even the Emperor, in
passing, has stopped his carriage, and has gotten out,
and is on his knees ! ! ! The French officers and
soldiers, I see, do not kneel. They simply raise their
caps. I am reading Prescott, I am ashamed to say, for
the first time. Of course, yon, who have read every
thing in all the languages of Babel, have read it. Don't
you think it a remarkable book? Such great research
and such beautiful style !

I dined yesterday with a party of Englishmen. We had
a most magnificent dinner — 7 o'clock : returned at-
12 m. I am really grateful for the kindness I receive.
It, in some measure, takes away the unpleasant part
of an exile's life. Write me, *as often as you can!* —all
the political news and conditions, as well as the social
and literary ! — *every thing, anything* — only write.

Adieu — yours ever,
H. W. A

Emperor Maximillian of Mexico

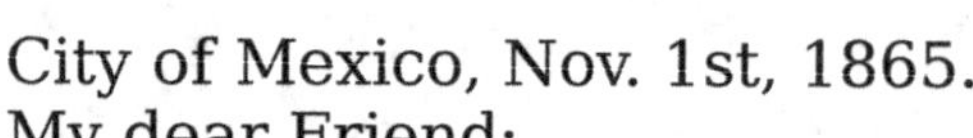

City of Mexico, Nov. 1st, 1865.
My dear Friend:

Your two letters, one dated July the 15th, and the other, Natchez, August 23d, have just been received. I read them with intense pleasure, for, my dear madam, you are the only living soul that has written me a line since I left Shreveport, on the 2d day of June last. I have now been absent from Louisiana five months, and strange to say, of all my hosts of friends, none have written — all have forgotten me except yourself! I assure you that 1 do from the bottom of my heart appreciate your constant, pure, disinterested friendship. Your beautiful, kind words, are invaluable, and most consolatory to me. Milles gracias, cara querida Senora ! I wish I knew as much Spanish as you do! But I am trying to learn, so as to read and speak the beautiful language with you, if we should ever meet again, which may God grant, though I see no hope now of my ever being permitted to return home ! Colonel ------ left me some two weeks ago. I gave him several letters for you, which I hope you have long since received. Well, my dear madam, I have turned editor, and am waiting impatiently for letters from you, to publish in "*The Mexican Times.*" Do write me often, and give me all the political and other news. Send me for publication a short history of General Lee and Stonewall Jackson. Write me some poetry, and send me any good pieces of original poetry you can get hold of! I shall send you the paper regularly — if possible. Please let me know how to send it. My whole time is taken up. I labor twelve hours every day, for I have to write all my editorials, and then see to getting up the paper. I can't afford to employ an assistant. My health is not good. I suffer much from my old wounds, and am sometimes so lame that I can hardly walk to my office. But, my dear friend, I ought not to tell you this, it will only distress you : you can give me no relief I have long since shut out from my heart all hopes of aid or sympathy from any source. Sometimes my spirit sinks a little, but not for long. My wounds make me feverish. Confinement, you know, is always irksome; and when I am sick in this lonely chamber, and I pass hours and hours with no one but my Mexican servant to listen to the impatient ravings of a fevered brain, oh, then, I think of those dear ones I have left in Louisiana, of home, of all whom I love so much. But, my dear friend, enough of this, though it is a relief to be able to write you so freely! Yet I must not wantonly and selfishly distress you. I do not see how I can ever return to Louisiana! I cannot ask a pardon. A parole I would gladly accept. Perhaps a general amnesty may come — if not, I cannot with honor go back and ask pardon for what I don't consider a crime. Let my properly go to those who have seized it— I can make another fortune. I am very, very thankful to my friends for their interest in my behalf. If I could ever serve the people of Louisiana, in any, the smallest degree, I will gladly, gladly do so. I will return eagerly to the people who have ever been so good, so true to me.

I go to the opera every night — being an editor, I have free admittance to all the theatres and operas. Last night they performed my favorite, the Trovatore. It was beautifully rendered, and I could not keep from shedding tears. Music has upon me now a strange effect. It takes me back to the scenes of my childhood and my early manhood — to the pleasant days I have spent with the warm hearts from which I am now forever parted — and leaves me for a while sad, and almost broken-hearted. I have made but few acquaintances in Mexico, but those few are select, and very agreeable. The Emperor and Empress have been very kind to me. I wish you could see "our Carlotta." She is a noble woman, the fast and good friend of all unfortunates, such as we poor Confederates! She is so charitable ! — a real *woman*! This is All Saints Day. The whole of Mexico is in a ferment of pleasure and pleasure seeking. High Mass at 8, bull-fights at 4 p. m., operas at night. I go to all, as much as I can, and have become quite a good Mexican. Give Mr. S , General Wm. T. Martin, and J. S , my kind regards; they have ever been my good friends. Good-bye. Pardon this melancholy letter. Write me often — your letters are inexpressibly comforting to me. That *was* a lovely extract from in the last! How thankful I should be for such a friend — *indeed* I am.

Ever yours,
Henry W. Allen.

City of Mexico, Dec. 25, 1865. R. C. Cummings, Esq., Shreveport, Louisiana:

My dear Friend — Your letter of the 9th ultimo is just received, under cover of letter from Messrs. R. C. Cummings & Co., of New Orleans, and accompanied by a draft on London, in my favor, for the sum of one hundred and seventy-nine pounds sterling, the re-ceipt of which has been duly acknowledged.

This is Christmas Day, and it does seem as if a kind Providence had so arranged it, that I should receive this material testimonial of regard from my devoted friends in Louisiana, as a Christmas present. Be pleased to express to those kind friends, who have joined you in this act of liberality, my sincere, my heartfelt thanks. But few men have had the good fortune to be blessed with so many good, true, and devoted friends, as have fallen to my lot. That Heaven would bless you, the State of Louisiana, and bring her citizens safe through their many trials and troubles, has been my constant prayer ever since I left her borders. I can never, never forget her ! As for your-self, sir, this is not the first time that I have been placed under obligations to you. Accept the grateful thanks of an exile, with the hope that some day he may be able to repay, in part at least, the many acts of kindness rendered him by you. My friend, it is true, beyond the possibility of a doubt, that there is such a thing as friendship beyond the grave. If, therefore, we should never meet again— if it should be denied me to see my friends in Louisiana again on this earth — oh! I have the assurance that we shall meet again " beyond the skies." When it shall please God to con-sign this mutilated body to its last resting-place — be it among strangers in Mexico, or friends in Louisiana — I will want no better epitaph inscribed on my tomb than the sentiment contained in the closing part of your letter:

" Your friends are proud to know that Louisiana had a Governor who had an opportunity of securing a million of dollars in gold, and yet preferred being honest in a foreign land, without a cent."
My conscience tells me that *I did my duty* — that I protected the people, and remained faithful, to the last, to the high trust confided to me. I have always believed, and now I know, that the good people of Louisiana have not forgotten — no, never will forget — him who was ever true to them.

With grateful feelings of undying friendship, I am, dear sir,
Yours truly and faithfully,

Henry Watkins Allen.

" CHRISTMAS COMES BUT ONCE A YEAR "

Published in Allen's *Mexican Times,* December 25th,
1866

Before this issue of our paper readies most of our
readers, the anniversary of our Lord and Saviour will
have arrived. It is a day of rejoicing for the rich and
the poor, the bond and the free, in all Christian lands,
and even the captive in his lonely cell, if not permitted to participate in the festivities of this sacred and
joyous occasion, will have pleasure in the recollections of the past.

Christmas day ! On this day how many young hearts
will leap with joy ! how many mothers and fathers will
call round them their children, and, kneeling before
the throne of the great Jehovah, thank Him for His
continued blessings ! how many widows, clad in
weeds of mourning, will gather their little ones close
to them, and in humble supplication commune with
the God of the fatherless ! how many exiles in foreign
lands will kneel in prayer and ask their Heavenly
Father to protect their wives and children, and their
dear, dear friends far away!

On last Christmas we were seated in our executive
chair, the chief magistrate of the great State of
Louisiana — the Governor of a noble constituency of
lovely women and brave men. The Christmas before
that we were a Brigadier-General in the field. On the
next previous Christmas we were confined to our bed,
given up to die, and suffering all the agonies of terrible wounds.

Today we are in this great city, editing this humble
paper, and coining our brain into daily bread ; but,
thank God, in good health — as it were rejuvenated —
and now enjoying the hospitalities of the good and
generous people of Mexico.
God bless the exiles, wherever they may be, in this
wide world of sorrow; and may they, on the coming
Christmas day, with grateful hearts thank all who

have been kind to them in the land of the stranger. That heaven may bless our native land, and bind up the bruised and broken hearts, and dry every mourner's tear — is our sincere, our fervent prayer.

Immigration Appeal

Excerpted from Allen's *Mexican Times,* Published in English in Mexico City

Come and settle where you can grow sugar-cane, coffee, indigo, cotton, cacao, and tobacco, with all the tropical fruits. Come where the climate is an eternal spring and where, strange to say, there are no fevers-no epidemics of any kind, except in the tierra caliente of the seacoast. Bring with you, your engineers and mechanics, and such implements of husbandry as may serve as patterns for others. Here you will find iron, steel, copper, and timber all ready to be turned into such utensils as you may want. The more precious metals- the silver and the gold-are here in great abundance, awaiting the reward of your industry and enterprise. . . . The best article of cotton is grown in every part of the Empire-the sea-island being very productive on the Gulf and Pacific coasts. . . . The lands in the tierra templada yield large crops of Indian corn, wheat, rye, barley, oats, and potatoes, which always find a good market at the door. The tobacco planters are making fortunes-the coffee and cacao haciendas are still more productive, yielding large profits to their own.

To those in the United States whose fortunes have been swept away by the terrible tempest that has so long raged in that afflicted land, to those who have drunk the cup of bitterness to the very dregs, we say, come to Mexico. Here you can get homes without money and without price. Here you will find a shelter as did the Huguenots who fled to England, as did the Puritans who came to the bleak shores of America.... The fortunes which you have lost can be regained here by a few years of industry and enterprise. Come then, and bring with you your families and your household goods. Let the maid and matron, the aged sire, the tender son, and hired servants-all come.

City of Mexico, Jan. 1st, 1865.
My dear Madam:

I send to-day by a friend three packages of -------, and slips that you asked for, and a long letter for you. My friend will mail them in Havana. In the mean time, I send you this line by mail. Do you get wearied of my frequent epistles? I am afraid sometimes you may; but I hope not. I write not only to gratify my own selfish heart, but to provoke your replies, which are so valuable to me. How good you are to write so often and so frankly! I am so grateful to you! I laughed heartily over your description of -------. The political position is rather lugubrious! It is well that you are amiable, with such a sense of humor, such power of satire, and so much learning as you have crammed in that little head of yours ! This has been a great day in Mexico; for I, like all others, have spent the day visiting, and am now (8 o'clock at night) very tired. I have been to the British Minister's, to Marshal Bazaine's, to Count De Nones, and other places, till my poor wounded limbs ache terribly. Please send me a letter every month for publication. Don't be too severe in your criticisms on my poor verses to the Empress. You know I am afraid of your laughing satire! The *Mexicans liked my poetry*; they say it "is good;" but as they are not finished *English* scholars, I have some misgivings. *I don't know.* My dear friend, I am writing for *bread,* and am happy to inform you that I am making a living, a good, respectable living. I think I have obtained the respect and confidence of the

people of this great city. The Empress has been very
kind; and I felt every line of the verses, "I*f they do
limp.*'" She is a great woman; every one loves her. * *
* I am keeping house; my printers are living with me.
We have Mexican servants, and I am learning to
speak the language. I give English lessons, which
helps me to get along. Yes; I have " *lived for weeks* on
25 cents — one meal — per diem." *Who told you*? But
that is all over now; don't fret about it. How could I
complain, "*and tell you of it*." how could you aid me?
As to what Buckner says about the climate, I can
understand; it is delightful, though ! I mn going away
— going to Paris in May. My wounds trouble me
greatly.
* * * * * * * * * *

If you should ever meet Miss ----- again, please say to
her that I have no matrimonial engagement with the
lady she mentioned, nor with any other. My dear
friend, what would I do with a wife? I can hardly
support myself in my exile. I always thought *that
marriage* a mistake, ill-judged. I am sorry about it: I
liked them both. But it is all a lottery, and who draws
a prize is lucky indeed. This is the carnival season in
Mexico ; the city is filled with maskers, and music of
all kinds. I send you a flower, and a piece of Cortes'
"Tree of weeping;" it is a huge cypress-tree. What
lovely paintings you would make of these flowers! You
would make a book superior to your Louisiana one. I
am very impatient to get " The Illumination," that
song of Moore's. I like it so much! and, illustrated by
your skilful pencil, how valuable it will be ! Last
evening, I went to hear the opera of Martha, when, at
tlie close, "The Last Rose of Summer" was sung. I had
to quit the theatre, almost in tears ; associations were
too strong for me. It carried me back to Louisiana. * *
* *

If you should see " Vallery," tell him " howdy' " for me.
He is a faithful and good servant, honest and true.

Ever yours,

H. W. A.
" I have just had a letter from Sandidge. What a
friend he is ! Give Governor H----- my regards. I am
delighted to see him a director of the Citizens' Bank.
The right man in the right place. *If there ever was an
honest man, Governor H----- is one.* I have made the
acquaintance of but few ladies — I have no time :
with me, it is work, work, work; my daily bread
depends on it. My paper is a success, but does not
bring in much money yet; but my wants are few, and I
am comparatively happy. Don't worry about me — you
can't help me. They say I will get relief in Paris. I am
going to try it. Yes ! the women are "*like the Havan-
ese,*" they are many of them " very fat," but at the
same time pretty. "Don't I remember old Mrs. Com-
monfort?" Of course I do, and the pretty girl with the
dark eyes, and fire-flies. How little I dreamed, in
those days of sunshine, I should be here an exile in
their native land ! The British Minister (Mr. Scarlett),
has been very kind to me. I have received many
courtesies at his hands. Thanks for the clippings from
the papers. How considerate you are! My regards to
your good husband.

Ever your friend,

Henry W. Allen

City of Mexico, February 10th, 1866.
My Dear H. :
Your letter of the 20th January is just received, enclosing a memoir of Stonewall Jackson, by Mrs. -----.
I shall publish it in the *Mexican Times* with the greatest pleasure. What a wonderful woman she is! How
learned, how gentle, and kind, and warm-hearted !

Well, ray dear friend, I have read, with tears of gratitude, your entreaty for me to return to Louisiana. I
would cheerfully do so, for I know that my friends are
true and sincere but I cannot until I am assured of a
pardon, or a guarantee is given that I shall not be
cast into prison, or otherwise persecuted. As much as
I love Louisiana and her people, I would not voluntarily go into a loathsome prison, and be compelled to
get on my knees and ask for pardon, for the privilege
of seeing my old friends again.

Mrs. D writes me that there is no hope of my being
permitted to return. I therefore shall make my
arrangements to reside permanently abroad : still, I
shall never expatriate myself, but shall live and die an
American citizen. On the 8th of April, I will be in
Havana on my way to Paris, in order to have an
operation performed on my wounded limbs, for I am
suffering tortures every day. I have written to Colonel
----- to meet me with a few friends on that day in
Havana. My paper will go on, under the charge of an
able and discreet editor. I have sent you many copies
of the Times, and hope they have gone safe to hand.
My dear H, I often feel sad and depressed, although I
have such a buoyant disposition; you will say, " as the
hart pants for the water-brook," so must I earnestly
long for the land of devoted friends. I have, however,
so much to do, my time is so thoroughly occupied,
that the " melancholy mood" soon passes off. I send
you several copies of my paper to-day. * * * *

Our good friend, Mrs. D, writes me that she proposes
to write my life. Now, my dear friend, I must ask the
favor that you will review and correct the work before
publication. Mrs. D will be delighted to have your
assistance; you have known me so intimately, so well,
that I feel that my reputation, which must now go
down to posterity, will be safer in your hands than in
those of any other. Our friends in exile here are all
making a living. Some farming, some employed on

the railroad, some in counting-houses, stores, &c., &c. All, I am glad to say, are conducting themselves very properly, and are highly esteemed by the Mexicans. The colony at Cordova bids fair to do well. Judge is the agent of the Government there, and is well satisfied with his prospects for a fortune. I consider this empire perfectly secure, France, and Spain, and Austria can't back out. Their honor is at stake. Your people are not prepared to go to war at present ; for the South, although overwhelmed, is not conquered. The spirit of the people cannot be subdued, although they willingly accept the new order of things, and will act in good faith. However, it is useless to disguise the fact, there is no good feeling between the two sections of the country. They can never again love one another, unless the persecuting spirit of the Radicals should give way to better feelings on their part. Adieu: may God bless you.

Your sincere friend,

Henry W. Allen.

Vera Cruz, March 15th, 1866.
My dear Friend :

Your letters of February 16th, 18th, and 22d, with enclosed clippings from the New Orleans press, and letters for friends at Carlotta, all came safely to hand to-day. Many thanko for the same. I have already forwarded the extracts to the city of Mexico, to my paper. By the way, I regret so much you don't get the Mexican Times regularly. I know it would please you to have it. * * * *

I return to the city of Mexico to-morrow, — in a few days will start for Europe. I go to consult a surgeon about my wounds, for I suffer a great deal, and there seems no remedy. I do not know how long I shall be gone. It will depend on circumstances ; but after the surgeon gets through with me, I am determined to visit Jerusalem and the Holy Land, if possible, before I return. You shall receive letters from me written on the banks of the "Jordan flood."

" Sweet fields beyond the swelling flood,
Stand dressed in living green."
Don't you remember the hymn ?

I have a strange, romantic longing to bathe in the waters of that river, and to stand where Moses stood, and " view the promised Land."

I always had this desire. Do you think it is superstitious? I am pretty certain you sympathize with me ; so I don't fear your laughing. I am anticipating great pleasure in writing you the longest letters from all the interesting places. My paper will go on as usual. I will correspond with it, and also with the ----. My signature is -----. By this means I get the money to travel. Mr. ----- pays me so much per letter. This is a secret. Under this pay I hope to be able to travel twelve months, after getting through with the surgeon. I have received the letters you wrote about, but for a long time have had none from -----. When you write to Dr. Martin again, say to him that I have written him often since I left, and that I write him again to-day. There is an opera here at present— last night we had the Trovatore. There are so many pleasant recollections connected with it, that I enjoyed it very much. May Heaven bless and preserve you, my dear friend, is the prayer of

Yours truly,

H. W. A.

P. S. — I shall send you a wooden cross made out of cedar of Lebanon, for your mantel-piece. You will like that.
Vera Cruz, March 16th, 1860.

Immigration is setting in fast to Mexico, in earnest. Every vessel brings many passengers as emigrants, from Tennessee, Georgia, Mississippi, Louisiana, South Carolina, and Missouri. There is land enough for all the South, but they are slow in surveying it; and all those who come here should bring some money. I fear there will be much misery among those colonists who come here without money. They had better stay at home. I am here for a few days on business. I find this a very agreeable place. Fish and oysters very good. I write this sitting in the window of my hotel, which looks out upon the sea. The view is beautiful. Old ocean roaring at my feet, and the great castle in front, keeping " watch and ward" in the deep blue sea. I shall be in Havana very shortly — shall expect letters there. We had Lucia di Lammermoor last night, and the melancholy music still rings in my ears, " Fra poco— me, ricovero." How sad it is ! * * *

I have just received a package of books from New York ; among them Poe's works. I opened it at the Raven. I find myself continually repeating this verse, — its melancholy sentiment is most agreeable to me at times :

"Be that word our sign of parting, bird or fiend, I shrieked, upstarting — Get thee back into the Tempest and the Night's Plutonian shore ! Leave no black plume as a token of that lie thy soul hath spoken ! Leave my loneliness unbroken. Quit the bust above my door — Take thy beak from out my heart, and take thy form from off my door ! Quoth the Raven, Never more."

What a strange thing it is ! You can get my book of Travels from and ,
if you want it. Adios.

H. W. A.
Vera Cruz, March 17th

To Vallery : City of Mexico, April 4, 1866.

I have just received a letter from Mr. Texada, in which
he mentions your name, informing me that you were
working at the State-House, and doing well. I am very
glad to hear it, for you deserve to do well. I am also
glad to hear that you have not forgotten me, for I
think of you very often, not only as my faithful servant
in former days, but as my companion in arms, and on
the battle-field. God bless you, Vallery. I don't know
that I shall ever see you again, for it is possible I may
never return. I am now just about starting on a long
and painful journey to Paris, to see if I can't get well.
I would like so much to have you along to assist me
and cheer me up in my exile, but I have not the
means to pay your expenses. You must be temperate,
and prudent, and industrious, and save your money. If
I am ever a rich man again, I will help you and make
you comfortable for life. If you should see any of our
people again, tell them that I send them all my love. I
hope in God that I shall meet them all once more.

Good-bye, Vallery. Remember my advice. You were
ever true to me, and I will never, never forget your
services. God bless you.
Truly your friend,
Henry W. Allen

City of Mexico, April 2d, 1866.

My dear Friend —
I avail myself of the departure of Colonel , of New Orleans, to write you this. He has been to Mexico to look about for land for himself and relatives, and returns without accomplishing his purpose. This I much regret, for he would have been a great accession to our colony. Many come out here, and return dissatisfied. I don't blame them, for with all your drawbacks, there are a thousand more comforts in the States than here. Those who have comfortable homes in Louisiana, should never leave them. Since I wrote you last, nothing of interest has transpired. We have just got through with Holy Week, and, my dear friend, such mummery you never saw or heard of! For two days no carriage nor horse could appear in the streets; no amusements of any kind could be indulged in: this was on Holy Thursday and Friday. But on Sunday we had bull-fights, and operas, and theatres in full blast ! ! ! I have, however, gotten used to all these things. Mexico is, I believe, the only country where living representations of the Crucifixion are given. On Friday we had a naked Indian on the cross, as Jesus Christ ! The Indian was tied between two others, representing the thieves ! This tableau was surrounded by others representing the Roman centurion and soldiers, with Pontius Pilate, dressed up, on his throne. All this mummery pleases the people very much, but the burning of Judas seemed to delight them much more.

I took a trip to Vera Cruz and Cordova a week or two since, but did not enjoy the trip much, as I became sick, and suffered very much; am still quite unwell, and suffering terribly from dyspepsia. I hope to get off during this month, and will write you from Havana. Judge P. is well, and pushing finely ahead with his coffee-farm: he blacks his own shoes, and feeds and curries his own horse. He expects his wife and daughter in the fall. My regards to Mr. -----. Believe me,

Very truly, your sincere friend,

Henry W. Allen.

P. S. The only recreation here is to go to the theatre or opera, or some show at night. The semi-barbarous people have no higher conception of social amuse- ment : when I am able, I go too, but it grows weari- some. I would give the world, if I had it, to listen an hour to intellectual conversation ! !

City of Mexico, April 7th, 1866.

My dear Mrs. -----
Your letters of 1st and 6th March, with their enclo- sures, letters for Judge , etc., have been duly received. I am glad you like that little poem, " The Beggar's Petition," which was published in my paper. It was well received here, and complimented by *her Majesty the Empress.* And now that it receives your approbation, I am satisfied. I read the letters to -----, as you requested, and forwarded them to him to-day. My health has become wretched; *I do not know what a well day is.* The climate is too cool. In this high altitude no one perspires without most violent exer- cise. Then the air is so rarefied that I cannot get my breath easily, at night, which disturbs my sleeping. As I wrote you, I am promised a permanent cure for my wounds, and all other ills, by going to a celebrated Doctor in Paris. I will leave this city during this month. Write me no more letters to Mexico. I will write you from Paris. I regret that my time has been so occupied that I could not prosecute my Spanish studies as I desired. I have, however, made some progress, and now speak the language a little, and read it much better.

* * * * * * * * *

I am now finishing Buckle's " Civilization of England."
It is a wonderful book. If you have not already read it
(and what book is there that you have not read ?) I
recommend it to you. A good Catholic Priest from
Louisiana — a chaplain in our old C. S. army — comes
to see me very often, and we discuss *polemics* very
freely. I gather much information from this learned
and good man.

A newspaper, however, is a jealous spouse, and exacts
every attention to itself. I have labored faithfully and
zealously as an Editor for eight months, and look
forward with great pleasure to the time when I shall
have a good holiday. In relation to my returning, it is
useless for you, my dear friend, or any one else, to
press this matter on Mr. Johnson. A parole I will
gladly accept, but I would not beg for pardon at the
hands of any mortal power. I bend the knee only to
God. I don't think I have done wrong. I would like to
return home, and would be a law-abiding citizen, if I
could; but I hear the matter has been decided against
me. My friend. Colonel Sandidge, of Shreveport, sent
me, a few days since, a copy of a letter which he had
written to the President in my behalf. I replied, that
whenever I could return with honor and safety, I
would do so most cheerfully; *and so I will*! I am more
than anxious to see the good people of Louisiana, who
have honored me so much. At the same time, my dear
friend, I must live, *I must work*! and make my
arrangements for the future, without waiting any
longer. Good-bye : my regards to Mr. -----, and to your
Uncle John, when you write him; he is a noble speci-
men of humanity. — I hope we may meet again. Truly
your friend,

Henry W. Allen.

We have some American celebrities here. General -----
has a most accomplished daughter. She is just out
from England. She has the very finest voice out of
Italy. She is a prodigy, and sings better than any
Prima Donna I ever heard. Mr. Grayson, from
Louisiana, is here, painting the Birds of Mexico. He is
equal to Audubon. The Empress patronizes him, and
will, at her own expense, publish his work. Young
Chapman, the son of the American painter, now in
Rome, is here, busily engaged in sketching the ruins
of Mexico. He bids fair to rival his gifted father.
H. W. A.

I shall positively be in Paris on the 1st of June. Write
me there, care of -----
* * * * * * * * * *

I have written you a long, long letter, and no doubt
annoyed you excessively, by its scrambling style; you
will pardon it, as it is *the last for many weeks*!

Truly yours,
H. W. A.

5

Ex-Governor Allen to Horace Greeley

To Horace Greeley, Esq., Editor of the New York Tribune :

Sir : In your valuable paper of the 22d ult., and in subsequent numbers, we are pained to see several articles written against the unfortunate exiles from the United States. We think it a very unfair, ungenerous and unkind spirit. The men of whom you have spoken so flippantly and so lightly are many of them of your age, and deserve, to say the least, a respectful notice at your hands. We regret this the more, Mr. Greeley, because we always believed you to be honest in your political views, and above the miserable prejudices of the hour. That, while differing in political opinions from your brethren of the South, you had manliness enough to attribute to them equal sincerity of purpose. You upbraid us and abuse us for quitting our native land and coming to Mexico, when you knew very well that there was full many a Federal prison "gaping to receive us." When we left our country, all the Governors of the seceded States had either been arrested, or orders to that effect had been issued. It was also generally believed that every Confederate general and statesman would be arrested and turned over to the tender mercies of a court-martial. We can safely say that if a guarantee had been held out that we would not have been disturbed, none of us would have expatriated ourselves. You, Sir, would have done just as we did, unless you had been desirous of wearing the martyr's crown. You first abuse us for being rebels, and then denounce us for settling in Mexico. Where else, in the name of Heaven, could we go? We could not go North, nor East, nor "West ; we were compelled to come South, as the only outlet for those who would seek refuge in a foreign land. When the Irish, Canadian and Cuban patriots — when the Hungarian, Polish, and Italian exiles fled to your shores, you. Sir, have opened you heart, and with true Christian philanthropy, you have extended to them your warmest sympathy ; but when your own countrymen, stripped of all their earthly goods, are expatriated, and laboring with their own hands for an humble living — for bread with which to keep life afloat — strange to say, you can find in your heart no sympathy, no word of encouragement — but rather the cold sarcasm and the ribald jest.

We have been very kindly received by the Emperor Maximilian and the Empress Carlotta. They have permitted us, poor and penniless, to remain in this Empire, and to breathe the fresh, pure air of the lovely climate. They have exhibited to us the same generous sympathy which you and your government have ever shown to all exiles from foreign lands. For this we are deeply sensible, and will ever feel grateful to their Majesties. Still, none of us have entered into the military service of the Empire. To our personal knowledge, many have applied for service, but the Emperor has invariably declined. Out of the large number of Confederates now in this Empire none are heard to denounce their native land. There are no juntas or secret gatherings to plot against the land of their birth. You have never seen, nor never will see in this paper — the *Mexican Times* — an editorial denouncing the United States Government. Now, Mr. Greeley, why can't you let us alone? Sir, Christian charity, common decency and fair play would say, " Let them alone: we are free of them: let them live and die in peace." We have never injured you; we don't know you; we have no desire even to form your acquaintance; but we beg you to let us alone. We know that you hate us, and that if you had the power, you would not only persecute us to death in this world, but consign us to that lake in the next, "which burneth with fire and brimstone forever!"

The man who has once been a slaveholder, and a rebel, can never enter "your heaven." In this very charitable judgment of yours, we believe that the Christian world will beg leave to respectfully differ; for in their opinion George Washington and Stonewall Jackson stand to-day as well justified in the sight of Almighty God, as George the III. or Abraham Lincoln. We believe that the soldiers of the Federal and Con-federate armies, who fell in battle or died of disease, will stand at the bar of God and be judged alike, irrespective of their political tenets. You, sir, have arrived at the age allotted by the Psalmist, and must, in the general order of things, be soon gathered to your fathers. You will die rich — rolling in wealth, while the unfortunate men whom you daily abuse, will leave behind them scarcely enough to secure a decent burial.

We say that the time will soon come when you shall die and be buried. We will meet, for each must appear before the Great Judge, to answer for the sins com-mitted on this earth. You will stand forth as the wealthy Mr. Greeley, with a copy of the late Tribune — the work of your long life — and you will thank God that you are not like the rebel slaveholder, at whom

you will point with scorn and contempt. We will
appear with our broken sword in hand, and kneel for
pardon at the mercyseat. God will judge us both.

Now, Mr. Greeley, we must part till that great day —
the day of wrath — when we shall meet face to face.
There was once in the classic land of the East, a
prophetess who foretold the downfall of her native
land, but her countrymen refused to believe her until
too late, when her prophecy was accomplished. She
said

> " The day shall come — that great avenging day—
>   When Troy's proud glory in the dust shall lay:
>   When Priam's power and Priam's self shall fall,
>   And one prodigious ruin swallow all."

The text is in Homer; you can make your own commentary. We have seen the aged grandsire, not like
Belisarius, begging in the streets, but working with
his own hands for his daily broad; we have seen the
noble, middle-aged soldier, -who had faced death on a
hundred battlefields, toiling- from "early morn to
dewy eve," to earn a few dollars to send back to his
young wife and babes. We have seen men who had
filled high political stations and been aa honor to
their country, submit, without a murmur, to all the
discomforts of cruel poverty and exile. We have seen
the brave exile stretched upon his dying bed, and as
his hour of dissolution approached, we have witnessed his tears of affection, and heard his farewell
words and messages sent to kindred and friends in
fatherland. But for all this you have no sympathy. You
will answer with a ribald sneer, or a " fool-born jest."
You may have been right in suppressing the Revolution, but no man or woman who has one particle of
Christian charity left in his or her bosom, will sustain
you in persecuting the conquered South, or pursuing
with such vindictive hate the patriot exiles.

We have the honor to subscribe ourselves, respectfully, your obedient servant,

Henry Watkins Allen.

Horace Greeley: Editor of the *New York Tribune*, Failed "Liberal" Republican Presidential Candidate in 1872